From Great Wilderness
to
Seaway Towns

From Great Wilderness to Seaway Towns

A Comparative History of Cornwall, Ontario, and Massena, New York, 1784–2001

Claire Puccia Parham

State University of New York Press

Published by
State University of New York Press, Albany

Printed in the United States of America

For information, contact the State University of New York Press, Albany, NY
www.sunypress.edu

Production by Marilyn P. Semerad
Marketing by Anne M. Valentine

Library of Congress Cataloging-in-Publication Data

Parham, Claire Puccia.
From great wilderness to Seaway towns : a comparative history of Cornwall, Ontario, and Massena, New York, 1784–2001 / Claire Puccia Parham.
p. cm.
Includes bibliographical references and index.
ISBN 0-7914-5981-0 (hc : alk. paper)
1. Cornwall (Ont.)—History. 2. Massena (N.Y.)—History. 3. Northern boundary of the United States—History, Local. 4. Saint Lawrence Seaway—History. 5. United States—Relations—Canada—Case studies. 6. Canada—Relations—United States—Case studies. I. Title.

F1059.5.C67P37 2004
971.3'75—dc22 2003058127

10 9 8 7 6 5 4 3 2 1

Contents

Acknowledgments

I wish to thank the many people who assisted me with this project. I am indebted to my husband, Edward, whose love and support made this book possible; to my parents who have always believed in me and encouraged me to pursue my dreams; and to my daughters, Eve and Annabelle, who are daily inspirations to me. I am also grateful to the residents of Massena, New York and Cornwall, Ontario and the numerous Seaway workers who shared their life stories with me and invited me into their homes. Special thanks also go to the St. Lawrence County Historical Society, the Power Authority of the State of New York, and David Mercier who provided the cover art and design. I would like, finally, to thank my long-time advisor, Dr. Robert Weir, for his guidance during my years of work on this project.

Acknowledgments

Introduction

Cornwall, Ontario and Massena, New York are two towns separated by a narrow expanse of the St. Lawrence River on the northern New York–Canadian border. Besides being close geographical neighbors, the locales were both settled in the closing decades of the eighteenth century. In 1784 United Empire Loyalists and their families who were no longer welcome in the former colonies relocated to Royal Township #2, later renamed Cornwall. Massena's founding fathers were northeastern farmers who left family homesteads in New England and New York in search of cheap and abundant land on the newly opened frontier. Initially, both groups of settlers struggled to become economically self-sufficient and to foster cultural and political institutions among a widespread and often transient population. Religion proved to be the common link that brought the members of these communities together. Settlers' shared spiritual beliefs gave them the strength to endure the harsh frontier conditions and enhanced their relationships with their neighbors.

In terms of industrialization, the progress of both towns was tied to their location near a navigable waterway and the subsequent development of hydropower. Following the construction of power canals on the St. Lawrence and Grasse Rivers during the second half of the nineteenth century, Cornwall and Massena became major regional manufacturing centers. Cornwall's initial factories were textile mills financed by wealthy Montreal entrepreneurs. By the early twentieth century these enterprises were joined by more than a dozen manufacturing operations including a paper mill and a men's clothing factory. Massena's first major manufacturing firm was an aluminum processing plant constructed by the Pittsburgh Reduction Company in 1903, later known as the Aluminum Company of America (Alcoa). Prior to World War II Alcoa was the only producer of aluminum-based goods in the continental United States and was the largest employer north of Syracuse. The workers recruited by the owners of these large enterprises altered the population of Cornwall and Massena and increased the number of local residents employed in manufacturing. Following World War II, however, both towns experienced economic downturns and high unemployment. The much anticipated St. Lawrence Seaway and Power Project was touted by local officials as the key to Cornwall and Massena's economic revivals.

In the 1950s Cornwall and Massena served as their countries' respective headquarters for the international rapids and power dam segment of the St. Lawrence Seaway project. The waterway, completed between 1954 and 1958, was the culmination of a century-long dream by the two nations to improve inland water transportation and to provide much needed cheap hydroelectric power for both nations' growing populations and industry. During the duration of the construction, the two towns experienced economic prosperity, population expansion, and religious diversification. However, once the Seaway was completed, most workers moved on to the next project and the two areas did not derive any of the long-term financial benefits promised by local and national politicians. Modern technology now allowed the transmission of electricity over long distances and made the locating of manufacturing enterprises near major power sources unnecessary. Since 1958, the unemployment levels on both sides of the border have risen, as many of the major manufacturing enterprises have either closed or downsized their facilities. Collectively, the history of Cornwall and Massena adds a new dimension to the debate over the differences between Canadian and American society.

The long-standing debate among Canadian and American scholars over the similarities and differences between the residents of the two nations has tended to reflect two broad schools of thought. One school argues that all sectors of Canadian and American society historically differ because of the countries' contrasting organizing principles. Canadians are more class conscious, law-abiding, elitist, and collectively oriented, while Americans pride themselves on living in an egalitarian, classless society and thrive on individualism and personal achievement. These values can be traced back to the outcome of the American Revolution and have continued to influence behavior and institution building in the two neighboring countries for more than 200 years. Regardless of the increasing similarity of the economies and popular culture of Canada and the United States since World War II, these fundamental developmental differences ensure that the two nations will never be economically, socially, or politically identical. The second school of thought views Canadians and Americans as holding similar values and beliefs based on their close geographic location, particularly among the inhabitants of border towns.

The groundwork for the first hypothesis, known as the value-orientation theory, was set down by Seymour Lipset in his article, "The Value Patterns of Democracy: A Case Study in Comparative View," published in 1963. His most recent work, *Continental Divide: The Values and Institutions of the United States and Canada*, is a recapitulation of the sociologist's 30-year analysis of the cultural and institutional differences between Canada and the United States.[1] Lipset makes specific assertions about the economic, social, and religious values that influenced the establishment of businesses, personal relationships, governments, and churches by Canadians and Americans. Economically, he indicates Canadian entrepreneurs are more cautious and conservative than their American neighbors. They, therefore, are unwilling to take the financial risks necessary to develop new technology and industry whose products could successfully compete in the global marketplace.[2] Socially, Lipset argues that Canadians are more accepting of foreigners and their unique cultures based on their long-term coexistence with French Canadians. Americans, on the other hand, want immigrants to assimilate and cast aside their native values and cultures. Politically, Lipset insinuates that Canadians desire a strong paternalistic government and defer to authority.[3] In the United States citizens explicitly reject monarchical rule and ascriptive aristocratic titles.[4] Therefore, Canadians formed governments run by the elite, while Americans established democratic political structures staffed by the common man. Religiously, according to Lipset, most Canadians are members of the Roman Catholic, Anglican, and United Churches, while Americans remain under the strong influence of Protestant sects whose preachers support egalitarian and evangelical practices. American worshipers value their personal relationship with God and retain control of their congregations' financial affairs. Throughout his career, the validity of Lipset's value-orientation approach was debated by many scholars who questioned its relevance in explaining cultural changes in Canada and the United States after World War II.

In 1973 Irving Horowitz challenged the contemporary merits of Lipset's theory based on the growing economic and cultural similarities between Canada and the United States. In his essay, "The Hemispheric Connection: A Critique and Corrective to the Entrepreneurial Thesis of Development with Special Emphasis on the Canadian Case," he argued that the behavioral and value differences between Canada and the United States were not historically linked to the nations' conflicting revolutionary ideologies, as Lipset suggested, but were instead based on a lag between the two countries' social development. Once Canada completed its social and economic evolution, Horowitz stated, the country would become more like the United States and less like Great Britain. This transformation began following World War II as the increased level of crime, education, and religious participation in Canada narrowed the cultural gap between Canada and the United States. Horowitz, therefore, concluded that "Lipset's thinking is premised on a continuation of pre–World War II tendencies rather than post-World War II trends."[5] This assertion was supported by S. D. Clark in his book, *Canadian Society in Historical Perspective*, who also criticized Lipset for "not sufficiently recognizing that what was true of the nineteenth century and early twentieth century Canadian society is not true of post second World War society," and for relying too heavily on historical sources.[6]

Beginning in the 1980s a new generation of scholars emphasized the similarities between the values and experiences of Canadians and Americans and criticized the empirical evidence that Lipset presented in support of his ideological inferences. At the center of this debate were three studies conducted by Stephen Arnold and Douglas Tigert, James Curtis, Robert Lambert, Steven Brown, and Barry Kay, and Craig Crawford and James Curtis.[7] All utilized empirical data and numerous public opinion surveys that spanned several decades to test Lipset's conclusions. Arnold and Tigert conducted two independent surveys the results of which contradicted the very foundations of Lipset's arguments regarding the influence of Canadian conservatism and American individualism on the two nations' values and institutions. The authors concluded that "there have been more similarities than differences in the institutions and cultural patterns of the two countries."[8] Curtis, Lambert, Brown, and Kay tested Lipset's hypothesis on the differing level of involvement of Canadians and Americans in voluntary associations. They determined that most of his assertions were flawed when compared with the data collected by several polls between 1960 and 1974. "In different comparisons, Canadians as a whole are similar to Americans in involvement level."[9] Finally, Curtis and Crawford employed extensive empirical evidence to test Lipset's central value-orientation thesis and its four main supporting assertions and to encourage more research on the subject.

Recently borderland scholars have offered Canadian and American historians a new conceptual framework for analyzing the lives of the residents of the nations' border towns. Anthropologists and political scientists have explored the unique cultures, values, and lives of border town inhabitants across the globe and defined certain characteristics which are common to all of these individuals. The most groundbreaking study in this new genre is Oscar Martinez's *Border People: Life and Society in the U.S.–Mexico Borderlands*. Martinez outlines a set of criteria to evaluate the uniqueness of border town life and uses oral interviews to prove his theory. His most useful tool for historians is his argument that inhabitants of border towns function in an environment called the "borderlands milieu." These circumstances are defined as "unique forces, processes, and characteristics that set borderlands apart from interior zones."[10] They include facing the constant threat of foreign invasion, dealing with heterogeneous populations, interacting with foreigners, and feeling separated or isolated from their countrymen. What is lacking is a local study of two towns on the U.S.–Canadian border that employs the methods of borderland studies to determine an actual set of values and beliefs that test Lipset's thesis.

This work compares Cornwall and Massena at different historical moments from 1784 to 2001 and disproves Lipset's concept of a "continental divide." It argues that the two towns' respective histories and comparable borderland locations in a capitalist-world system led them to follow comparable patterns of social and economic development that contrasted their more homogeneous rural neighbors and their compatriots in other areas of the country. These border town settlers created similar social, political, and economic institutions because of their peripheral locations and their inherent congregational and democratic values. As former American colonists, both area residents wanted to develop towns similar to their former communities. The founders of Cornwall and Massena and their descendants, therefore, challenged national values and beliefs and developed a distinctive society and culture of their own.[11] In contrast to Seymour Lipset, who argued that the organizing principles made the two countries different, my research suggests that Louis Hartz was closer to the mark when he stated "the differences between the two countries are less significant than the traits common to both."[12]

The materials for this work were drawn from diverse sources. Local histories and newspapers provide invaluable accounts of the experiences of settlers in both Cornwall and Massena. The transition from subsistence farming to early industrialization and commercial farming and the era of large corporations emerges from consulting local directories, company histories, and statistics, while the Seaway years are recorded in three document collections donated to the St. Lawrence University archives. Included in these files are newspaper articles, government reports, memoirs, pamphlets, and correspondence, as well as economic and social statistics from the United States and Canada. Oral interviews of past residents, Seaway workers, and government officials either support or refute the information contained in published sources. The incorporation of these narratives with secondary accounts enhances the understanding of social and cultural changes that occurred in Cornwall and Massena between 1784 and 2001, while providing a glimpse into the lack of development of the local economy. This study begins with a general description of the settlement of Cornwall and Massena before delving into specific historical moments that illustrate the towns' similar historical trajectories.

Chapter 1 explores the settlement of Cornwall, Ontario and Massena, New York from 1784 to 1834. It traces the origins of the early settlers and describes their struggles to achieve economic self-sufficiency and develop permanent social and political institutions. The analysis of the founding framework of the towns provides essential data for later juxtaposition with information regarding the subsequent societal and economic variances in Cornwall and Massena. A comparison of the towns illustrates that the settlement experience of Cornwall and Massena residents was similar based on their mutual peripheral location and their heritage as residents of the former American colonies. They both established democratic and egalitarian political and social organizations that exemplified their comparable values and beliefs.

Chapter 2 explains the transition of the towns' economies between 1834 and 1898 from subsistence farming and petty retail to commercial agriculture and early industrialization. Both towns industrialized late due to their distance from commercial centers. However, Cornwall and Massena's locations near canal projects meant they experienced cultural, religious, and ethnic diversification contrary to other regions.

Chapter 3 analyzes the era of large corporations in Cornwall and Massena from 1900 until 1954. Industrialization made the two towns manufacturing centers, which was a contrast to the agrarian lifestyle in adjacent towns. Factory operatives diversified the population and established new religious congregations. Cornwall and Massena's cultural and ethnic diversity forced residents to deal with outsiders sooner than their neighbors and resulted in interethnic conflict.

Chapter 4 describes the construction of the St. Lawrence Seaway and the demographic and ethnic impact of workers on Cornwall and Massena from 1954 to 1958. The town residents blamed these new arrivals for an escalation in crime and overcrowded schools. The St. Lawrence Seaway project had a similar social effect on both towns and illustrated how environmental factors and location on an international border played a determining role in shaping the lives of area residents.

Chapter 5 traces the long-term financial impact of the Seaway on the two communities and brings the study to the present day. It explores the national and local elements that hindered the economic advancement of Cornwall and Massena and analyzes why neither area experienced the prosperity local and national experts predicted prior to the commencement of the Seaway construction. Similar to other border towns around the globe, Cornwall and Massena remained underdeveloped due to their peripheral location.

CHAPTER ONE

The Early Settlement of Cornwall, Ontario and Massena, New York, 1784–1834

The towns of Cornwall, Ontario and Massena, New York were established by pioneers on the U.S.–Canadian border at the end of the eighteenth century in a previously untamed wilderness. The northernmost part of New York State and the southern border of British North America were labeled the "Great Wilderness" by cartographers on maps drawn prior to 1772. The region was isolated from established commercial centers, inhabited by Indians and covered by dense forests. The area, therefore, was unattractive to many frontiersmen until after the American Revolution when the forced exile of British loyalists and the limited availability of fertile land in New England encouraged the settlement of this formerly desolate borderland. The founding fathers of Cornwall and Massena faced starvation and economic uncertainty during the first years of settlement due to their geographic isolation.

The permanent settlement of Cornwall, Ontario and Massena, New York, while twenty years apart, was demographically, socially, religiously, and politically similar. Early pioneers from New England and other former American colonies cooperatively built houses and churches and worshiped together at Sunday services. The rigors of frontier life, economic and social isolation, and an agrarian economy prevented the development of social differences among settlers and the ascension of elites to power. Regardless of the fact that they now lived on opposite sides of the border, the loyalists and Massena settlers still harbored comparable social and political goals and values. The founding fathers of both towns were collectively oriented, distrusted the state, and developed voluntaristic and egalitarian religious traditions. The border location of Cornwall and Massena forced residents to become self-sufficient, made them vulnerable to foreign invasion, and encouraged them to develop different social and political institutions from those in the heartland regions. The settlement and early struggles of families in Cornwall were more similar to those of their neighbors in Massena than to residents in other areas of Canada.

Cornwall

Cornwall, Ontario was settled in 1784 by United Empire Loyalists and their families as one of five new royal townships. During the Revolutionary War, many British sympathizers left homesteads in New York, Pennsylvania, and New England, joined royal regiments, and fought on behalf of King George III. Once the war was over, loyalists pressured British government officials for new land and financial compensation as repayment for their allegiance. For defense purposes British officials wanted some of these families settled close to the United States border. The male residents of the royal townships provided an experienced militia force in case American officials attempted to extend their property further northward in the future. Following the signing of the Treaty of Paris in November of 1783, Sir John Johnson, commander of the King's Royal Regiment, and several of his fellow military leaders traveled down the St. Lawrence River and negotiated land deals with the St. Regis Indians for property in a previously unsettled area of Upper Canada. Once the deal was signed and the necessary surveys conducted, experienced French-Canadian bateaux captains brought loyalists and their belongings to their new homes along the St. Lawrence. The first settlers arrived in Royal Township #2 in 1784.[1]

Cornwall's isolated location forced the loyalists to become self-sufficient and create a unique community based on environmental factors. Prior to Sir Johnson's agreement with the St. Regis, the area where Cornwall is situated was largely an untamed wilderness. The French had long occupied the eastern region of Canada ending at the present Ontario–Quebec border. Explorers and missionaries had journeyed further inland and some of the islands and rapids still bear the names of those pioneers.[2] In the past, central Canada was also considered as a location for a trading or military post by French government officials. But, according to a local reporter, it was "unlikely that more than half a dozen white men had ever gazed upon the place where the future Cornwall was situated."[3] When the former soldiers arrived to claim their new plots of land along the St. Lawrence River, no roads or means of communication existed to connect the area with major commercial centers like Montreal. Therefore, many of the township's early settlers relied on home production and the local exchange of foodstuffs for basic subsistence.

Royal Township #2 was the most popular settlement among loyalist soldiers because of its fertile agricultural land, favorable climate, and good timber.[4] The area was described by a geographer as 10,231 square miles of forest and farmland laced with sparkling lakes and streams.[5] Cornwall's climate was also well suited for farming. The 163-day growing season and 70 degree average temperature were similar to the conditions the loyalists were accustomed to in New York and New England. The monthly rainfall of three inches was ample for most crops.

The indigenous fir trees and hardwoods were valuable resources for the early residents. Wood accumulated by settlers during land clearing was chopped and processed into potash or lye and sold for cash for use in soap and other products in Canada and overseas. Farmers simply designated burning areas on empty lots of land and sold the ashes to traveling dealers. Additionally, lumbering was a source of off-season employment for many farmers. There was a local and regional market for wood, as settlers were constantly arriving in the royal townships and constructing new homes and churches. Lumbering bees were also held by farmers to rid their land of unwanted trees. Several men gathered to cut down massive amounts of pine, maple, oak, and elm and drag the trunks and branches to a clearing to be burned.[6] While the arable land and timber were initially seen as assets to the loyalist soldiers, the physical isolation and frontier conditions they experienced fostered a unique community that often put them at odds with national officials. However, it was forced exile that initially brought the early settlers to Royal Township #2.

The original 516 settlers arrived in Royal Township #2 with minimal supplies and faced years of hard work and possible starvation. Upon their departure from military camps in Montreal, Pointe Claire, Saint Anne, and Lachine in the fall of 1784, loyalists were given a tent, one month's worth of food rations, clothes, and agricultural provisions by regiment commanders. They were promised one cow for every two families, an ax, and other necessary tools in the near future.[7] For the next three years, bateaux crews delivered rations to the township, after which residents were left to fend for themselves.[8] Military officials distributed small amounts of beef, pork, butter, and salt to the head of each household. The total allotment of each item was based on the number of family members.[9] Financially, most male settlers shared in the $500,000 compensation package paid to former soldiers, while a minority of the officers were awarded a pension of half pay for life. In 1787 British government officials discontinued the food rations, financial compensation, and agricultural implements extended to the loyalist settlers. Most Cornwall residents were not self-sufficient in terms of food production and faced starvation. Additionally, merchants had not yet established stores and mills to sell or process goods that could not be produced by settlers at home.[10] Life for the founding fathers of Cornwall was primitive and unpredictable even though they owned large amounts of property.

The loyalists were awarded land through a lottery system. Each participant drew a number out of a box that corresponded to a similarly labeled parcel of land. The size of the allotment was based on the military rank of the individual. Noncommissioned officers received 200 acres, while the highest-level field officers were awarded 5,000.[11] The acreage included one plot of land with river frontage for planting and water access and another further inland for housing. Some former officers who participated in the lottery never settled in the area and many of the acres remained uncultivated. According to Edgar McInnis, "Large tracts of land in the most desirable locations lay waste, and new settlers had either to pay excessive prices or locate in areas remote from markets and transportation."[12] These circumstances stunted the population growth of Cornwall, since no property was available for purchase by newcomers at a reasonable price. The ownership of more land by the former officers did not socially or economically separate them from the rest of the population.

While some officers, including Samuel Anderson and Major James Gray, received substantial amounts of waterfront property, this did not make these former regiment commanders wealthier than the rest of the early Cornwall residents. They were not able to hire other men initially to build their houses and continually tend their grain fields and vegetable gardens. The harsh conditions of frontier life, lack of appropriate tools, and the area's remote location prevented the immediate development of a wealthy landowning class. All residents depended upon the help of their neighbors to build shelter, plant crops, and share supplies during bad harvests.

The settler's primary task was preparing his land for the next year's harvest. Male pioneers cleared, seeded, and harvested their acreage and crops by hand with a ship ax, as no oxen, horses, or machinery were available. With these primitive implements, the process of clearing the land was slow and arduous, with most families managing to clear about two-thirds of an acre after six months of work.[13] Therefore, settlers augmented their food supply with the ample fish and game in the area. They also set up a bartering system to exchange goods and services. Although many were experienced frontiersmen, the hardships they faced in Upper Canada were often extreme and insurmountable due to the area's isolation.[14] As M. A. Garland and J. J. Talman noted, "Life in the bush had a tendency to demoralize the settlers. The task of clearing his land and providing the necessities of life was a hard and monotonous one."[15] Building temporary housing was also difficult in this isolated location.

For shelter, loyalists constructed wood huts with the assistance of neighbors. William Catermole wrote, "With respect to new settlers, they always find their neighbors ready to assist them in putting up their houses."[16] The typical pioneer erected a shanty by placing round logs on top of each other to a height of seven to eight feet with an elm bark roof. The walls were mortared with mud and small sticks. Builders cut two small openings into opposite walls for a window and a door. Settlers used blankets or wooden boards for doors and cut squares of oil paper to serve as windows. The floor was comprised of split logs or dirt. The only piece of furniture most loyalists brought with them was a bed. Tradesmen crafted all the other furniture, including tables and chairs, after arrival. The most unique feature of the early log homes was the large fireplace used for heating and cooking. Some of these were big enough to accommodate 6-feet long logs.[17] According to William Catermole, these primitive dwellings cost male settlers a total of £10 to £12 to complete.[18] Women spent most of their time in these shanties performing their domestic duties.

Loyalist women had to be hardy, strong, and adaptable to the simple and primitive living conditions in the Royal Townships. They, along with their children, performed many tasks usually carried out by men in other communities during planting and harvesting, including thrashing wheat and cutting wood. Women's primary responsibilities were cooking, cleaning, and childrearing. A typical dinner cooked by pioneer women included pork, cornmeal porridge, vegetables, with a wild strawberry pie for dessert. In the autumn, women made candles to provide artificial light for family members to read by during the winter months. The candles came in two varieties. The first, molded, was formed by pouring melted tallow into tin frames. The other, wicked, was made by repeatedly dipping pieces of yarn tied to a long stick into hot vats of tallow. Female settlers also produced the family clothing and woolens. They often gathered in small groups and processed wool and flax into cloth and woolen material. While one woman spun the wool on a wheel into yarn, another would weave it into cloth on a handloom. Housewives or tailors then cut and sewed this material into a variety of garments, including shirts, pants, and skirts.[19]

Settlers also held many bees to husk corn, sew quilts, prepare apples for drying, and construct barns, mills, and churches.[20] In her book *Roughing It in the Bush*, Susanna Moodie observed that "people in the woods, have a craze for giving and going to bees and run to them with as much eagerness as a peasant runs to a race."[21] The logging bee was the most common event held by farmers who wanted to strip their land of unwanted trees. All men within a 20-mile radius were invited and most brought their axes and oxen. Once the men arrived, someone was placed in charge of supervising the work. Initially, several men cut down the timber and dragged the trunks and branches to a clearing where another group of men stacked them into piles. A third team was charged with burning the logs and scooping the ashes into bins for processing into potash. Once the work was finished, the party began. While the men drank whiskey and cider, the women served food and the young people danced and socialized. Bees often involved all ranks and nationalities of society. Thomas Need, a saw mill operator in Victoria County, described the raising of his facility in 1834 in the following way: "They assembled in great force and all worked together in great harmony and good will not withstanding their different stations in life."[22] These gatherings exhibited the lack of aristocracy in the rural loyalist settlement along the St. Lawrence River and residents' disregard for individuals' former social standing or lineage.

In 1812 the majority of Cornwall's male inhabitants were self-sufficient out of necessity and still clearing land and plowing soil with primitive tools. The harshness and isolation of frontier living prevented the development of an aristocracy and, instead, united all members of the community in a struggle for survival. Early loyalists, regardless of the amount of land they owned, depended upon the help of their neighbors to clear land, build homes, and share supplies and food during times of poor harvests. According to Edwin Guillet, "The life of pioneer settlers in Canada was one of hardship, but the difficulty under which they lived was to some extent relieved by cooperation."[23] These circumstances were similar to those of their American neighbors in Massena at that time. As Gerald Craig indicated, "In many aspects, life of the Upper Canada farmer differed little from that of the farmers on many another North American frontier."[24] The War of 1812, however, disrupted town life for several years.

The War of 1812 was a culmination of post-revolutionary tensions between Britain and the United States. President James Madison feared Canada as a growing military threat. He also resented British interference with the American settlement of its newly acquired western land and its restriction of neutral trade by capturing American merchant ships. Governor General James Craig of Canada renewed military assistance to Native Americans in the Ohio River Valley, hoping that the Indians could defend their territory and continue to trade with the British. During the Napoleanic Wars, Britain began seizing American cargo ships, including the Essex, which were carrying sugar and molasses from the West Indies to France.[25] This new British naval blockade threatened the profits of American merchants and revived anti-British sentiments. Attacking Canada seemed the only way to end British interference. For nearly three decades, Cornwall residents had avoided becoming entangled in any national disputes. However, their border location and the military expertise of many male residents forced them into playing a central role in what many historians refer to as the second war for American independence.

While many loyalists exchanged their muskets for hoes for several years, they were never far from their military past. In 1787 British officials divided the territory of Upper Canada into counties for both electoral and military recruitment purposes. The leaders of each county organized their own militia, which were charged with local defense and the training of soldiers to serve in national units. Two former loyalist commanders, Captain Archibald Macdonnell and Major James Gray, assembled and led the Stormont company. They recruited former regimental officers, including Jeremiah French and Joseph Anderson, to serve in their new units and promoted them to the next highest military rank.

In 1812 the Cornwall militiamen joined the national forces in defending the dominion's border against foreign invaders.[26] According to the *Old Boy's Reunion Brochure* in 1926, "Never forgetting their military experience, it needed but the declaration of war by the American Congress in 1812 to muster the pioneers and their sons round the old flag once more."[27] While the brunt of the war took place in the western part of Canada, near Chateaugay, guards manned several outposts above and below Cornwall protecting vulnerable land and water crossings. These troops were involved in several key battles, including the Battle of Crysler Farm. This victory prevented American soldiers from invading Montreal and maintained the national flow of munitions and food down the St. Lawrence River.[28]

Unlike Massena, whose residents who were not directly affected by the battles of the War of 1812, Cornwall served as a relay post for supplies, munitions, and troops, making it a prime target for American troops. Therefore, town residents were put on a constant state of alert. According to Lieutenant Colonel Ralph Bruyeres, who was sent to determine the vulnerability of the supply route between Prescott and Montreal in 1812, Cornwall was located in one of the hardest regions in Upper Canada to defend due to its close proximity to the American border.[29]

The invasion of the American troops eventually took place on November 11, 1813 at the commencement of the Battle of Crysler Farm. Three thousand five hundred ground troops under the command of Colonels Brown and Wilkinson descended the St. Lawrence on foot, accompanied by 300 others in boats. Brown's troops camped outside Cornwall from November 10 through 12, while Wilkinson's units marched on to Crysler Farm for a battle with British and militia troops. The British commanders claimed victory on November 12 with the loss of 93 Americans and another 237 wounded. When Brown's troops camping near Cornwall heard of the loss, they boarded their flotillas and headed for home. The victory at Crysler Farm prevented an occupation of Montreal and the possible destruction of Cornwall. After November 1813 no other attempt was made by American forces to invade Cornwall.[30]

The war's aftermath revealed that Cornwall was not as economically diversified as neighboring Kingston, where residents had begun developing transshipment and shipbuilding businesses and had constructed several small factories. While Cornwall's economy remained more agriculturally based, it still showed some signs of advancement. Farmers cleared larger amounts of land for pastures and partially converted their operations from wheat farming to dairying. Lumbering and potash production remained male inhabitants' main sources of cash. Many families also moved out of log cabins into framed dwellings that cost between £1,000 and £2,500 depending on the style.[31] A traveler in 1832 reported seeing fewer log homes and more brick and frame structures in the St. Lawrence River settlements.[32] By 1845, Cornwall's population of more than 1,000 was housed in 321 framed, 45 brick, and 129 log homes.[33]

The original Cornwall settlers were predominantly regimental soldiers and their families who were compensated for their loyalty to the crown with substantial lots on the St. Lawrence River. While many were farmers in the old colonies, they reluctantly faced the overwhelming task of clearing vast, untamed forests. Many were no longer young and had already experienced frontier life in their former homes. Male inhabitants, regardless of the amount of land they owned, labored with primitive tools and faced starvation if their crops failed. Through cooperation, male settlers lessened some of the stresses associated with pioneer life in an isolated location. As David Rayside suggested, "The harshness of conditions in the countryside made social standing and size of land grant less significant."[34] Cornwall residents developed a unique community based on environmental factors and separation from their Canadian compatriots who populated the heartland. Therefore, the early lives of Cornwall residents paralleled the future development in New York more than those of other loyalist settlers in Upper Canada at the end of the eighteenth century. As Gerald Craig put it, "In many respects Upper Canada was an American community."[35] This extended even to religious practices.

During the first fifty years of settlement in Upper Canada, dedicated worshipers formed a broad spectrum of religious congregations whose governing bodies and services were greatly influenced by the congregational and democratic religious and political beliefs fostered in the former American colonies. According to S. D. Clark in *Church and Sect in Canada*, "The American connection was decisive in determining the form taken by religious organization in Canada during the early period of settlement."[36] Many worshipers saw religion as a stable institution and their faith as a way to deal with the harsh conditions and isolation of frontier living. Like the pioneers who settled the American West, the loyalists experienced starvation, financial uncertainty, and loneliness. They gained a new respect for individualism, self-sufficiency, and social equality. These values became a permanent aspect of Canadian religious ideology and were different than the basic Anglican teachings.

The first obstacle many Cornwall settlers faced was the lack of congregations to attend. While most were affiliated with the more structured faiths of Presbyterianism, Anglicanism, and Roman Catholicism, Cornwall families were left in charge of their own spiritual lives based on their isolated location. They were unsuccessful at recruiting full-time ministers and priests, as many members of the British clergy viewed Canada as an unsettled frontier and its parishes as an undesirable assignment. Therefore, settlers started their own congregations and conducted their own services without the guidance of a minister. Lay readers not only presided over sporadic services, but also performed weddings and funerals. In *A Concise History of Christianity in Canada*, Terence Murphy indicated that "local initiatives of this kind were crucial to the early development of religious institutions."[37]

The Presbyterians were the most prominent faith in the area from the early days of settlement and traditionally one of the most nationally organized religions. The Cornwall congregants constructed the town's first public building on Pitt Street, which was also used as a barracks and courthouse. They were also initially put under the watchful eye of ordained minister, John Bethune, who also ministered to worshipers in the surrounding settlements. This was an attempt by British North American Presbyterian officials to establish a traditional church organization overseen by a system of courts, synods, and general assemblies. But frontier life altered the deference of local worshipers to the authority of church leaders as it had in the former American colonies. While Cornwall Presbyterians still accepted the Book of Common Prayer and stressed ceremony and Christian discipline, they were determined to retain their ability to excommunicate members and to ordain their own minister. Bethune remained the only Presbyterian clergyman in Upper Canada for several decades and preached to followers in Cornwall for twenty-eight years until his death in 1812.[38]

Cornwall Presbyterians illustrated their independence from national rulers by hiring Joseph Johnston in 1817 to succeed Bethune. He had no official religious training or standing in the Church of Scotland. However, following five years without a leader, members of the Cornwall congregation invited him to conduct services anyway. In 1818 Johnston took orders in the Presbyterian church over the objection of national church leaders.[39] Soon after his appointment, Johnston spearheaded a crusade to raise cash for the construction of a new white frame church to replace the original log building. He secured a large amount of financial support from Presbyterians in Cornwall, Montreal, and Quebec, and managed to erect the frame of the church. Church elders, who thought Johnston's architectural design was too audacious, halted construction soon after its commencement. Having lost the confidence of his flock, Johnston accepted a post at the Presbyterian church in nearby Osnabruck in 1823.[40]

In 1827 the 113-member Cornwall congregation hired its first full-time minister, Hugh Urquhart, who created a permanent local governing body and educational system. This reflected a return of the congregation to a more traditional Presbyterian structure and the reestablishment of elite control over worshipers. In July 1827 eight elders—Archibald McLean, James Pringle, Adam and William Johnston, John Cline, Martin McMartin, John Clesley, and James Craig—were elected and developed a Kirk Session to manage church affairs. Urquhart also organized a Sunday School to educate the young members of the congregation on the fundamentals of the faith, in the hopes of fostering lifelong church affiliation. The long-term mechanisms he established guaranteed the stability and expansion of the Presbyterian faith in the area.[41] Terence Murphy suggested, "In the 1830s, church leaders formed church committees and started church schools as a means of making religion an integral part of people's lives.[42] By 1839 there were 961 Presbyterians worshiping at St. John's.[43]

The original Catholics who settled in Cornwall also did not implement the traditional parish structure headed by a priest. Instead, based on their isolated location, Francis McCarthy, Daniel McGuire, John Luney, and Captain John MacDonnell adopted a congregational method of organization also known as trusteeism. According to Sidney Ahlstrom, prior to 1791 there were few Catholic priests in North America. Therefore, Catholics independently established and maintained their own parishes. He indicated, "In a time when funds were lacking and when episcopal authority was weak or non-existent, trusteeism was a way of providing a church for people who wanted one."[44] Initially, Cornwall settlers traveled to St. Andrew's to worship in a modest log chapel constructed by Captain John MacDonnell, one of the most devout Catholics in the settlements. In 1806 the twenty-three Cornwall Catholic families began holding services in the Cornwall courthouse or private residences. Two decades later, Cornwall Catholics led by Donald Macdonnell, the town's longtime sheriff, and John Loney, financed the commencement of construction of St. Columban's on Fourth and Pitt Street. The Cornwall congregation remained a mission church of St. Andrew's until the completion of St. Columban's in 1834. In 1835, only one year after St. Columban's was dedicated, parish leaders recorded seventy-eight baptisms, eight marriages, and six burials. As local historian John Harkness noted, "St. Columban's Parish had finally taken root in a community that had grown to over 1,000 citizens.[45]

Adherents to the Church of England or Anglicans were also among Cornwall's founding fathers. Like their Presbyterian and Catholic counterparts, Anglicans periodically held services in the absence of an ordained minister. Initially, the Anglican bishops in Upper Canada lacked the number of clergy required to minister to the scattered population in the new settlements. Therefore, from 1784 to 1787, Anglican residents of Royal Township #2 were ministered to annually by Reverend John Stuart, the only Anglican clergyman west of Montreal. The approximately 100 Anglicans in Cornwall hired their first full-time minister, John Bryan, in 1787 and established the first weekly Anglican services in the royal townships. However, two years later he fled to the United States to avoid public censure. Cornwall residents later discovered that Bryan was an impostor who had forged his religious credentials.[46] Bryan's inadequacies support Terence Murphy's argument that prior to 1815 with the shortage of qualified clergy, British denominational leaders sent their problematic ministers to Canada.[47] From 1789 to 1801, the Anglicans were again without a leader, but continued to hold prayer meetings.[48]

The Reverend John Strachan was the preacher who revived the Cornwall Anglican congregation and built it into a stable institution. Upon his arrival in the township in 1803, he found the church building in shambles and many parishioners attending services of other denominations.[49] Other Canadian ministers had complained that their parishioners infrequently attended services, were not captive audiences, and had little respect for the Sabbath.[50] Therefore, Strachan's primary tasks were to raise funds for a new church, to reclaim the allegiance of many of the departed faithful, and to create a permanent church administration. He solicited £633 in private donations, government funds, and pew rents for the construction of a framed church. In 1806 builders completed the new Trinity Church, and male parishioners elected their first vestry composed of Joseph and Samuel Anderson and Jeremiah French to oversee church business. Six years later Strachan left the 850 members of the parish under the successive guidance of William Baldwyn, Salter Mountain, and George Archbold. In the next several decades, parish leaders created a Sunday School, enlarged the vestry, and established a church-sponsored school. Therefore, Strachan's administrative, spiritual, and educational practices were continued and improved by his successors. By 1839, with 891 members, the Anglicans were challenging the Presbyterians and Catholics for majority status among Cornwall worshipers and were soon joined by the Methodists.[51]

Methodism appealed to many Cornwall residents based on its simple doctrines and organization and its evangelical traveling preachers. John Wesley, the faith's creator, stressed the role of the individual in seeking salvation and preached that perfection was available to those who desired it with the aid of the Holy Spirit. While a superintendent oversaw and defined the circuits that traveling preachers serviced, it was the weekly class meetings that were the foundation of Methodism. Occasional camp meetings, held by two or more ministers, also served as a source of group consciousness based on shared spiritual values. These planned gatherings made settlers feel less isolated and part of a community. The sermons ministers preached spoke of attributes that were central to settlers' lives including self-sufficiency, social equality, and individualism. The conversion experience itself provided worshipers with a release from the anxiety and frustration associated with frontier life.[52] The social and emotional content of Methodism adapted well to frontier life.

From 1784 to 1790 Cornwall Methodists independently sustained their faith. Samuel Empury organized prayer meetings at his home and scheduled periodic services with traveling ministers. The weekly gatherings strengthened the faith of attendees through prayer, joint study, and testimony. In 1790 Reverend William Losee from the New York Methodist Association assessed the number of Methodists in Canada and outlined two preaching circuits for ministers. The first extended to the west of Montreal and covered Prince Edward Island, while the other encompassed the eastern portion of Upper Canada and ended at Cornwall. American itinerant preachers visited Cornwall Methodists sporadically until the War of 1812, when their border crossings were restricted by national officials. On Christmas Day 1817, Reverend Henry Pope, a representative from the Methodist Church of the United States, arrived in Cornwall and reopened the old circuits abandoned during the war. Six years later, a camp meeting organized by Reverend William H. William resulted in many converts. Subsequently, Cornwall Methodists took steps to establish a permanent congregation. Local worshipers instituted a fund drive to raise cash for the construction of a church, while church leaders formed a search committee charged with recruiting a permanent minister. In 1839, there were 160 registered Cornwall Methodists.[53]

While the majority of Cornwall residents belonged to three religions that were traditionally hierarchically structured and administered—Catholicism, Anglicanism, and Protestantism—their isolated location and experiences in the former American colonies encouraged them to establish congregational organizations. In the absence of ministers, Cornwall residents took charge of their spiritual lives. They were successful at independently conducting meetings and saw no need to relinquish any control over church affairs to preachers or vestry members once they were hired or elected. Methodist ministers also built a strong congregation in Cornwall, as their style and beliefs complemented frontier living. The itinerant preachers' message of social equality raised the self-confidence of members of the lower classes and fueled their desire to overthrow the traditional social and political authority of the elite. The congregational method of governing churches had also strengthened the common citizens' willingness to criticize political officials and the government structure. In Cornwall, men led by Patrick McNiff challenged the authority of the former regimental commanders and created a contentious political atmosphere. As Sydney Ahlstrom stated, "A new epoch in the history of religious freedom had opened a new realm of political participation."[54]

The attempt to establish an organized governing structure in Cornwall exposed the differing political beliefs of the former military commanders and common citizens. Many Cornwall settlers cherished the participatory form of government they had established in the former colonies and wanted the same mechanisms developed in Upper Canada.[55] However, the former regimental commanders wanted to maintain their arbitrary rule. Beginning in 1784, Cornwall was ruled like a regimental camp. Former military leaders, including Sir John Johnson, Major John Gray, and Captain Alexander Macdonnell, supervised the allotment of land, settled grievances and disputes, and distributed government-sanctioned supplies. These revolutionary heroes also served as magistrates in the early court sessions. However, many of the loyalists resented the power assumed by former military leaders whose homes they had helped build and whose land they had cleared. As they were equal economically, they felt they should be on the same footing in the political arena. According to political historian Edgar McInnis, this distrust of military leaders and a desire of settlers with an American background for a system of representative government caused this informal governing system based on deference to fail.[56] Common citizens and regimental soldiers also clashed over the establishment of a permanent town government.

National government officials, Sir Guy Carleton, the head of the Canadian government and Stephen DeLancy, the inspector of the loyalists, first attempted to formalize the structure of town governments by ordering settlers of the royal townships to hold town meetings in 1787. The two leaders sent a letter describing the proper procedure for executing a town meeting and the election of town representatives. In Cornwall a conflict arose between former military leaders, including Captain Samuel Anderson and local activists led by Patrick McNiff, over who should conduct the meetings and be eligible for election as town delegates. Both Anderson and McNiff supporters campaigned for their candidates and distributed outlines of the inaugural meeting's agenda. When the gathering was held on July 12, 1787, Samuel Anderson, the current town magistrate, presided over the proceedings. Anderson and his counterparts hoped that the election of officials would take place without incident. However, McNiff and his supporters stood up and began to shout about the dictatorial power of the military leaders, calling for their removal and murder. Anderson and his fellow officers left in response to this verbal abuse. The citizens who remained at the meeting elected ten representatives, including McNiff, William Impey, Jonas Wood, and Donald McDonnal. After the votes were cast, the meeting was adjourned, and McNiff sent a list of the new officials to Sir Carleton.[57] However, Anderson and the other regiment commanders challenged the election results in a letter sent to Sir Carleton and De Lancy. In response to the controversy, Sir Carleton set aside the idea of locally appointed officials administering town affairs and instead created a regional and national political structure that controlled town affairs from above.[58]

In 1788 Sir Carleton established a provincial government headed by a lieutenant governor and supported by a popularly elected legislative assembly and a parliamentary appointed council. The main goal of the new provincial government created by Lord Dorchester was to keep popular movements and protests like those staged by McNiff in check by strengthening the authority of the government. During the nineteenth century, these officials collectively authored and implemented all provincial public policy.[59] The fundamental element of the new governmental system was the Court of General Quarter Sessions. Members were charged with managing the legal and financial affairs of four newly designated districts in western Quebec.

Until the 1830s members of the Quarter Session, who met biannually in each district, had jurisdiction over all criminal matters and town administrative duties and were presided over by six magistrates. Session officials also approved funds for road construction, collected taxes, and appointed various town officials and committees to perform certain daily municipal duties or complete special projects. Typical criminal cases handled by the sessions were petit larceny and the selling of spirits, which carried a light sentence of several lashings or a small monetary fine. While the names of many of the magistrates were recorded, transcripts describing the specific actions of the early sessions do not exist.[60]

The democratic political beliefs held by many Cornwall residents were different from those cherished by the settlers of Alexandria, Ontario, who were governed by a ruling aristocracy composed of former military officers and clerics. David Rayside noted that residents in Alexandria realized that the only way that their community would survive was if the majority of male settlers relinquished their political power to these upper-class men.[61] The initial protests of Patrick McNiff illustrated the support of the majority of Cornwall male citizens for the development of a participatory and egalitarian political system. The loyalists wanted a local government administered by elected officials who were responsible for completing municipal infrastructure projects and mediating financial disputes. Therefore, the attempt by British officials and Church of England leaders to stop American ideals from surfacing in the political arena initially failed.[62] In reality according to Gerald Craig, "The province is still overwhelmingly American in origin. The tone of communities is as republican and Yankee as across the river."[63] The town's geographic isolation and financial hardship affected Cornwall inhabitants regardless of their lineage or previous military rank and made the values of the early loyalists more similar to those of their neighbors in Massena.

Massena

New York State officials encouraged the settlement of Massena, New York following the American Revolution to prevent the British from expanding their present territory. The region was first discovered by Jacques Cartier on his exploration of northern waterways in 1536. Following the Revolutionary War, New York State officials purchased land in the last unsettled part of the state from the Seven Nations of Canada.[64] The New York State legislature subsequently offered land grants to revolutionary soldiers and sold the remaining acreage at public auction. Alexander Macomb, a land speculator and adventurer, purchased 3,670,715 acres in 1787, including the present location of Massena, and divided the property into ten townships. Macomb had his land surveyed and sold plots to the highest bidder.[65]

The first permanent Massena settlers were predominantly young men and their families from nearby Vermont and New England searching for available land on the newly opened frontier. As Leonard Prince indicated, "Word of cheap land along the northern border of New York State filtered into New England. Young men were eager to move westward and northward or wherever they could secure cheap land."[66] Most of the area was covered by dense forest, occupied by roaming Indians, and characterized by explorers as having a rugged and severe landscape.[67] Therefore, during the first decades of settlement, life was filled with hardship and disease and conflicts with the Indians over property boundaries. These unpleasant conditions killed off entire families and influenced others to leave the region.[68] However, the land disputes were eventually resolved through treaties between the St. Regis Indians and the state government. Remaining settlers achieved self-sufficiency and developed social and political institutions among a widespread and often transient population.

Massena lies on the far or distant periphery of New York State. Originally comprising 30,671 acres, Massena was the last unsettled part of the state at the end of eighteenth century. The only access to the region was via poorly marked trails. Therefore, the original settlers arrived with all their personal belongings and necessary supplies, as they anticipated never returning to their old homesteads. The waterways became the main local and international transportation routes traveled by passenger boat and barge captains. Settlers also constructed mills to produce building materials and grind wheat and corn into meal and flour. Therefore, Massena was characterized by longtime local residents as a self-reliant small town with a shifting population. It was initially the fertile land, potential waterpower, and accessible timber that made Massena an attractive area for settlement.

Geologists considered Massena's climate and soil as being favorable for certain types of crop cultivation. The 150-day growing season was similar to the average in the central part of the state. The annual rainfall of 29.1 inches provided an ample water supply for most crops, while the nearby rivers provided alternative irrigation during times of drought.[69] Most soil in Massena was clay loam, which was rich in nutrients and could support a variety of vegetation. The most fertile land was along the riverbanks where the recession of water had left abundant mineral deposits. Until the 1820s, wheat was the staple crop harvested to feed livestock, including sheep and poultry, while potatoes and corn were planted for human consumption. However, the clearing of land by male settlers exposed fertile soil for growing hay for dairy cattle.

Many of the early settlers were also lumbermen. The dense forests of pine that originally surrounded the town were excellent sources of shipbuilding timber. Manufacturers in Montreal, a nearby shipbuilding center, provided a ready market for the processed wood. Spars ranging from 80 to 110 feet were floated down the river to other areas of Quebec for use in furniture manufacturing. In 1810 it was estimated that $60,000 worth of timber was rafted to Canadian cities annually by local lumbermen.[70] Locally, the founding fathers used the wood to build log cabins and construct churches and bridges. The lumbering business ebbed with the progress of settlement around 1828. Many residents turned to farming or business ownership as a way to earn a living. While the land along the St. Lawrence River was well-suited for farming, it was the swift current of the area's waterways and timber that attracted the initial pioneers.

Amable Foucher was the first individual to reside in the previously unsettled region of New York State, now known as Massena. In 1792 the French-Canadian entrepreneur left his hometown of Old Chateaugay near Montreal and traveled across the U.S.–Canadian border in search of a location for a sawmill. He leased land from the St. Regis Indians for $200 per year and built a dam and a sawmill on the Grasse River, where he processed lumber for shipbuilding. Foucher recruited workers and their families from Canada, including Francois Boutte, Jean Deloge, and Joseph Dubois, whom he housed in a log cabin settlement bordering the mill.[71] For almost a decade, Foucher's cluster of cabins and a mill were the only settlement and manufacturing operation in the area. Foucher operated his mill until 1808 when New York State officials bought the property and, in turn, sold it to Lemuel Haskell.[72] Haskell was among the many migrants who came to Massena in search of cheap land. He was joined by one of Foucher's workers, Antoine Lamping, who was one of the few lumbermen to make the transition from transient worker to permanent resident and was involved in gaining a town charter.

The official founding of Massena, New York was related to the establishment of St. Lawrence County in 1802.[73] Residents of the original ten townships wanted a county seat closer than Plattsburgh in Clinton County to conduct legal and financial transactions.[74] With more than 100 miles of rough trails and dense forest between some of the townships and the original administrative center, male residents found it difficult to pay taxes and attend court sessions. Therefore, in 1802, 156 men including Anthony Lamping, Amos Lay, and William Polley, signed a legislative petition requesting that a county be organized by New York State lawmakers along the St. Lawrence River.[75] On March 3, 1802, the New York State Legislature designated St. Lawrence County as the state's thirty-first county. The initial structure of the county consisted of four townships: Lisbon, Oswegatchie, Madrid, the new town of Massena, and a county seat located in nearby Ogdensburg.[76] Massena's isolated location forced each family to build its own house and raise all necessary food for people and livestock. Similar to their Cornwall counterparts, Massena pioneers' selection of land, development of homesteads, and initial crop selection followed a standard pattern referred to by agricultural historians Percy Bidwell and John Falconer as the "Yankee system."[77]

Daniel Robinson from Shrewsbury, Vermont was the most well-known example of an early Massena settler. In the fall of 1802, Robinson, in his early twenties, visited several areas in northern New York and Canada searching for a location for his new family farm. Before being directed to the fertile land in Massena by the St. Regis Indians, he visited Ogdensburg, New York and Cornwall, Ontario and found nothing suitable. When Robinson arrived in Massena, he selected a plot on the Grasse River and camped there for several days before returning to Vermont. He then journeyed to Utica to legalize his purchase of 1,400 acres at $3.00 an acre.[78]

In March 1803 Robinson returned to his newly acquired property with two men and two oxen, and cleared four acres of land by cutting down trees and burning the logs and the underbrush. Next, he planted corn and wheat for the year's harvest, constructed a log cabin, and erected fences around his property to keep out Indians and wild animals.[79] Robinson's first year progress of deforesting four acres was more than the national pioneer average of one to three acres per year. According to agricultural experts, it usually took a farmer four to five years to reach a level where he had cleared enough land to harvest adequate food and build appropriate shelter for his family.[80] In February 1804 Robinson traveled to Vermont and married 16-year-old Esther Kilbourne, whom he brought to his new home in Massena, along with his sister and brother-in-law, Mr. and Mrs. Elisha Denison, who had purchased a plot a mile away.[81]

The initial housing Massena's male settlers constructed was very primitive and offered little privacy to family members. Most log huts consisted of a single room, where family members ate and slept and where livestock was often sheltered in the winter. A first-hand description of a couple's first house in the nearby town of Hopkinton indicated, "The house consisted of one room in which they all slept and did all the work. Every night they led the cow in and tied her in the corner."[82] Men collectively constructed these shanties with wooden poles held together by notches on each end. They filled the gaps between the logs with clay, mud, and straw. The roof was composed of bark and split boards. Families heated their houses with a primitive fireplace comprised of a stack of stones piled in a circle in the center of the floor. Most log huts also had at least one window and a door cut in the wall. Wives often covered the former with a wooden shingle or piece of oil paper to keep the draft out. Men blocked the latter with heavy wooden doors fastened from inside with a metal bar at night. Storage areas were also built to hold grain and vegetables during the winter months, as most of the cabins were assembled without cellars.[83] According to a traveler in the late eighteenth century, "In such dark, dirty, and dismal habitations, the pioneer family lived for at least 10 to 15 years and often longer."[84]

In their first spring in Massena, the male settlers, similar to Cornwall loyalists twenty years earlier, cleared and plowed more fields for crop cultivation and deforested other areas to serve as pastures for horses, cows, and sheep. According to Bidwell and Falconer, "The early farm equipment was awkward, heavy, and poorly designed, which made land clearing and crop cultivation hard and tedious."[85] Franklin Benjamin Hough described one settler's efforts to clear his land. "In 1800 Daniel Harrington having commenced a small improvement the fall before, which consisted of a slight clearing on the bank of the river, where he sowed less than an acre of land to wheat; and having no team to assist him, he harrowed the grain with a hand rake."[86] Men also slaughtered livestock, which provided a major part of their diet, and supplied ingredients for medicinal, household, and building products. The settlers made calves' foot jelly for the treatment of ulcers and other skin irritations, tanned hides for boots and door hinges, processed tallow for candles, and stuffed pillows and bedding with goose feathers. As most Massena farmers had no steady income, local residents set up a bartering system with neighbors and Cornwall residents to exchange labor and goods. In return for assisting a neighbor in harvesting crops or building a new barn, local residents received a piece of livestock or assistance during the next year's haying season.

While the men were responsible for crop cultivation, construction of buildings, and managing financial matters, Massena women were in charge of the upkeep of the log cabins. According to Phoebe Orvis, a longtime resident of Hopkinton, her main domestic duties included childcare, cleaning, cooking, sewing, and washing and ironing the family's clothing.[87] Orvis also described in her diary how women gathered in small groups to weave flax into linen. The cloth was then sewn into garments for all members of the family. Sheep's wool was also carded, washed, and spun into yarn for sweaters and blankets. Female settlers produced all of their families' clothing and bedding. Bidwell and Falconer noted, "From his head to his feet, the farmer stood in vestment produced on his own farm."[88] However, a female inhabitant's most important daily duty was the preparation and presentation of the evening family meal. A common dinner consisted of hot or cold bean porridge, a bowl of vegetables, and some brown bread. The evening meal was the one time of the day when family members gathered around the table to eat and pray. Socially, women also organized and supplied food for various community gatherings. As Eleanor Dumas summed up, "Parties and dancing went hand and hand with barn raising, housewarmings and the long winter evenings when families could get together."[89] Massena settlers lived undisturbed in their isolated location for almost a decade.

Upon the outbreak of the War of 1812, Massena residents realized that their geographical location did not entirely isolate them from national conflicts. Regardless of their decade-long peaceful coexistence, many residents, including Robinson, feared raids or attacks by Indians or the British. Massena and the U.S.–Canadian border were guarded by 250 militiamen. However, town life was never really altered by the border conflict since no battle ever took place near Massena. The only local incident was the burning of the troops' barracks in September 1813 by a unit of 300 Canadian militiamen under the command of Major Joseph Anderson, who were stationed across the St. Lawrence River in Cornwall. As proof of their accomplishment, the militia commanders took several prisoners back with them to Cornwall and sank numerous boats anchored on the river. However, the American soldiers were released within a few days and no other invasion occurred.[90] While the War of 1812 had few ill-effects on Massena, its border location, like Cornwall's, made it susceptible to foreign invasion.

After the war, Massena residents moved out of log cabins and into framed homes. The new houses were grander than the first, with more rooms, elaborate entrances, and landscaped grounds often adorned with peacocks. In 1816 Montreal bricklayers built the first brick house in the area for Daniel Robinson with imported materials from Vermont. Many of Robinson's neighbors also constructed new homes out of more durable material.[91] From 1825 to 1833 Captain John Haskell, Benjamin Phillips, and John Belfield Andrews each built stone houses on Andrews, Phillips, and Tamarack Streets. Day laborers under the supervision of a foreman completed these homes in two years. Workmen chiseled the 10-inch-thick stone for the exterior walls from the bed of the Grasse River and dragged the slabs to each site with oxen. They then mortared the 30-inch walls with lime cured on-site in kilns. The houses also had wooden porches, cellars, four fireplaces, and 9-foot ceilings. A heavy front door opened into a central hallway with a large staircase.[92]

During the first decade of Massena, the life of early settlers was akin to that of Cornwall residents two decades earlier because of their isolated location. Men and women became self-sufficient, raised children, and built a small community based on mutual values and beliefs. Citizens cooperatively built homes, cleared land, and harvested crops. All male settlers faced the same struggles related to farming and crop cultivation in a previously unpopulated area, regardless of the amount of land they owned. As Franklin Benjamin Hough concluded, "If anyone needed a helping hand, his desire need but be announced to be heeded."[93] Massena settlers also initially established religious congregations as a means of creating shared spiritual experiences among a scattered population. Settlers brought with them religious beliefs and ideas about government that reflected their New England heritage and, therefore, created institutions that embodied these common values. Besides praying daily for good harvests and health, the male residents saw religion as a way to instill moral behavior in their children and control the actions of their fellow citizens.

The religious experience of Massena residents mirrored that of their Cornwall neighbors as they too organized congregational and voluntary associations. Their shared heritage and isolated locations challenged individuals on both sides of the border who wanted to practice their faith to independently conduct meetings and to develop spiritual organizations in the absence of traditional clergy. Between 1800 and 1840 Massena settlers met weekly for prayer services and were visited periodically by traveling preachers. These loosely organized congregations were the town's central social and cultural organizations. As Sydney Ahlstrom indicated, "To a lonely, scattered people, they brought vital fellowship of an intimate personal concern."[94] While loyalists created Presbyterian, Church of England, and Catholic congregations, the founding fathers of Massena adhered to the more sectarian and evangelical faiths of Congregationalism and Methodism. However, regardless of their denominational differences, religious worshipers on both sides of the border remained in charge of their own spiritual lives and the administration of their churches.

The Congregational Church was considered by historians as the first denomination formed in Massena and exemplified the establishment of a church based on the New England Puritan model.[95] Congregationalism was a mutation of the fundamental beliefs and practices of Puritanism. When the Puritan movement died, the evangelicalistic spirit within it was reborn in Congregationalism. The church had gained members after the American Revolution because of the appeal of its system of self-government to citizens who had just fought for political independence. The Congregationalists formed churches whose members determined who were saints, who should be disciplined, and who should be ordained as ministers. They suggested that the inhabitants of new settlements follow a typical pattern of development. Initially pioneers should form a church comprised of the town's visible saints. These men and women then added to their congregations by interviewing those who could give credible accounts of their conversion experience. Once a significant number of worshipers had been identified and a church organized, funds were raised to erect a meetinghouse. This building often then served as a location for the town's other civic and political gatherings.

Congregational missionaries from Vermont and Massachusetts accompanied settlers to their new homesteads in Massena and assisted them in establishing proper worshiping and living habits. Early congregation members were described by a church historian in a 1946 brochure as "resourceful, accustomed to hardship, generally God-fearing, and outspoken."[96] The original church pledge required the male head of a household to read the scriptures daily with his family, pray every morning and evening, and never allow dancing, excessive drinking, or gambling to occur in his presence.[97] As historian Mary Ryan indicated, it was "the duty of parents to educate and sanctify their children. God had appointed them as the head of the family and it was their responsibility to ensure their offspring remained faithful."[98] Massena settlers also periodically reaffirmed and strengthened their spirituality by observing days of fasting and humiliation. For four years, the Congregationalists held prayer meetings frequently in the homes of various members of the congregation. However, following the 1806 visit of Amos Pettengill and Boyd Phelps, two missionaries from Vermont, services were held on a more regular basis. From 1806 to 1817, Congregationalists attended weekly sermons by a minister from a neighboring church in Madrid.[99]

In April 1819 Wealthy Porter and Dr. William Paddock formally organized Massena's First Congregational Church. Reverend Ambrose Porter was the congregation's first full-time minister. Porter and his thirty-three worshipers created a formal administrative body composed of church elders, who were charged with setting and enforcing the strict guidelines of the faith, as well as judging the worthiness of new members. Massena residents, who wanted to join the congregation, appeared before the church elders, described their conversion experience, and professed why they believed in God. Only those who passed the test gained admission to the congregation.[100] For fourteen years the Congregationalists met in the town schoolhouse, recruited new members, and remained the largest denomination in the area. In 1836 the Massena Congregationalists jointly funded the construction of a 300-seat meetinghouse with members of the Baptist and Adventist churches.[101] The leaders of this faith offered Massena settlers some regularity in their lives, while still appealing to their desires to have a personal relationship with God. The town's founding fathers were also attracted to Methodism for similar reasons.

During early settlement the Methodists were the only challengers for the souls of the Massena faithful. Beginning in 1805 Massena Methodists were visited periodically by circuit riders who were charged with preaching to worshipers in northern New York. These ministers, who conducted services in private homes and schoolhouses, were described in church histories as "young men on horseback with hearts aflame who rode across the country seeking to light similar flames in the hearts of settlers."[102] William McLoughlin indicated that these men spoke the language of the common man, democratized religion, and broke down class lines.[103] Most riders traveled along established routes, and Massena was included on a circuit with Malone, Ogdensburg, and Potsdam. These preachers were very successful at gaining new followers because, unlike their Protestant counterparts, they were willing to venture into the backwoods areas and preach to members of the rural community. Comparable to their brethren in Canada, Methodist ministers reached every corner of America's new frontier and delivered spiritual guidance to their followers, including the male and female settlers of Massena. The class meetings also remained the central focus of local church life. From

1810 to 1834 the Massena Methodist lay readers conducted prayer meetings in spaces donated by various members of the community and continued to attract new members.

Both the Congregational and Methodist leadership created evangelical and sectarian churches whose practices related well to frontier life. Unlike in Rochester, New York where, according to Paul Johnson, manufacturers and business owners used religion as a means of establishing control over their workers, religious participation in Massena was voluntary and open to all members of society.[104] Similar to their Cornwall counterparts, Massena residents took charge of their own spirituality for most of the nineteenth century in the absence of full-time preachers.[105]

Massena settlers' egalitarian and congregational spiritual beliefs and their trust in the ability of anyone to govern influenced their early political life and allowed men from a variety of social and professional backgrounds to serve in public office. In 1802 the New York State Legislature passed the original county charter empowering the residents of Massena to establish locally based legal and political structures. The court of common pleas and circuit court were charged with deciding criminal and civil complaints, while town meetings administered by elected officials authorized the construction of roads, allotted funds for the poor, and dealt with other miscellaneous town matters.[106] Early town officials included a supervisor, town clerk, assessor, overseer of the poor, commissioner of highways, and superintendent of schools.

The first town meeting took place in Massena in 1803 at the home of Peter Tarbell. It is not known specifically who attended the meeting, except that those present implemented a traditional town government structure with a supervisor at the helm. During the course of the proceedings, the first roster of town officials was elected. They included: Matthew Perkins, serving as town supervisor; Ezekiel Colburn, filling the position of town clerk; Elisha Barber, Elisha Denison, and Jacob Chase fulfilling the duties of highway commissioners; and, John Wilson and John Reed overseeing the maintenance of the poor.[107] Massena residents were, therefore, ruled by successful farmers, professionals, and business owners.[108] An analysis of town supervisors from 1802 to 1900 revealed that the post was held by seven farmers, two lawyers, three lumbermen, one surveyor, one horse dealer, two innkeepers, one banker, and ten merchants.[109] In contrast to Cornwall, town meetings became a permanent fixture of the democratic, locally elected Massena government that concentrated on completing road projects and developing a social welfare system.

Similar to officials in most frontier towns, Massena's inaugural administration surveyed and constructed a system of passable roads and established a financial assistance program for the poor. The first Massena road was completed in 1803. The Middle Road to Hopson's Corner, as it was subsequently called, began at the mouth of the Racquette River.[110] With the town government in place, the commissioner of highways implemented a program of subscription to fund and to provide the labor to complete other roadways. Under the plan, each freeholder worked a number of days on highway construction near his property based on the amount of acreage he possessed. The landowner could either fulfill the obligation personally or send a substitute.[111] These men were also responsible for the long-term maintenance of these roads. According to Hal S. Barron in *Mixed Harvest: The Second Great Transformation in the Rural North*, this policy of financing road projects with labor instead of a cash tax was typical in northern rural towns until the 1870s.[112] Over the next several years, Massena male settlers completed a number of interconnecting roads, making local travel and journeys to neighboring towns more manageable.

Early town leaders also addressed the financial matter of maintaining the poor. Many new residents did not become self-sufficient because they could not afford to purchase a plot of land on which to raise cattle and harvest vegetables. These individuals, therefore, could not participate in the bartering system, an integral part of Massena's agricultural community. Additionally, the owners of sawmills and other small factories did not hire a substantial number of workers to man their operations, and there were few employment opportunities in neighboring towns. Furthermore, many orphans, widows, and men who were injured in crippling accidents required financial assistance. With no formalized program of state relief, town leaders kept citizens out of the poorhouse by offering them tax-funded cash allowances. In the first three decades of the town's existence, government leaders approved more than $1,000 in aid for the poor, including $500 in 1818 and $200 in 1820 to assist settlers in the new Deer River section of the village.[113] The willingness of individuals to have their tax dollars spent to help others exemplified the persistence of residents' community-oriented values fostered during the pioneer days. Most successful male residents, while motivated to prosper financially, never lost their sense of obligation to assist those less fortunate.

Male Massena residents elected government officials who embodied their mutual values and beliefs, and who concentrated on managing town financial affairs and instigating dispute resolution among residents while not infringing on their individual rights.[114] These included substantial landowners, merchants, entrepreneurs, farmers, and businessmen. All garnered the authority to direct town affairs and to decide criminal punishments because of the deference and respect of their fellow citizens. The democratic municipal government established by Massena male settlers was contrary to the achievements of their Cornwall neighbors, who shared comparable values and desires, but failed to implement a corresponding political institution until 1834. By the 1830s residents were making Massena their permanent home and were building social ties with other families.

In summary the experiences of Massena's early settlers were similar to those of the Cornwall loyalists because of their peripheral location and comparable environmental circumstances. Both settlements were far from commercial centers and were only connected to neighboring towns by dirt trails. Therefore, the founding fathers of Cornwall and Massena were forced to become self-sufficient. The fertile land and ample water supply allowed male residents to grow enough food to feed their families and livestock. The abundant trees provided lumber for log cabins and served as a commodity settlers sold for cash. Women produced all their families' clothing and organized social events to offer relief from the hard frontier life and to bring neighbors together. The original inhabitants of Cornwall and Massena also established independent congregations whose members held weekly prayer meetings. Due to their distance from major towns, they only saw an ordained minister annually, and were otherwise responsible for their own spiritual maintenance. Life for the founding fathers of Cornwall and Massena and their families, therefore, was very primitive. They struggled to develop a community and survive in a desolate area isolated from family and friends.

The border location of Cornwall and Massena also made inhabitants susceptible to foreign invasion. Both areas had been settled following the American Revolution to prevent territorial expansion by the neighboring country. Cornwall had always maintained a militia in case the border needed to be defended. Until 1812 Cornwall and Massena, however, were not involved in national conflicts between their untrusting nations. Instead, they had often assisted each other in times of need. In 1812 male residents of both towns were drawn into a national conflict and put on a constant state of alert. While Cornwall residents played a more major role in defending the border, life was disrupted in both areas for several years. The once interdependent and porous border temporarily became closed.

Finally, Cornwall and Massena pioneers were both citizens of the former American colonies and, therefore, harbored the same congregational and democratic spiritual and political beliefs. Cornwall settlers held contrasting values and goals from central government officials and those in the heartland. This often led to conflict. Many of the loyalists were recent migrants from the United States and they wanted the same political and religious organizations they had grown accustomed to in their former hometowns. These included congregational churches and a democratic local government elected by all citizens. These values and beliefs put Cornwall residents at odds with central government officials and former regimental commanders who wanted to establish a hierarchical and authoritarian government supported by an official state religion. While male settlers in both towns wanted a democratic and participatory form of government, only Massena residents succeeded in implementing town meetings overseen by popularly elected officials prior to 1834. After 1834 the two areas would continue along the same trajectory based on the completion of canal projects and the commercialization of agriculture.

CHAPTER TWO

The Canal Era and the First Manufacturing Boom in Cornwall and Massena, 1834–1900

The completion of canal and hydropower projects on the St. Lawrence River in the nineteenth century triggered the industrialization of Cornwall and Massena. Both areas were located near fast-running water. However, during the early decades of settlement, the areas' isolation, combined with their unharnessed waterpower, prevented economic growth. North American factory owners who traditionally situated mills near developed power sources and main transportation routes saw no advantages to establishing plants in either Cornwall or Massena. The economies of both towns, therefore, remained agriculturally based. Cornwall and Massena farmers were leaders in the production of cheese and milk, and cultivated grain and vegetables for local and regional distribution. Socially, the population in both areas remained ethnically unchanged. The economic and social makeup of the two towns, however, was altered during the construction of the Cornwall canal in 1843 and the Massena canal in 1898. While the canal projects were forty years apart, their conclusion signaled the advent of the industrial era in both towns.

During the construction of the waterways, Cornwall and Massena residents witnessed a diversification of the population and religious worshipers. Contractors on both sides of the border needed a large workforce willing to perform hard and often dangerous manual labor. Since this type of occupation did not attract many local residents, foreign workers were recruited from Montreal and New York City. Many did not speak English and most were practicing Catholics. The arrival of Irish and Italian canal and industrial workers diversified the Cornwall and Massena populations and engendered nativist responses. Therefore, manufacturers constructed separate housing for their workers, and church leaders organized new congregations in working-class neighborhoods. Catholic congregations surpassed the membership of Cornwall and Massena's other houses of worship, and competed with them for new worshipers and financial contributions. These new residents, therefore, altered and expanded the existing social organizations of both towns. By 1900 Cornwall and Massena possessed identical social, political, and economic structures.

The impact and timing of industrialization in Cornwall and Massena were comparable based on environmental factors and geographic location. Both towns attracted factory owners after the completion of canal projects. However, industrialization came later to these locales than to other areas due to their distance from commercial centers. Even with the construction of a canal in Cornwall, it took two decades for Montreal investors to risk their capital in ventures in this backwoods town. In Massena, only one manufacturer was willing to locate in this peripheral location. Both areas, however, experienced more ethnic diversity than their more homogeneous rural neighbors and more evangelical religious customs than their compatriots in the nations' cities. Evidence suggests that Cornwall and Massena remained similar to each other based on their isolated border location and waterpower. The construction of the Cornwall canal first introduced outsiders to the area, and later attracted entrepreneurs.

Constructed between 1834 and 1843, the Cornwall Canal was the third in a series of nationally funded projects built along the St. Lawrence River between Montreal and Cornwall. Each improved inland water transport and expanded the country's hydrogenerated power.[1] The members of the Upper Canada Parliament initially discussed the project in 1816 because of the difficulties military commanders encountered transporting their troops and supplies up and down the St. Lawrence River during the War of 1812.[2] In 1818 members of a provincially appointed commission studied the specific geographic and economic aspects of such an undertaking. Following lengthy parliamentary debates about the waterway's merit and substantial price tag, national officials authorized the Cornwall Canal project on February 13, 1833. A decade later, contractors completed the original 11½-mile-long canal.[3] However, soon after the conclusion of the project, the Canadian government's transportation minister realized that the water depth and width of the locks could not adequately accommodate the ships of the age.[4] Over the next fifty years, Irish workers undertook numerous expansion projects and committed several murders. This violent behavior put them at odds with Cornwall residents.

Cornwall's location near the canal forced residents to deal with foreigners sooner than their immediate neighbors. The Board of Works and private contractors employed more than 1,000 Irish laborers on the Cornwall Canal between 1834 and 1842. Most laborers lived in shanty huts near the canal site and shopped at the company store. Poor living conditions and high unemployment rates led to violence.[5] Historian J. F. Pringle notes, "Hundreds of men were employed on the various contracts and it was only natural that there should be a rough element who were constantly making trouble."[6] Local inhabitants distrusted the Irish canal workers and expected them to abide by the law and adopt Canadian religious and social values. As Oscar Martinez indicates, "In the case of isolated villages, discord with other groups may arise out of fear and resentment triggered by encroachment from outsiders."[7]

When canal workers murdered deputy sheriff Ewen Stuart in 1834 and former Lieutenant Governor Albert French two years later, animosity arose between the Irish laborers and longtime Cornwall inhabitants, and exposed the latter's fear and lack of tolerance for immigrants.[8] After the repeated violent crimes committed by canal workers, many residents considered the roads bordering the canal unsafe for travel and took alternate routes.[9] In September 1835 Cornwall magistrates applied to Lieutenant Governor John Colbourne for military assistance in maintaining order and public safety until the project's completion. According to a *Cornwall Observer* editor, "After this sacrifice of one of our most respected townsmen, Sir John Colbourne cannot refuse two companies at least to guard our jail and maintain our laws."[10] In 1836, the troops arrived and remained stationed in Cornwall until 1843.[11] Local congregation leaders also became involved in controlling the criminal behavior of canal workers, which they attributed to the Irishmen's heavy drinking. However, French's murder reinforced Cornwall residents' characterization of the Irish as unruly drunks.[12] The tolerance of local residents for outsiders was again tested when Cornwall's new mill owners employed French Canadians.

The peripheral location of Cornwall prevented industrialization for several decades, as Montreal investors preferred to finance manufacturing enterprises closer to the country's established commercial centers. Unlike their New England counterparts, they did not see the value in building mills in virginal locations. For almost twenty years following the completion of the new waterway, the dams along the canal exclusively provided a cheap source of power for locally owned flour and grist mills. Therefore, according to a longtime resident, "Cornwall (in 1850) remains stationary, the actual number of inhabitants being but 1506. . . . It is a neat, quiet old-fashioned place with several good houses. Cornwall is not a place of good business."[13] Most residents still earned a living as farmers.

Following the completion of the canal project, Cornwall farmers concentrated on improving their property and diversifying their crops. They purchased new farm equipment, cleared more land, and produced dairy products. Based on their successful marketing of vegetable, grain, and milk products, farmers bought larger amounts of land and met shifting consumer demands by altering their crop selections. Between 1861 and 1881, the census reported an increase in the number of Cornwall farmers who cultivated over fifty acres of land and split their efforts between grain and vegetable harvesting and maintaining dairy herds. In 1861, 649 residents occupied plots under fifty acres, while 419 farmers owned over fifty acres. By 1881, however, the number of agriculturists occupying plots of land under fifty acres declined from 649 to 399, but those who lived on farms over fifty acres rose from 419 to 508. The most substantial change was in the number of cows owned and the amount of butter produced. Cornwall dairymen owned 4,382 cows and yielded 400,756 pounds of butter in 1881, making them the region's leading milk and butter producers.[14] Cornwall farmers were driven by ambition and a desire to be financially successful. They took the risk of clearing more land and planting new crops as a means of becoming participants in the commercial market. The new industrialists who arrived in Cornwall between 1867 and 1890 also shared these values and business practices.

Cornwall's transformation from a farming community to a manufacturing town commenced as entrepreneurs sought favorable locations for factories near canals and dams. According to Jeremy Stein, the establishment of three mills in Cornwall between 1868 and 1882 was consistent with the growth of the consumer goods industry in the province of Ontario at mid-century.[15] After 1850 manufacturing became an increasingly important component of the Canadian economy, partially replacing agriculture and natural resource extraction.[16] The construction of a series of canals and the establishment of bonusing systems by government officials were the key elements for the expansion of the industrial bases of towns near the St. Lawrence River. The St. Lawrence canals also provided manufacturers a transport route for their raw materials and finished goods. Ian Drummond surmised that from 1870 to 1890 industrialists established plants in all parts of Ontario along the new canals. The most successful entrepreneurs were those who produced cotton textiles and woolens and received financial assistance from national and local governments.[17]

Cornwall leaders developed a municipal bonusing program to provide mill owners with start-up cash, tax incentives, and emergency loans. Andrew Hodge, a former mill operator and current town councilor, stated, "This municipal council duly recognizing the importance of manufacturing in this country . . . pledges to aid and assist all cotton, woolen and other similar factories which may be established within the municipality."[18] The extension of financial assistance to new companies was not unique to Cornwall. Federal government officials adopted a bonusing system to promote the development of new manufacturing plants. In 1870 the members of the Quebec legislature approved the practice of offering 10-year tax exemptions and cash bonusing to industrialists "for the purpose of encouraging the introduction and establishment of new manufacturing of all kinds."[19] Subsequently, the leaders of most municipalities copied this practice. Most offered company owners, who agreed to construct a new factory in their town and remain for a certain number of years, 3-year tax exemptions and other cash bonuses. The long-term success Cornwall's economy garnered from this practice was second to none. As Ian Drummond stated, "Where municipal assistance was forthcoming, the results could be spectacular."[20]

Cornwall's population was also increased by the arrival of French-Canadian factory operatives recruited from outside the area by mill owners. As in New England, French Canadians were the first and most important group of mill workers. Quebec's provincial farmers no longer had enough land to pass on to their male offspring. Therefore, employment opportunities in Cornwall caused an unprecedented migration. As in America, mill operators found the Quebecois ideally suited for unskilled textile work. They were characterized as docile, not overly ambitious, and primarily concerned with making a living for themselves and their families. Most also willingly sent their wives and children to work in the mills. French Canadians were the first employees of George Stephen at his pioneering textile factory. Stephen's success caused Montreal businessmen to recognize Cornwall as an advantageous location for plants. They, in turn, invested thousands of dollars in the construction and maintenance of two additional cotton mills and a paper mill. Like their New England counterparts, it was the water power and available land along the canal that initially appealed to manufacturers.

In 1867 Cornwall's location on a canal and its underdevelopment caught the eye of George Stephen, a young entrepreneur trained in textile manufacturing. Stephen, a native of Scotland, had emigrated to Montreal in 1850 to work as a clerk at his cousin's dry goods store. His cousin's best-selling items were home-crafted goods including tweeds and blankets. Stephen determined that there was a limited supply of these low quality products and was determined to open a manufacturing operation to mass-produce blankets. He first, however, had to learn the textile trade. Stephen, therefore, moved to Almonte, Mississippi in the 1860s to become a partner in a family-run woolen mill. After several years at the U.S. plant, he saw the potential for a similar operation in Cornwall, Ontario because of the area's accessible waterpower.[21]

Following the Waltham plan, Stephen found a favorable location for the plant along the Cornwall canal between Mack's flour mill and the pottery works and organized a joint stock company with several other Montreal businessmen to fund the endeavor.[22] The Cornwall Manufacturing Corporation became official in 1867. Sir Hugh Allan, the largest shareholder, was at the helm and Stephen served as vice president. Stephen's mill commenced production in 1868 and dominated the otherwise rural landscape. Having gained water rights on the canal, the factory was driven by waterwheels and produced Canadian tweed blankets and flannels for a national and international market. The facility included a dye house, storehouse, and tenant cottages for workers in addition to the main mill building.[23]

A fire destroyed Stephen's original mill in 1870 and forced Cornwall officials to adopt a program of industrial assistance. While Allan and Stephen vowed to rebuild the enterprise, they were unable to personally fund the reconstruction due to the large sum of their initial investments. They, therefore, solicited financial assistance from town officials. The members of the Cornwall Town Council created a tax-funded incentive program that lasted into the next century. In the initial agreement with Cornwall Manufacturing, town officials consented to a 10-year tax exemption and a $4,000 bonus paid over six years to the company's owners if they constructed a plant on the original site and agreed to continually employ at least 100 workers.[24] Employment levels peaked in 1887 when the company employed 750 workers with an average monthly payroll of $18,000.[25] Within thirteen years the machines at the plant were silenced.

The closure of the Cornwall Manufacturing plant in 1900 and its merger with the two other local cotton mills illustrated a trend in Canadian manufacturing. As R. T. Naylor notes, after the depression from 1892 to 1904, as mill owners' profits decreased, many combined their operations. Until 1890 the Canadian industrial structure was comprised of small firms with local orientation and investors mostly producing consumer goods. After the turn of the century, the owners of large integrated manufacturing operations created by mergers prevailed in controlling domestic competition and prices.[26] Regardless of Cornwall Manufacturing's short existence, local historians Elinor Senior and J. F. Pringle credited its founder, George Stephen, with expediting the development of a bonusing program by Cornwall government officials and with encouraging other entrepreneurs to locate facilities on the canal.[27]

Based on the success of Stephen's mill, Andrew and Robert Gault opened the Stormont Cotton Manufacturing plant in 1870. Similar to Stephen, the Gaults were dry goods merchants from Montreal who wanted to manufacture woolen products to sell wholesale and retail. The brothers purchased a mill from John Harvey in 1869 and replaced his operation with a new factory. Fire also destroyed their plant in 1874. The Gaults subsequently solicited $10,000 from local lawmakers to cover rebuilding costs and insisted on a long-term tax exemption. A public vote at a November 11, 1878 town council meeting approved the cash grant and tax reprieve by a large margin of 222 to 23.[28] When builders completed the new building in 1880, it housed 250 looms operated by 300 employees, who produced gray sheeting, gingham, and denim. The following year an addition to the new structure doubled the number of looms and increased the workforce to 520.[29] In 1892 former competitors Stephen and the Gaults merged their operations under the name Canadian Colored Cotton Mills Limited with Archibald Gault as the president. According to R. T. Naylor, "It was clear that merger was the only solution to the stabilization problem and for cotton, with it interlocking directorships, merger was a relatively easy step."[30]

Bennett Rosamond, a partner of Stephen's in Mississippi, Montreal businessmen Edward MacKay and Donald Smith, and Cornwall mill owner John Harvey, financed a third cotton plant under the name of Canadian Cotton Manufacturing that proved to be the most technically advanced. They arranged financing for the initial construction of the plant and then turned over the management of the facility to Allan and Stephen. In 1872 Rosamond and his associates received cash bonuses, tax exemptions, and land from Cornwall officials. The red brick building was four stories high, 310 feet in length, 90 feet in width, and bordered the canal. The 20,000 spindles and 500 looms gave the facility the capacity to employ 400 workers. Cotton workers made sheeting, shirting, and seamless bags for flour and grain. Rosamond also erected several boardinghouses for operatives near the mill, whose landlords charged women $8 and men $10 monthly in board. By 1879 the seventy-nine employees worked 12-hour shifts from 6:30 A.M. to 6:30 P.M. for $1.75 to $3.00 per day in wages.

Rosamond and his associates continually installed the latest technology to remain competitive with New England and southern textile manufacturers. In 1882 the company constructed the largest weave shed in the world. The 500 by 120-foot building housed 231 workers and was equipped with advanced firefighting and electric-lighting systems. The mill underwent several expansions during the next two decades and by 1893 boasted 864 looms, a gas works plant, a dye house, and several warehouses. In 1903 Stormont mill owners merged their operations with the other two mills. The three facilities were subsequently purchased by Canadian Cottons Limited. In that year the supervisors of the three mills employed 1,463 workers, produced goods valued at $1,647,347, and paid $446,588 in wages.[31] Initially, Cornwall's astonishing growth was based exclusively on the textile industry. The establishment of a paper mill by outside investors broke this trend.

John Barber and a group of Toronto investors were the last to locate a major manufacturing enterprise in Cornwall because of the area's ample waterborne power. The Cornwall canal provided Barber with waterpower for his machinery and paper processing. The waterway also offered him a direct transportation route for his raw materials from northern Ontario, and for his finished product to various ports, including Montreal. In 1882 Barber completed construction of a $141,674, 33-acre facility on the north end of the Cornwall canal. He also purchased $126,397 of the latest water-powered machinery and hired 100 employees.[32] Surprisingly, Barber received no bonuses or incentives from the town.[33] His new operation was so successful that he ran his paper machines 24-hours-a-day, six-days-a-week.

An accelerating demand by United States newspaper owners for paper, while good for Barber's profit margin, drained the Canadian rag supply needed to produce pulp and caused him to upgrade his factory. Barber decided that constructing a sulfite mill was the only way he could remain competitive and fill his customers' orders. He heard that Austrian scientists had uncovered a way to use sulfuric acid and lime to break down pulp fibers.[34] In 1886 Barber and his vice president, Charles Riordan, traveled to Austria to investigate the Rittner-Kellner process, and obtained the exclusive rights to use this method in Canada. They ordered two steel digesters, a key component of the process, from a manufacturer in Duisberg, Germany. The parts were shipped to the Cornwall mill the following year. In May 1888 the Toronto Paper Mill employees produced their first batch of pulp at the new facility and within months the plant's staff processed fifteen to eighteen tons of pulp daily.[35] In 1891 Barber employed fifty male and forty female operatives who produced $122,322 worth of paper and were paid $28,147 in annual wages. The supervisor of his neighboring sulfite mill provided jobs for twenty-five men, who produced $36,146 annually and earned $9,200 in wages.[36] The Toronto Paper Mill remained the area's most prosperous and technically advanced facility well into the twentieth century.

Cornwall's local shopkeepers also shared in the prosperity and became the town's new political leaders. In the closing decades of the nineteenth century, Cornwall's streets were lined with a variety of stores. Area residents no longer had to drive to Kingston or other neighboring towns to purchase ready-made clothes, home furnishings, or hardware. The availability of this merchandise also decreased the amount of clothing and shoes made by women in home production. In the 1870s John McIntyre and W. J. Kirkpatrick established a dry goods store and specialized in the sale of imported and Canadian-made products, including carpets, curtains, and blinds. The two men were so successful they built a new business block in 1879 to accommodate their store and provide space for other retailers. Both McIntyre and Kirkpatrick were also active in town politics. The former served as mayor and the latter as reeve. McIntyre and Kirkpatrick were joined over the next ten years by H. A. Weber, who established a stationary and book store; M. A. McDonald, who owned a furniture company; J. E. Snetsinger, who sold dry goods and ladies clothing; R. J. Pitts, who peddled hardware; and, G. W. Armstrong, who supplied groceries. Besides being successful merchants, these men all served on the town council.[37] The establishment of specialty stores to serve the needs of new arrivals made the lives of Cornwall residents less isolated and more similar to their countrymen in urban areas, since they were finally able to buy the same consumer goods.

The final effect of industrialization on Cornwall was an increase and diversification of the population. From 1870 to 1891 many French Canadians from surrounding towns and impoverished British subjects from overseas came to Montreal in search of employment. During these decades many areas of Canada were in the midst of a recession. In contrast, Cornwall welcomed three new mills, whose employment needs exceeded the local supply. With the poor conditions in the surrounding rural areas, it was not surprising that many French Canadians were attracted to these new factory jobs. As Rudolph Villeneuve stated, "With the increase in population came a transformation in the ethnic character of the town, as more and more French Canadians moved to Cornwall to work in the cotton mills."[38] By the turn of the century, 1,105 individuals had emigrated to Cornwall, with 466 new residents arriving between 1881 and 1890. The town's total population had increased from 5,081 in 1871 to 6,790 in 1891.[39] As in the New England mill towns, French Canadians were the first group segregated by language. They relied on each other for financial and spiritual support and security. In Cornwall the Quebecois became active members in the Catholic Church as a means of dealing with their new unfamiliar surroundings.

The arrival of Irish workers, canal laborers, and French-Canadian mill workers altered the religious makeup of Cornwall and expedited the organization of permanent parishes. For the Irish and the French Canadians, religion was part of their cultural heritage and became an institution that allowed them to resist assimilation. As in New England, the establishment of a French neighborhood church was one of their first priorities. These new citizens also demanded parochial education for their children. This encouraged priests to establish a separate school board and schools by the 1840s. Between 1834 and 1900 Catholicism overtook Presbyterianism as the area's dominant religion. All local parish leaders dealt with bilingual congregations, pew overcrowding, and competition from new faiths for the minds and donations of their worshipers. Cornwall congregations also became more stable institutions housed in larger buildings and overseen by permanent ministers and vestries. The more hierarchical administrative mechanisms implemented by local inhabitants reflected an era of spiritual maturity and structural reorientation in Canadian churches. As Terence Murphy indicated, "After 1840, churches had evolved from struggling and scattered missionary outposts into mature ecclesiastical institutions."[40] While residents still valued congregational organization and democratic governance of their faiths, they hired prominent reverends to oversee the expansion of their houses of worship to accommodate all the area's worshipers.

During the second half of the nineteenth century, the Cornwall Presbyterians remained one of the area's most hierarchically structured faiths and attracted many of the town's new industrialists. They hired nationally renowned preachers, who established the area's wealthiest denomination, attracted prominent members, and built an ornate church. Under Reverend Hugh Urquhart, the congregation increased its financial standing by renting large amounts of land to businesses and individuals during the canal project.

In 1819 a wealthy worshiper had donated over 100 acres of property to St. John's. By 1866 the annual rent paid by the land's tenants equaled $600.[41] The congregation's biggest challenge with the arrival of the area's new industrialists was to construct a new church that reflected the town's new found prosperity. In 1886 the church elders gave in to Reverend John MacNish's demands for the construction of a bigger church and purchased a lot on Second Street. To finance the undertaking, MacNish sold several prime building lots and solicited donations from several wealthy parishioners. A renowned architect designed and supervised the construction of the new house of worship. The 700-seat stone building, expansive social hall, and Sunday School rooms opened in March 1889. Both parishioners and national church leaders referred to the $36,000 church as the "finest ecclesiastical structure in the eastern district."[42] When MacNish retired in 1903, he left behind a 300-member Presbyterian congregation with strong financial and spiritual foundations.[43]

In the nineteenth century the membership of St. John's congregation splintered, based on conflicting administrative philosophies. In 1843 the Church of Scotland separated into two parts—the Free Church and the Auld Kirk—as adherents disagreed over patrons' rights to place ministers in charge of congregations without their consent. Following this official decision, leaders of the new Free Church were sent to Cornwall and other neighboring towns to gain Canadian supporters and converts. Several St. John's congregants were attracted to the new Free Presbyterian Church because it left worshipers in charge of their own spirituality and allowed them to chose their own ministers. Therefore, beginning in 1846, they held services at private homes and elected a building committee to research the possibilities of constructing a new church. The elders of the new congregation purchased a building lot in 1848 and initiated a donation campaign to support the construction of a Free Church. Builders completed the Knox Church in 1851. Within three decades the congregation had outgrown its original church and, in 1882, members of the building committee launched a subscription campaign and purchased a new building lot on the south side of Second Street.[44] The congregation held its first service in its new facility in 1885. Six years later the Canadian census takers recorded 1,113 Presbyterians in Cornwall.[45] The large membership of this faith was only exceeded by the area's Roman Catholics.

With the arrival of Irish canal workers, St. Columban's, Cornwall's Roman Catholic congregation, experienced a period of rapid expansion and ethnic diversification. Priests struggled to meet the spiritual needs of new worshipers, strove to control the unruly behavior of their membership, and improved the local social welfare and educational systems. As the number of parishioners grew, members cast aside their trusteeism and replaced it with a more structured church administration. In 1834 the parish was awarded its first permanent priest, James Bennett, as the number of Sunday mass attendees reached an all-time high with the arrival of Irish Catholic laborers to work on the canal project. He eased the tensions between longtime Cornwall residents and Irish laborers by curbing the latter's unruly behavior. Bennett believed that drunkenness was at the root of all Irish bad behavior and, therefore, visited the town taverns, sought out intoxicated canal workers, and sent them home with a sober escort to keep them out of trouble.[46] He also encouraged these men to attend Sunday services with their families. However, when many heeded Bennett's suggestion and attended weekly mass, the pew capacity of the 20-year-old church was taxed. In 1856 ground was broken for a new church. Parishioners and their priests now turned their attention to meeting the spiritual, educational, and social welfare needs of their new diverse membership.

The biggest dilemma the members of St. Columban's faced after 1870 was dealing with the language barrier between old worshipers and their new French-Canadian brethren. Father Charles Murray met this challenge by creating a separate school board, opening two Catholic schools, and establishing a French language parish.[47] The latter accomplishment occurred in 1887, when all male church members unanimously approved the request of French-speaking parishioners to have their own parish. Later that year the Nativity of the Blessed Virgin Church was completed on Montreal Street across from the French language school, L'Ecole Du Bois, built a year earlier. Father J. J. Kelly, a bilingual priest, oversaw the new congregation and French language school. When Father Murray left St. Columban's in 1889, he was described as "an instrument used by God to promote Catholic education in Cornwall."[48] Uniquely, Catholics also addressed the social welfare problems created by an increasing population.

Father George Corbet served the parishioners of St. Columban's for forty-two years and during his tenure undertook the most extensive social service agenda in the history of the Cornwall Catholic Church. Among his many accomplishments were the building of a hospital, home for the elderly, orphanage, and high school.[49] Besides completing the initial financial and physical structures, he also solicited funds to support the long-term economic maintenance of these buildings and recruited religious orders to staff them.[50] According to Brian Clarke, "This cradle-to-grave care by Catholics was a national trend, which explained why lay people gave such generous donations to their parishes."[51] In the decades preceding a formal government-sponsored social service system, church leaders and their parishioners were charged with caring for the old and less fortunate members of their community. In 1891 there were 3,741 practicing Catholics in Cornwall, an increase of 577 adherents in the last three decades.[52] The Church of England, like the Catholicism, became so popular during the canal and industrial era that church leaders were forced to construct a second church.

Cornwall's Church of England congregation attracted many new members after church officials secured full-time ministers who revamped the church's financial affairs and gained the respect of local citizens by challenging canal contractors' work rules. The Anglicans' first two long-term pastors in the nineteenth century, George Archbold and Reverend Alexander Williams, tackled some difficult church and town issues brought about by the area's canal project and the influx of Irish canal workers. Archbold arrived in Cornwall in 1830 and assumed the leadership of the 850-member congregation. From 1834 to 1844 he enlarged the church's seating capacity, established a mission in Moulinette to service canal workers, and increased the number of congregants. In an 1834 report to the bishop, Archbold stated that an average of 250 worshipers were attending the parish's two weekly services.[53] Archbold was succeeded by Reverend Alexander Williams. During his three years of leadership, Williams challenged the vestry to take a harder stance in collecting pew rent and organized the Parochial Association of the Eastern District.[54] His most publicized campaign was his criticism of the sacrilegious work rules of canal contractors. Most required employees to report to the job site on Sunday or be fired on Monday. Williams' comments appeared in a letter published in the *Cornwall Observer* in 1843 and were applauded by residents and canal workers alike. In 1844 Williams, frustrated and worn out by his extensive parish duties, resigned his post and returned to England.[55]

During the transitional years between the end of the canal project and the industrial era in Cornwall, the Trinity congregation began a campaign to build a new facility in honor of its most famous leader, the Reverend John Strachan, and the parish became a regional leader in the Anglican Church. Reverend Henry Patton led the congregation during these uncertain decades. Patton successfully campaigned for the new Strachan Memorial Church building after the legendary reverend's death in 1867.[56] The Strachan Memorial Church remained unfinished until the vestry borrowed $11,000 to complete the construction in 1875. The other important occurrence during Patton's leadership was the return of the Trinity parish to a prominent role in the regional church structure based on the redistricting of the parishes of the Canadian Anglican Church. Trinity now came under the jurisdiction of the new diocese of Ontario and, by 1871, with a membership of 867, was the largest congregation in the diocese.[57]

In the 1880s the renewed popularity of Anglicanism in Cornwall encouraged Trinity members to create a second congregation, the Church of the Good Shepherd, in the French-Canadian neighborhood. The new congregation met in several temporary locations until 1886, when J. S. Mountain, a local retired priest, donated $3,000 to purchase a lot for a permanent church. A year later the parishioners held their first service at the Mountain Memorial Church, also known as the Church of the Good Shepherd. For two years the congregation remained under the authority of the pastor of Trinity, but in 1889 the membership of the Church of the Good Shepherd became independent and self-supporting. By 1893, when area manufacturers hired more factory workers, the wooden structure became too small to accommodate all worshipers at Sunday service, and Mountain again financed the construction of a new building and the renovation of the old structure into a church hall.[58] In 1891 the publishers of the *Census of Canada* reported 1,201 adherents to the Church of England.[59] The traditional structure and sacraments of the Anglican Church were a stark contrast to the innovative Baptist faith.

The Baptists represented the first evangelical and fundamental church established in Cornwall and appealed to many new and old residents because of their emphasis on personal holiness and unlimited atonement. Like the Methodists, the Baptists attracted local worshipers who had always harbored congregational and democratic religious values. Comparable to residents of other North American towns, many Cornwallers wanted to remain in charge of their own spiritual lives. In 1881 two Baptist women, Jane MacArthur and Jennie Hamilton, moved to Cornwall and found no congregation or formal church structure. MacArthur and Hamilton met once a month on Sunday afternoon to pray with ten other worshipers. By 1882 the prayer group had grown to sixteen members and began to meet every Sunday at the homes of various worshipers. In January of that year a meeting was called at the home of Mr. and Mrs. William Andrews to initiate the organization of an official church. The association first needed to gain acceptance to the Canadian Baptist Council, and then locate a permanent meeting place. In June 1882 the Cornwall Baptists were recognized as a regular church by a council of ministers, elected three deacons, and nominated a treasurer and clerk to manage church finances. The deacons were charged with finding a building lot for a church, collecting money to fund the endeavor, and hiring a full-time minister. In August the congregation invited Reverend P. H. McEwan to become the church's first minister. Later that year the twenty-six members purchased land for a church, started a Sunday School, and welcomed nine new members to the faith after the congregation's first official baptism ceremony. In September 1884 the Baptists held their first service in their 260-seat church on York Street.[60]

During the remainder of the 1880s the Baptist congregation struggled to maintain the allegiance of its worshipers based on the inability of the congregation's leadership to sustain a full-time minister and its enforcement of new strict membership guidelines. In 1886 the congregation was without a minister and resorted to holding prayer meetings. This caused many members to leave the congregation and attend the services of other faiths. The church leaders also began to take an active role in monitoring the everyday lives of parishioners and excommunicating those who were convicted of violating church rules. Punishable offenses ranged from frequent nonattendance at services to picking strawberries on Sunday. For over a decade the number of congregation members who were thrown out or left of their own free will greatly outnumbered new followers.[61] The Baptists' abandonment of their congregational beliefs almost led to the congregation's demise.

From 1834 to 1900 Cornwall's churches remained the town's central social and moral organizations, and were the only stable institutions in citizens' ever changing lives. Members of most denominations no longer shared ministers with neighboring towns. Instead, parishes were awarded full-time preachers, who were actively involved in overseeing the moral and social lives of town residents. The town's new, more elaborate churches also served as havens for new and old residents, who strove to deal with their new industrial and ethnically diverse environment. While the Cornwall worshipers abandoned their forefathers' congregational and democratic practices in the religious arena, they finally established a local, participatory government.

After Cornwall was officially incorporated as a town in 1834 by the Upper Canada Parliament, residents established a democratic local government under the auspices of a Board of Police. Geographically, the town was divided into two election wards. The occupants of each ward selected two members to serve on the 5-man board. During the inaugural election on April 1, 1834, Phillip Vankoughnet and Martin Caman were appointed by voters in the western ward and John and Peter Chelsey were victorious in the east. All these men were local merchants and had gained the respect of their fellow citizens based on their financial success.

The Cornwall Board of Police first met on April 21, 1834 and chose Archibald McLean as its fifth member. At their April 26 gathering the board members appointed McLean, the son of a United Empire Loyalist and member of the provincial assembly, as the board's first president. The five men also hired John Perkins as the board's clerk, James Pringle as treasurer, and Horace Spencer as street surveyor and high constable. At the May 6 meeting board members fulfilled their final required task by outlining and publicizing prohibited and unacceptable behavior in the town's new bylaws. These improprieties included serving alcohol to children, apprentices, or servants without their parents' permission, public drunkenness, swearing, and using insulting language in public. Individuals were also prohibited from gambling or displaying obscene pictures or posters in public. Violating these regulations resulted in a $50 fine or thirty days in jail.[62] From 1834 to 1846 the Board of Police remained in charge of all town financial and legal matters.

In 1846 the provincial government amended Cornwall's charter, allowing residents to institute a new municipal government structure led by a mayor and supported by a popularly elected town council. The nine town councilmen, three from each ward—east, west, and central—were elected by the area's eligible male voters. The councilmen initially chose one of their own to serve in the capacity of mayor. George McDonnell, a lawyer, became Cornwall's first mayor in 1847. The inaugural councilmen included: grocers,

P. E. Adams and D. W. McDonnell; jeweler, Robert Atchison; cabinetmaker, Vincent Annable; and, iron manufacturer, Austin Cadwell. In 1859 the provincial government again revised its policy authorizing the mayor to be directly elected by local voters. Dr. Charles Rattray was the first to hold the office under this new law.[63] These new forms of self-government gave citizens more control over selecting local officials and afforded councilors a greater ability to make administrative decisions that met the needs of their particular constituents and businesses.[64] Male Cornwall residents had finally achieved the democratic municipal government that many of the loyalists had desired.

The establishment of new manufacturing enterprises by outside investors and the large number of immigrant workers they employed altered the economic, social, and political life of Cornwall residents. After 1850 the town's economy was transformed from a small farming community to a manufacturing town. Montreal businessmen, who were ambitious and prepared to take financial risks, invested their life savings in local factories and hired immigrant workers to man their machinery. These entrepreneurs expanded their facilities over the next several decades and developed new products based on government subsidies and tax exemptions. The new workforce employed by George Stephen and John Barber encouraged current store owners to expand their product lines and new businessmen to set up retail outlets. The mill workers also changed the religious makeup of Cornwall, increasing the number of Catholics and forcing most church leaders to enlarge their facilities. Politically, town residents instituted a democratic, popularly elected local government staffed by new industrialists and merchants. This illustrated citizens' respect for those who were ambitious, took risks, and were financially prosperous. Therefore, the values and beliefs of Cornwall residents remained similar to those of their Massena neighbors from 1834 to 1902. Cornwall's borderland location and waterpower made the lives of residents more comparable to their Massena neighbors than to their Canadian compatriots.

Massena

For most of the nineteenth century, Massena residents, based on their isolated location, remained self-sufficient farmers producing all their necessary food stuffs and building materials. The town's significant distance from nineteenth-century American commercial centers and inadequate transportation routes hindered the development of regional or statewide networks for the exchange of manufactured and agricultural goods. From 1834 to 1900 Massena farmers, like their Canadian counterparts, diversified their crops, increased the amount of land under cultivation, and concentrated on dairy farming. In the 1830s wheat was the staple crop harvested by Massena farmers to feed their livestock, while potatoes and corn were planted for human consumption. By

1850 local landowners planted a wide variety of grain and vegetable products to serve their own needs and meet the changing demands of consumers. Many harvested more oats to sell to stagecoach operators and railroad contractors as horse feed. According to New York State census takers, the number of bushels of oats cultivated by Massena farmers increased from 19,201 in 1855 to 56,005 in 1875.[65] Conversely, farmers decreased the number of acres they devoted to wheat from 15,457 to 4,549.

Between 1840 and 1880 most Massena agriculturists also reinvested their profits in their farms and began to function more like businessmen. Many recognized the expanding market for dairy products and focused on shifting some of their operations to this endeavor. David Ellis noted, "The rise of the dairying industry was the most significant development in the agricultural history of the state between 1825 and 1860."[66] By the 1850s Massena's main industries were butter and cheese making. Other male residents earned livings as merchants, hoteliers, and manufacturers.

While the majority of male residents in the last five decades of the nineteenth century remained farmers, many Massena merchants established stores that catered to the seasonal needs of Massena Springs visitors and the year-round demands of local residents. Local inhabitants opened various retail outlets to sell all types of products. By 1845 five inns and taverns, five retail stores, one grocer, and five merchants were listed in the census.[67] Over the next several decades, skilled craftsmen established several blacksmith shops, a wagon factory, a brick factory, four tanneries, and a tailor shop. By 1873 the author of the *Massena Gazetteer* listed thirty-eight entrepreneurs, including twenty merchants, who owned and operated jewelry, clothing, hardware, and grocery stores. These included Hiriam Russell's meat market, Mrs. John O. Bridges' ladies' clothing store, and William Wilson's general store. Like Cornwall merchants, these Massena citizens invested all their income back into their businesses, carried a variety of merchandise to meet the changing needs of local residents, and constructed business blocks as a way to convince other residents to open new stores.[68] Their business practices and values were shared by the area's hotel owners.

The marketing of the sulfur springs located at the edge of town and the completion of the Massena canal were the two developments that breathed some life into Massena's floundering nineteenth-century economy. The Massena Springs, described by Leonard Prince as "two springs only a few feet apart, one hot and one cold,"[69] had historically been used by Indians as a cure for disease and as an alleviator of discomforts associated with external sores and ulcers. It was not until 1822, however, when Captain John Polley, one of the original settlers of Massena and a veteran of the War of 1812, purchased forty acres of land and built a hotel, that Massenans realized the value of exploiting this natural resource. A visitor to the facility in that year predicted, "Soon the Springs will become a delightful resort for the healthy as well as the sick."[70]

Between 1828 and 1858 David Merills, Benjamin Philips, and Parsons Taylor opened three other hotels and several cottages, and town officials hired contractors to construct a bathing house covering the springs. In addition, local residents established a bottling plant where workers packaged the water for national distribution. For more than fifty years, an estimated 1,500 to 2,000 visitors from around the globe flocked to the springs annually. The Massena Springs resort owners also hired local citizens every summer to serve as bellhops, cooks, housekeepers, and gardeners. However, following the deaths of many of the original promoters and hoteliers, their children showed little interest in modernizing the property that they inherited, and consequently, the bathhouse and hotels fell into disrepair.[71] The economic prosperity of resort owners was also shared by several local manufacturers.

Massena residents also established small factories in the area after 1834. Similar to Cornwall industrialists, these were ambitious men who were concerned with community advancements. Each was an active member of a religious congregation and strove to improve the physical and economic health of Massena in the nineteenth century. Two of Massena's most successful nineteenth-century manufacturers were Uriel Orvis and Judson Hyde, who owned several mills, and were well-known religious and educational benefactors. In terms of business, Orvis operated a saw mill in addition to the general store he owned with his partner, James McDowell. Between 1830 and 1848 he constructed several more small manufacturing establishments, including a stone and brick mill, a cement factory where he produced materials for Cornwall canal contractors, and an ashery and tannery where he processed tree pulp and animal hides. Politically, he held a variety of positions, including tax assessor, overseer of the poor, commissioner of the highways, and co-author of the town bylaws. Orvis was also an active leader in the Massena educational system, serving as a trustee and inspector of the common schools. In the 1830s he erected a meetinghouse for various congregations, and his wife later donated land to the Baptist Church for a parsonage and a church expansion.[72] Orvis' financial and political success was rivaled by that of his counterpart Judson Hyde.

Judson Lyons Hyde, Massena's other prominent manufacturer, began his professional career as a store clerk and, at the time of his death in 1904, was the president of the First National Bank. For twelve years he worked a farm on the outskirts of Massena and transported his own butter, cheese, and farm produce and those of his neighbors to merchants and dealers in Boston. During his visits to Boston, Hyde developed a professional relationship with the owners of Simpson and McIntyre, a large dairy distribution firm, and became one of the company's main stockholders. In 1880 Hyde, along with his son, Frederick, opened a creamery in Massena on Center Street in affiliation with the Boston firm. Prior to 1902 this establishment was the only major industry in Massena. For several decades the workers at the Hyde's creamery processed 100,000 pounds of milk daily from area farms. Politically, Hyde was an active member of the Republican Party and a member of the Union School Board. He was also a lifelong member of the Congregational Church and an organizer of the Pine Grove Cemetery.[73]

The resort owners and Orvis and Hyde personified Seymour Lipset's characterization of the American businessman, who "worshipped success and was achievement oriented."[74] Like Cornwall industrialists, they were willing to invest their life savings in new ventures, thereby improving the town's financial outlook and enhancing local employment levels. Even with the lack of train service to the area, the resort owners maintained large hotels with restaurants and large gardens that attracted annual visitors. The entertainment and personal service the resort employees provided rivaled those of the state's top spa in Saratoga Springs. Even though these hotels closed at the turn of the century as Americans changed their vacation patterns and Orvis' and Hyde's businesses ceased operation, the financial initiative and imagination of these local investors has never been matched again. Instead, Massena's new manufacturing operations were funded by outside investors. Massena residents and politicians would have to wait several decades until the completion of the power canal in 1902 to further expand the town's economic base.

For much of the nineteenth century, Massena residents harnessed the current of the Grasse River to power mills and discussed plans to construct a canal between the Grasse and St. Lawrence Rivers. In 1808 Calvin Hubbard and Stephen Reed built the first dam to power machinery at a tannery, grist mill, and woodworking shop. In the 1830s settlers considered digging a canal to bypass the Long Sault Rapids.[75] The first attempt by local politicians to gain legislative approval for the Massena canal was in 1833. Prior to presenting its plan to state officials, a group of Massena residents—D. C. Judson, William Ogden, N. F. Hyer, H. Allen, and M. Whitcomb—circulated a petition at a meeting of area politicians in Canton, New York in December 1833 to prove the regional support for the project. In the document the men outlined the construction of a $200,000, 6-mile, 35-feet-deep canal project linking the Grasse and St. Lawrence Rivers. The group presented its proposal and petition to the members of the legislature, who subsequently approved funding for an initial survey and feasibility study. The canal project, however, never progressed past the planning stages, as the Canadian government solved the navigation problems by constructing locks and canals on the north side of the St. Lawrence River between 1830 and 1843.[76]

Henry Warren, a Massena real estate magnate, resurrected the canal plans in the late nineteenth century and shifted the focus of the project from navigation to power generation. Warren realized the merits of constructing a powerhouse and canal in Massena in 1890 during a trip to the Niagara Falls hydropower project. The 45-foot drop in elevation from the St. Lawrence River to the Grasse River was similar to the natural conditions present in western New York. He was, therefore, determined to convince local officials and investors of the Massena canal's long-term benefits. In 1891 Warren conducted a preliminary survey to verify his hunch and to give his sales pitch more weight. Two years later he met Albon Mann, a former engineer and surveyor, and an annual visitor to Massena Springs, and discussed canal plans with him. To reinforce his argument, Warren took Mann on a carriage ride along the banks of the two rivers. Mann was convinced of the legitimacy of Warren's suggestions and performed his own personal survey. For the next three years, the two men worked on collecting private funding for the project and soliciting the support of local politicians and entrepreneurs.

Senator George R. Malby and Assemblymen Martin Ives reintroduced the Massena canal bill to the New York State Legislature on February 27, 1896. By this time, Warren and Mann had acquired the financial support of three partners—M. H. Flaherty, C. A. Kellog, and Charles Higgins—had sold $3 million in foreign bonds to English investors, and purchased the property rights to 1,624 acres of land along the river bank.[77] Chapter 484 of the Laws of New York of 1896 authorized the St. Lawrence Power Company to build the canal, send and transmit power, acquire land by condemnation, and change the location of streets.[78] Construction began the following fall.

The 300-feet-wide, 40-feet-deep, 3-mile-long power canal project took two contractors and more than 2,000 workers to complete. The initial contractor, Lehigh Construction Corporation of Pennsylvania, broke ground on August 5, 1897. A month later Lehigh employed 600 men, 40 mules, and 150 horses.[79] The removal of eighty cubic yards of earth was required to produce an average canal depth of forty feet. Seven steam shovels and dredges removed the dirt from the ravine and lowlands separating the Grasse and St. Lawrence Rivers. Workmen then dumped the unwanted material into railroad cars, pulled them off site, and emptied their contents. The slow, arduous process of removing barge loads of earth and the mixing and pouring of tons of concrete took its toll on workers and managers alike. By the winter of 1897 the owners of Lehigh construction realized they lacked the machinery and money to fulfill their contract and relinquished the remainder of the work to T. A. Gillespie.[80]

In June 1898 T. A. Gillespie resumed work on the project and completed the canal and powerhouse in 1902. Before beginning construction he took out ads in the local paper asking for 100 draft horses and their owners to help with the dredging. Gillespie received few responses to his request, since none of the farmers in the area or their draft horses were experienced in performing this type of hauling and transportation work. Therefore, Gillespie bought 150 draft horses used on the recent Erie Canal improvements. He also purchased machinery, tools, and a machine shop from Lehigh and transported three more steam shovels, four locomotive cars, and a ditch shovel to the Massena site. Next, Gillespie hired workmen to complete the project.

In terms of labor, Gillespie and his foreman had no problem recruiting workers. The canal and powerhouse were the biggest construction projects in the state following the 1893 depression. Construction jobs were hard to find, and many immigrant men came directly from Ellis Island to Massena by train. Like his predecessor, however, Gillespie never overcame the housing problems associated with accommodating a large number of temporary workers in a small town. The apartment buildings constructed by Lehigh could not shelter the entire workforce employed on the canal and local boardinghouses were already full. These circumstances resulted in the erection of unsanitary temporary shelters.[81]

In 1897 Lehigh Construction managers promised town officials that the canal workers and their families brought to Massena to work on the waterway project would not negatively affect the surrounding community. Company officials were determined to be self-sufficient in terms of housing and supplies. The company constructed Camp Bogart on the north side of town. This complex contained a dining hall, kitchen, and several 20 by 50-foot buildings, which each housed up to three workers and their families. As the project progressed, there was not enough room at Camp Bogart for the increasing number of workers, and many were forced to live in shacks or sand dugouts made of old boxes and lumber near the canal site. The cluster of primitive buildings, referred to as White City, was located on North Main Street, and extended from the town border to the canal site. According to a local journalist, Anthony Romeo, life during the canal days was appalling. The living conditions endured by foreigners and their families were similar to those experienced by the area's early pioneers. Most spent subzero winter nights in tarpaper shacks with no running water.[82] The living conditions had not improved in the summer of 1898 when Gillespie brought 125 Italians to town to work on the project.

The canal workers and their families altered the ethnic makeup of Massena. Many workers arrived in New York City on boats from various ports in Europe and were immediately hired by Lehigh's and Gillespie's recruiters. They then boarded a train to Massena. Most of the Italians and Hungarians who arrived in the area from 1897 to 1902 were single and could not speak English. Those who were married usually left their families behind until they found appropriate housing. The change in the ethnic makeup of the Massena population was documented in the 1875 and 1905 New York State Census returns. In 1875 census takers reported the presence of only one European in Massena. Three decades later 127 Italians and 37 Hungarians resided in the area.[83] According to one local historian, "When the waters of the St. Lawrence River rushed to meet the Grasse, they brought with them a break with the past and an exciting new vision of social and cultural change."[84] However, this euphoria was soon replaced by fear. Town residents became increasingly worried about the surge in crimes committed by canal workers, much of which was reported in the local newspaper.

Canal workers not only got into frequent skirmishes with each other, but also with the St. Regis Indians. This behavior reinforced Massena residents' aversion to foreigners. While no constables were added to the Massena police force, as most job foremen preferred to personally deal with the indiscretions of their workers, several incidents described in the *Massena Observer* required the assistance of law enforcement personnel. For example, a 1901 article explained the circumstances surrounding the theft of a wallet containing $140 during a party at an Italian boardinghouse. The owner of the wallet, Rocco Schimizzi, dropped it during the celebration. The thief, Guiseppe Pulimeni, picked up the wallet and hid it initially in a stone wall and later under the foundation of a nearby building. Schimizzi told his story to the Massena police and Pulimeni was charged with grand larceny pending the return of the money. The following year, a clash between Indians returning on the noon train from the lumber camps and Italians at the train station occurred. Even though these violent acts were not directed at members of the general public as they had been in Cornwall, they aroused a great deal of fear and concern for public safety. The longtime residents of Massena had established social and religious protocols that they expected all citizens to abide by. The goal of all Massena parishioners remained the establishment of a godly nation where churches not only converted individuals, but remade society.[85]

Massena's religious institutions and church leaders continually played a central role in the development of social opportunities, much as in Cornwall, Ontario. Many residents still lived on scattered farms. Religious services were the one time every week that many saw individuals outside their immediate family. They also viewed their congregations as the one stable establishment in their evolving lives. According to Winthrop Hudson and John Corrigan, "From the beginning of national life, religion had served as a bond of unity and generated a common loyalty and sentiment."[86] Therefore, after 1834, the Massena faithful built permanent structures and recruited full-time ministers. New arrivals also recognized the area's evangelical tendencies and established Baptist and Adventist associations. Members of all Massena faiths, similar to their ancestors and Cornwall neighbors, remained in control of their spiritual lives and the financial affairs of their congregations, even with the introduction of more formal administrative structures, including vestries and the hiring of full-time reverends. However, most Massena residents realized the need to have more organized congregations to deal with the ever changing spiritual demands of town's residents.

In 1834 the Congregational Church remained Massena's largest denomination based on its loose structure and emphasis on personal holiness. The importance of these elements to certain members caused them to organize a second association in 1833. According to the minutes of the First Congregational Church, William Paddock Jr. and a group of prominent members of the original parish, including Silas Joy, John B. Judd, and William H. Paddock, disagreed theologically with church elders. On July 31, 1833 Paddock and his followers held their first meeting at the Harrowgate House and unanimously voted in favor of starting a second parish. In 1834 they appointed a building committee comprised of William Paddock, Reuben Dutton, Silas Joy, John B. Judd, and Samuel Tracy. Paddock solicited donations from members to finance a new 200-seat church at the corner of West Orvis and Church Streets. After contractors completed the building in 1844, Paddock sold pews to other members to cover the remaining construction expenses. In 1883 the First Congregational Church closed its doors, as many members had been attending services at the new chapel for several years.[87] Throughout the remainder of the nineteenth century, Congregationalism remained the area's leading evangelical faith and recruited new members based on their congregational philosophy. Methodists still remained the Congregationalist's main rival in terms of membership.

The Methodists, the other congregation established by the area's initial settlers, continually appealed to Massena residents because of their democratic theology and emotional camp meetings. As the century progressed, Methodists abandoned their loose structure and began to assign full-time resident ministers to all established congregations. In 1836 Massena Methodists were still ministered to by traveling preachers. However, in 1841 William Hawkins and Allen Castle conducted a successful revival, and the number of local Methodists rose to sixty-four. Over the next four years, the spiritual frenzy lingered. So many Massena residents were converted to the religion by 1845 that they were awarded their own full-time minister. This increase in spiritual supervision did not mean that the Methodists completely disregarded their congregational values and governing structure. Massena Methodists were granted permission by conference members to elect their own elders to govern church affairs and to hold quarterly meetings to discuss church policy and financial concerns.[88] The first board consisted of John Payne, William Bayley, John Magovin, and Alfred Magowan. Under its second leader, Elisha Pease, the Methodist congregation constructed a brick chapel in 1848 that housed weekly services and Sunday School classes for twenty years. In 1868, following several decades of growth, the Methodists erected a new church with greater seating capacity and classroom space. By 1878 the Methodists recorded

225 members and 130 Sunday School students.[89] The Methodists were soon competing for new members with the Baptists, who had gained popularity during the Second Great Awakening.

As in Cornwall, the Baptists developed a stable organization in Massena prior to 1850 because of their spiritual vitality and individualistic emphasis on conversion. Initially, visiting preachers who traveled to Massena on horseback conducted services for local worshipers in area homes. After 1825, settlers from Massena and visiting lumbermen attended services in Louisville preached by a resident minister.[90] When the Louisville service area became too widespread, twenty-nine Massena Baptists, including Ephriam Hyde and Earle Stone, were sent to form a church in their own town. They congregated at the meetinghouse constructed by Uriel Orvis. In 1843 officials from the Baptist Minister's Council sent church officials to Massena to test the religious knowledge of Nathaniel Martin and his fellow worshipers. When all the parishioners passed the examination, the St. Lawrence Baptist Association recognized the Massena First Baptist Church as an official parish, and awarded the congregation a full-time pastor, Reverend Elias Goodspeed.[91]

In November 1858 Massena's First Baptist congregation was officially incorporated under the direction of trustees Stephen Squires, Peter Ormsbee, Allen Russell, and Joseph Orvis. In 1859 the 150 Baptists built their present church on property bestowed to them by Mrs. Laura Orvis and established a Sabbath School. The board members who oversaw the project were Hiriam Fish, Moses Russell, and William Garvin. In 1875 when Mrs. Orvis donated another adjacent parcel of land, a session room and baptistery were added to the church. By 1878 parish leaders recorded a total membership of 147 with 70 enrolled in Sunday School.[92] Baptists, similar to the Congregationalists and Methodists, developed a formal church administration structure and erected a permanent meetinghouse, but they remained in control of church financial affairs and never abandoned their emphasis on personal spirituality. Catholics also established an association in Massena in the 1830s and offered residents a more regimented spiritual experience.

The Roman Catholic Church was the final congregation organized by Massena residents prior to the mid-nineteenth century, and represented the first hierarchically administered church established in the area. As in Cornwall, parishioners were initially in charge of their own spiritual maintenance. With few Catholic priests in this isolated location, trusteeism prevailed. In 1830 Alexander McDowell, a priest from Kingston who was vacationing at one of the Massena Springs hotels, said the first Catholic mass in Massena. While in Massena, McDowell also established a Sunday School and conducted weekly masses for the duration of his stay. For the next ten years, the twenty Massena families conducted their own masses and constructed a small church at a cost of $140. The first trustees of St. Peter's were John Flaherty, William McQuinn, and Dennis McCarthy, who oversaw the financial and spiritual needs of the parish in the absence of a full-time priest.[93] In 1871 St. Peter's merged with worshipers in two neighboring towns, organized a building committee and, by 1875, completed a new church under the name Sacred Heart. The 400 members were finally designated an independent parish and awarded a full-time priest by diocesan administrators in that same year.[94] The arrival of canal workers in 1898, who attended services at Sacred Heart, solidified the parish's new role as Massena's leading denomination. Two other denominations, the Episcopalians and the Adventists, evolved based on Massena's commercial success.

The Episcopalians with their traditional governing structure and sacraments gained membership from the Massena Springs hoteliers and their guests, as well as the area's growing number of entrepreneurs. This small congregation hired full-time preachers to administer the sacraments, and elected a vestry to raise funds for an elaborate church. While occasional summer services were held by ministers visiting the springs, Reverend John Winkley, rector of Grace Church in Norfolk, conducted the first official service at the town hall in 1868. He returned to the area periodically over the next several months.[95] In September 1869 the Massena congregation was admitted to the Episcopalian Union as the Church of the Great Shepherd. Subsequently, the elected wardens hired Reverend Winkley as the congregation's first full-time rector and held services in the town hall for several years. In 1870 the worshipers purchased the old Methodist chapel with donations from three vestry members: Henry Clark, an entrepreneur; John Clary, a general merchant; and, John Bridges, a dry goods dealer. Together they renovated the facility with funds raised by parish women.[96] After Winkley resigned his post in 1871, he was succeeded by E. Gregory Prout and Henry Hutching, who each saw the position as an annual appointment.

In 1875 the St. John's congregation finally hired a clergyman, Reverend Joshua Goss, who made a long-term commitment to improve both the spiritual and financial status of the 70-member parish. Goss remained in Massena for twelve years. During this time the congregation recorded more than ten confirmations annually, and outgrew the old Methodist chapel. To deal with the space issue, Goss organized a building committee and named himself chairman. The committee's mission was to solicit funds and locate a lot for the new church. The efforts of this committee progressed slowly based on the apathy of many Massena residents toward the project. The new building remained incomplete in 1885, and Henry Clark overtook the fund-raising duties. He approached Massena Springs vacationers, who regularly attended weekly services during their stays, for donations to the building fund. Clark's efforts were more successful than earlier drives and the church was finally completed in 1887.[97] The Anglicans remained one of the smallest, but richest, Massena parishes. They were joined by the Adventists, whose loose organization and innovative philosophy were stark contrasts to the stodgy Episcopalians.

The Christian Adventists were the final congregation with origins prior to the completion of the Massena canal project. This faith evolved out of a new concern for Christ's Second Coming and had existed in several disorganized forms since 1837. Adherents studied the apocalyptic portions of the Bible, the very sections that Roman Catholics and other Protestants ignored.[98] The establishment of the Massena church was, in many respects, accidental. Reverend Cornelius Pike, a resident of Fort Edward, New York and a traveling evangelist, visited Massena on a tour of northern New York in the early 1870s and, surprisingly, found many believers. "In Massena we found some of the best brethren and sisters we have ever met with. . . . We had no idea we should meet such a people north of the Adirondack Mountains and south of Canada."[99] Pike spent eleven days in Massena in 1871, and forty people attended his last service. For the next year, his followers met at the Union Church in Massena Center. In 1872 Pike returned with his family and became the Adventists' first spiritual leader. He started a subscription paper in 1873 and asked for pledges to build the congregation's first church. Donations were received from Massena residents ranging from $50 to $500. Pike purchased a building lot with the proceeds in 1874. Contractors finished the church in November of that year, and the seating capacity easily accommodated the 60-member congregation.[100] Like the Congregationalists, Methodists, and Baptists, the Adventists were an evangelical congregation. The unstructured church and its reliance on individual responsibility for one's spirituality attracted many members both during and after the canal years.

In 1900 churches remained the center of Massena residents' social and moral lives. As Herbert Schneider stated, "The church building was physically the center of the community and the parish was the central, vital institution of religious activities."[101] Members of Massena's religious congregations still cherished their congregational and egalitarian values and beliefs and retained their personal relationships with God, even as their churches became more structured. While members of the Congregational and the Methodist parishes constructed permanent churches and hired full-time ministers, they remained in control of their own personal spirituality and showed their distrust for hierarchical rule. The Congregationalists went as far as starting a second association to uphold their spiritual freedom. Area residents also established new evangelical Baptist and Adventist congregations. These churches were examples of the long-term impact of the Second Great Awakening on local residents. Massena residents still rejected elitism and social privilege and believed in equality. These values and beliefs determined whom local voters elected to public office.

From 1834 to 1900 Massena residents, comparable to their Cornwall neighbors, were ruled by a democratically elected town government staffed by merchants and farmers. Town records indicate that in the last six decades of the nineteenth century, Massena voters elected four farmers, seven merchants, three innkeepers, one banker, and one horse dealer to fill the town supervisor's seat.[102] In 1886 Massena residents were awarded a town charter by the New York State Legislature and chose their first mayor. From 1886 to 1900 town voters elected four mayors: J. L. Hyde and John O Bridges, both merchants and businessmen; William Paddock, a farmer; and, Henry Warren, a canal and business promoter.[103] The selection of these men by Massena inhabitants to hold public office reflected their inherent respect for personal achievement, not family heritage. Resembling their Cornwall neighbors, voters elected local businessmen and merchants, who they thought were the right men for the job, based on their success in the private sector. Voters supported a popularly elected, democratic government that protected individuals' rights and addressed the social issues of the community.

In summary, even though the economic development of Cornwall and Massena differed between 1834 and 1900, residents of both towns lived in a unique environment based on their border location. Their distance from commercial centers hindered growth, even with the completion of canal projects. Cornwall and Massena political leaders struggled to attract manufacturers and the areas remained underdeveloped due to their peripheral location. However, while the underdevelopment made them different from the heartland at the beginning of the nineteenth century, it was their rapid commercial and industrial growth that set them apart from their rural neighbors at the end of the century. The harnessing of waterpower attracted industry to the region that was not available in adjacent towns. By 1900 Cornwall and Massena residents realized they were different from their immediate neighbors because of their unique physical assets.

The Cornwall and Massena canal projects and the area's subsequent industrialization also made the two towns more ethnically diverse than other nearby rural towns. Massena residents, like their Cornwall neighbors, experienced an increase and diversification of the population during the canal construction. Citizens' reaction to these newcomers illustrated their unaccommodating attitudes toward foreigners' cultures and their exposure to outsiders sooner than their neighbors in other areas of northern New York and eastern Canada. The influx of Irish, French-Canadian, and European immigrants exposed local residents to foreign cultures and religious traditions. The homogeneous populations of both towns resented and feared these outsiders, who spoke different languages and worshiped at the Catholic Church. When immigrants committed crimes and drank heavily, they seemed to justify residents' misgivings.

Finally, from 1834 to 1900, Cornwall and Massena residents retained similar financial, social, and political values. Economically, while Massena remained agrarian, Cornwall and Massena's economies were driven by industrialists and merchants who strove for their own financial gain and the success and prosperity of the community. Local entrepreneurs risked their life savings to construct factories, canals, and hotels. This was in contrast to other Canadians who were often cautious and prudent in terms of investments. Religiously, while both areas' worshipers constructed permanent churches and established governing bodies, they were still attracted to congregational faiths where members remained spiritually independent and in charge of church financial affairs. This was exemplified by the popularity of the Baptist and Methodist churches. Politically, Cornwall and Massena residents exhibited their egalitarian beliefs and respect for men who were materially successful by electing merchants and entrepreneurs to public office. Cornwall and Massena residents retained their community orientation, respect for success, belief in a democratic government and spiritual independence. Their relatively isolated borderland location caused the residents of these two communities to cherish values and lifestyles that were often contrary to those of their countrymen in the nations' population centers. The conclusion of the Massena canal project in 1902 was the beginning of a long-term parallel between the two towns' economic development.

CHAPTER THREE

The Era of Large Corporations in Cornwall and Massena, 1900–1954

In the first half of the twentieth century, Cornwall and Massena became regional manufacturing centers. From 1900 to 1954 the political leaders of both towns convinced the owners of several companies to locate plants in the area, and many farmers left their land to take better paying and more stable jobs at these new facilities. In 1924 the British owners of Courtaulds, a large rayon producer, built a facility in Cornwall to manufacture material for the Canadian market. The Courtaulds, Toronto Paper Mill, and Canadian Cotton personnel officers recruited French-Canadian operatives to man their machinery and employed numerous local residents. The managers of all three companies also expanded their product lines in the first half of the twentieth century to meet changing consumer needs. Also prior to 1954 the textile workers employed at Courtaulds, Canadian Cotton, and the Cornwall Pants Company formed a labor union. The leaders of this new organization achieved union recognition, better working conditions, and united all Cornwall clothing workers into one local.

Similarly, in 1902 Pittsburgh Reduction Company investors (better known as the Aluminum Company of America or Alcoa) constructed an aluminum processing plant in Massena and purchased power from the owners of the St. Lawrence Power Company. Alcoa employed former canal workers and local residents to operate its facility's potlines. Over the next five decades, the company increased its production levels, hired an increasing number of immigrant laborers, and earned the distinction as the largest employer north of Syracuse. Subsequently, other industrialists established a silk mill and an intimate apparel factory in the area, and hired the wives of Alcoa workers. Massena's economy made the final transition from an agriculturally based one to one whose financial security depended on industrialists' tax payments and employment levels. Alcoa employees, like their Cornwall counterparts, also joined labor unions to improve their working conditions and wages. The collective activity of American industrial workers in the 1930s represented a weakening of management's control over their employees' behavior because of the declining impact of welfare capitalism programs. Therefore, from 1900 to 1954, the economic and social growth of Cornwall and Massena was tied to the production and employment levels set by local plant owners.[1]

From a religious standpoint Cornwall and Massena residents still regarded their congregations as the areas' central social and moral institutions. With the influx of factory workers, the Catholic parishes on both sides of the border increased their membership. Congregants of all area faiths developed voluntary associations to raise money for church expansion projects and to foster new social bonds among worshipers. Cornwall and Massena men and women also established fraternal and social welfare organizations to meet the social and healthcare needs of old and new residents. In terms of population, both areas gained new citizens from diverse ethnic backgrounds, with Cornwall receiving more French-Canadian and British residents, and Massena gaining predominantly Italians, Eastern Europeans, and Jews. The longtime citizens of both towns displayed their dislike of foreigners by constructing separate housing and churches in working-class neighborhoods. The economic and social lives of Cornwall and Massena residents, therefore, remained comparable.

In the first half of the twentieth century, the geographic location of Cornwall and Massena resulted in unique economic and ethnic characteristics. From 1900 to 1954 both towns became major manufacturing centers because of their cheap hydropower. This contrasted with the agricultural lifestyle of residents in adjacent towns. Factory workers from a variety of European countries also made the populations increasingly diverse. Cornwall and Massena residents also retained different social, political, and economic values from their compatriots in the heartland based on their isolated borderland location. They remained community-oriented, ambitious, driven by success, and morally guided by their spirituality.

Cornwall

Cornwall, Ontario had grown up with and around the textile industry. The commitment to this industry did not change in the first half of the twentieth century. While prior to 1920, local industrialists opened seven new factories in the area to manufacture furniture and brew beer, only one, a pants shop, endured and prospered. National and local governmental officials had tried to diversify the country's production facilities by offering industrialists financial assistance. This made no impact on Cornwall based on its isolated location.

With its extensive shipping business and ample foreign labor force, Montreal remained foreign investors' chosen location for new production enterprises. Even with the continual success of the Toronto Paper Mill, Cornwall's economic future remained dependent on the ebb and flow of the textile market. However, the values that guided George Stephen in the 1870s still influenced the owners of the area's corporations and they continually improved their facilities. They reinvested their revenue in the latest technology, funded research and development projects, and created new divisions and products. Therefore, from 1900 to 1954, Cornwall's economy was still driven by the owners of Courtaulds, Canadian Cotton, and the Howard Smith Paper Mill.

By the turn of the century, with two major cotton mills and a paper plant, Cornwall earned the distinction of one of Ontario's preeminent factory towns. The manufactories became "the backbone of the town."[2] Cornwall's industrial base continued to expand and diversify after the turn of the century with the addition of seven new industries by 1920. However, from 1902 to 1920, the package of tax exemptions and bonuses, while still an effective vehicle for attracting new entrepreneurs, proved less successful at sustaining manufacturers' long-term economic viability. As local historian Elinor Senior noted, "Out of the seven industries attracted to Cornwall between 1902 and 1920, five received substantial help from the town in terms of money and tax exemptions, and yet only one survived without suffering early bankruptcy."[3] Cornwall Furniture, Cornwall Brewery, Ives Bedding, Canadian Linoleum and Oilcloth, and McGill Chair were all incorporated between 1900 and 1919, and each ceased operation before 1941. Only the Cornwall Pants Factory survived and prospered along with the cotton and paper mills.

The Cornwall Pants Factory, founded in 1911 by future Cornwall mayor Aaron Horovitz, was the only profitable Cornwall business owned and operated by local residents. Aaron and his brother, Louis, emigrated to Montreal in 1910 from their native Romania and decided to locate their business in Cornwall, based on the large pool of textile workers and cheap real estate. They rented a building on the corner of Water and Marlborough Streets, and employed twenty-five workers to manufacture men's and boys' pants. Twelve salesmen supervised by Louis Horovitz traveled across the country to sell clothing to individuals and store owners. In 1920 the Horovitzs outgrew their original workshop, moved their facility to the Plamonden Hotel, and added the Prince Clothing division to their operations. In 1934 the company's staff produced 1,000 pairs of men's pants and 250 boys' suits and overcoats daily. During World War II when their material supply lines were cut off, half of their employees sewed uniforms for the Royal Canadian Air Force and Navy. In 1952 the Cornwall Pants Factory employed 245 workers and reported annual sales of $1.5 million.[4] In a country where most of the factories were financed and operated by foreigners, the Cornwall Pants Factory was a unique local success story.

Cornwall's three cotton and woolen facilities, now under the umbrella of the Canadian Cotton Corporation, continually upgraded their facilities and remained competitive with their New England and southern rivals. For the first five decades of the twentieth century, the mills produced textile products, maintained a steady employment of 1,500 workers, and increased the value of their production from $1,647,397 to $6,000,000. Plant owners also renovated and retooled their facilities. Based on the competitive nature of the cotton business, supervisors constantly improved the quality of their denims, flannels, blankets, and shirtings to retain their market share. During World War II Canadian Cotton employees produced uniforms for the Royal Canadian Air Force and Navy and sheets for military hospitals and medical tents.[5] However, after the war when the demand for certain products declined, the owners of Canadian Cotton, like numerous owners of consumer-based facilities, centralized their operations and closed down their peripheral plants. The Cornwall facilities were no longer able to compete with textile producers in the American South and around the globe who had lower operating costs. According to Steve Dunwell, "Cotton mills flourished in several southern states, then surpassed and finally suffocated its northern parent."[6] In 1959 Canadian Cotton officials closed their three Cornwall plants.[7] The company's demise forecasted the impending deindustrialization of the town.

The Toronto Paper Mill prevailed as one of Cornwall's most profitable facilities because of John Barber's commitment to technical innovation and product quality. In the first two decades of the twentieth century, he purchased a third sulfite digester, an additional paper machine, and erected two steam plants. By 1904 the mill employed 130 men who operated the plant's machinery, maintained the equipment, and focused on power generation. For the next eight years, Barber sustained a steady level of production and retained his entire workforce. In 1913 his orders declined due to increased foreign competition. However, with the outbreak of World War I, Barber received large orders from Canadian and U.S. newspaper publishers and stationery dealers who could no longer purchase paper from foreign corporations. He also began to sell goods to merchants in war-torn nations whose previous suppliers were concentrating on war production. World War I, therefore, opened markets for Barber that had previously been the domain of European manufacturers. In 1914 the Toronto Paper Mill employed 348 workers and reported assets of $490,245 and liabilities of $130,706.[8]

In 1919 C. Howard Smith purchased the Toronto Paper Mill and immediately authorized a general overhaul of the company's production facilities and equipment to make the mill more competitive. Over the next three decades, Smith built a new sulfite and chlorine plant, purchased two additional paper machines, and erected a vanillin factory. In 1951 he employed 1,622 workers and installed a new $2.5 million paper machine.[9] The continual success of the mill was based on the owner's investment in new technology, new products, and the exploration of new markets. The mill's prosperity contradicted Seymour Lipset's argument that the typical Canadian manufacturer failed to develop new technology and industry and become involved in research and development.[10]

The establishment of a rayon production plant in Cornwall by Courtaulds reflected the increasing amount of foreign investment in Canada. In 1924 the owners of Courtaulds, an English company that specialized in the production of artificial silk or viscose rayon, constructed a large factory in Cornwall. Prior to locating in Cornwall, Courtaulds had sold its Canadian customers products made at its American plant in Pennsylvania.[11] When Canada's consumer and corporate demands for rayon increased in the 1920s, Courtaulds officials erected a plant in Cornwall to take advantage of cheap electricity, a plentiful supply of water, and a large number of workers with textile experience.[12] The factory was the second smallest in the corporate chain, which included five other facilities located in England, France, Germany, and the United States. The Cornwall factory's 600 employees produced twenty million pounds of rayon annually.[13] Over the next decade three additional mills were constructed, the number of weaving machines increased to 200 and the plant's production level of textile yarn grew from two million pounds to ten million. By 1942 Courtaulds' Cornwall plant managers recorded sales of $7,444,000 with a payroll of $2,509,538.[14]

During World War II, Courtaulds, like other Cornwall manufacturers, converted the equipment in one of its mills to exclusively produce tire yarn, a strong fiber used in the manufacturing of tires and drive belts. Defense contractors increasingly demanded this material since their assembly of military vehicles was at an all-time high. Courtaulds shipped its products to the operators of the Canadian army's supply depots, as well as to their counterparts in England. The British armed forces' commanders continually replaced their equipment, as it was being destroyed daily by the enemy. As Edgar McInnis wrote, "The mechanization of modern armies meant a vast increase in the demands that the war made on all branches of production."[15]

In the postwar years, Courtaulds expanded its product line at the Cornwall factory because of its declining market share in the rayon market. Corporate officials authorized the construction of a new mill and the permanent addition of three new products: tire yarn, staple fiber, and textile filament.[16] The new facility also housed machinery for the production of cellulose film, a transparent plastic wrap commonly used in food packaging. The employees of TCF, a subsidiary of Courtaulds, rolled and boxed the film for sale to commercial and private customers. However, Courtaulds' executives struggled with financial setbacks, even with their numerous attempts to diversify their company's product line.

During a 1954 tour of the Cornwall facility, Sir John Hanbury-Williams, chairman of the board of directors, stated that the Courtaulds' plant was not turning a profit. Similar to the Canadian cotton mills, American and European imports offered customers cheap alternatives.[17] These unfavorable trading conditions resulted in a severe national depression in the textile industry and caused the shutdown of the Cornwall textile filament division for several months annually between 1951 and 1953. Each time the division closed, the human resource manager laid off more than 1,000 workers. According to the facility's general manager, Drummond Giles, this curtailment of production was reflected across Canada, as thirty textile mills ceased operations between 1951 and 1954, putting 27,000 of the industry's 100,000 total workforce out of a job.[18] After the market recovered in 1954, Courtaulds' production rebounded the following year and most of the workforce was eventually rehired.[19] In that year the supervisors of the TCF division employed 300 men and women, while the managers of the rayon department employed 1,891 operatives.[20]

During the early decades of the twentieth century, Cornwall made the final transition from an agricultural to an industrial community. With the expansion of existing plants and the addition of several new companies, including Courtaulds, a majority of the town's population became employed in manufacturing. Over five decades, John Barber, C. Howard Smith, and the other plant owners expanded and upgraded their plants by purchasing the latest equipment. However, plant supervisors did not increase workers' wages or improve their working conditions. Therefore, during the 1930s, union organizers easily recruited all of the area's textile workers into an affiliate of the United Textile Workers' union.

Between 1936 and 1939 workers at Courtaulds, the Cornwall Pants Company, and Canada Cotton formed unions under the guidance of Arthur Laverty, Frank Love, Alex Welch, Ellis Blair, and Percy Laurin. Each of these men had union or employment experience which gave them an insight into the specific concerns and financial goals of textile workers. From 1931 to 1935, Arthur Laverty worked at Courtaulds and discretely organized his 1,100 co-workers into the Cornwall Rayon Workers Industrial Union.[21] Love, an electrician, was fired from his job at the Gallinger Electric Shop on Pitt Street because of his efforts to gain union recognition for his co-workers. After his dismissal he became a full-time organizer for the United Textile Workers of America.[22] Prior to relocating to Cornwall in 1936, Alex Welch was a member of the Worker's Unity League and an organizer for the United Textile Workers' Union. Ellis Blair and Percy Laurin, the two other key figures in the organizing drives and strikes of Cornwall textile workers in the late 1930s, both had worked in the Cornwall mills as teenagers and had personal knowledge of the working conditions within these facilities.[23] Based on their practical experience, these men convinced Cornwall textile workers to unite and fight for better wages and working conditions.

In 1936, female Courtaulds' workers staged the area's first twentieth-century strike. Women employed in the reeling department walked out after company officials fired four of their co-workers because of their slow work habits. Within twenty-four hours of the inception of the protest, the department managers agreed only to suspend the women for one week. However, the protesters wanted the women reinstated immediately. When the managers refused to meet its demands, the plant's entire work force met with Frank Love, the organizer of its fledgling textile union, and decided to stage a company-wide strike. Love was not in favor of this proposal based on the newness of the union, but since the women had already started the process, he reluctantly agreed to the walkout.

The Courtaulds' strike lasted for several months, as union representatives and management could not agree to terms. On August 6 Love and his fellow organizers asked the company's representatives for union recognition, a 40-hour work week, a five to ten cent increase in hourly wages, and improved working conditions. Management officials counterproposed a company union comprised of a worker's council. Love presented management's offer to a meeting of 800 workers who rejected the proposal and instead voted to join the United Textile Workers of America. On August 11 the men in the spinning department left their machines and were joined by members of the rest of the workforce. The following day 2,000 workers picketed the plant to prevent the delivery of raw materials by outside suppliers.[24] On September 28, after four weeks of bargaining, the factory workers agreed to return to work. While some of the union demands were met, including a two-cent-per-hour raise for all male employees, shorter working hours, and the investigation and correction of dangerous plant conditions by general manager Hugh Douglas, the issue of union recognition was tabled. However, by 1937, the Rayon Workers Industrial Union became the official bargaining unit for Courtaulds' workers.[25]

After the Courtaulds' victory, Laverty and his fellow union officials focused on organizing workers at the Canadian Cotton and the Cornwall Pants factory into the all-inclusive United Textile Workers' Union. Laverty's efforts at Canadian Cotton initially met with management resistance. On July 12, 1937 he gave a memo to Canadian Cotton's managers stating that the Textile Workers Union represented 80 percent of the plant's workforce. The union, therefore, demanded a 20 percent wage increase for all workers, overtime pay, promotions based on seniority and efficiency, and union recognition. When Canadian Cotton officials refused to meet Laverty's requests, he called a strike on July 30.[26] Within three weeks he had reached a temporary settlement with Canadian Cotton in which company officials promised wage increases and better working conditions. On August 20 workers returned to the assembly line, but they staged periodic walkouts until 1938, when all their demands were met, including the implementation of a closed shop. The establishment of a closed shop in all three Cornwall mills was the first such agreement negotiated by the leaders of any Canadian textile union.[27]

The addition of employees of the Cornwall Pants factory to the United Textile Workers' Union was the final successful union action of the 1930s. On September 4, 1937, Aaron and Louis Horovitz fired four of their employees for union activity. Based on these dismissals, 275 workers walked out of the plant. By September 19 Laverty had secured workers a 40-hour work week, time and a half for overtime, and arranged for the rehiring of the four fired workers. The victory at the Horovitzs' facility meant that the Textile Union represented all Cornwall clothing workers.[28] Elinor Senior pointed out, "The picture that emerges from this lookout at Cornwall's industrial growth, its workforce, and the strike action of the 1930s is that of a town bursting with an increased population, expanded industry, and a militant and triumphant union movement."[29] The success of the Cornwall union organizers was also phenomenal based on the area's ethnically diverse workforce.

During the first half of the twentieth century, the workers who operated the machines at Cornwall's manufacturing plants were predominantly of French-Canadian or British descent. Most had emigrated to the area during the two stages of industrial expansion from 1871 to 1891 and from 1921 to 1931. In 1901, 1,807 residents listed France or French Canada as their origin, while 3,454 reported Great Britain. By 1921 these numbers increased to 2,542 of French descent and 3,318 of British descent. In 1951, on the eve of the commencement of the construction of the St. Lawrence Seaway, Cornwall's total population of 16,899 remained dominated by those of French and British origins. The census reported 8,301 British and 7,073 French men and women residing in Cornwall. These new arrivals lived across town from existing houses in the working-class neighborhoods and eventually worshiped at new churches constructed by the area's leading congregations. Cornwall residents did not mind living in the same town as immigrants, they just did not want to have them as neighbors or share a pew with them during Sunday church services. Local inhabitants turned to their religious leaders to help them deal with their changing economic and social circumstances.[30]

From 1900 to 1954 members of all Cornwall religious congregations established moral crusading and social activist agendas to deal with problems related to industrialization, specifically, poverty, declining social bonds, and the new immigrant population. The faithful believed that if they improved the social and living environments of these new arrivals and encouraged their moral regeneration through religious worship, immigrants would naturally alter their cultures to adhere to the dominant Protestant values. Worshipers also viewed community service as a new road to sanctification. Men established voluntary associations to enhance their own spiritual lives and those of young male worshipers. Women raised money for church renovation projects and gained a new dominance over their congregations' financial affairs. According to Marilyn Whiteley and Lynne Marks, "Women could control church leaders' financial decisions because they could refuse to let reverends use the proceeds from their fund-raising events to bankroll unnecessary construction projects."[31] Women also became involved in improving their own education and the lives of immigrants by founding various charitable organizations. The goal of all Cornwall congregants was to retain their harmonious spiritual community by controlling the new foreign element of the population and instilling lifelong moral values in their children.

During the first five decades of the twentieth century, the leaders of St. John's Presbyterian Church established active voluntary associations and struggled over the controversial church union debate. Reverend N. H. McGillivray, who served at St. John's from 1904 to 1910, championed the membership of congregants in various voluntary associations as a way of strengthening their social bonds and their spirituality. He also encouraged current members to invite friends and family to attend the Presbyterian services. McGillivray's efforts resulted in a number of new converts and brought the congregation's total membership to 291. His successor, Reverend A. B. McLeod, also recorded an increase in service attendance, attracting an average of 200 worshipers to each communion service with his flamboyant preaching style. In addition he promoted the importance of young Presbyterians participating in Sunday School classes and youth activities as a way of instilling lifelong values and faith.[32]

The most charged issue of twentieth century Protestantism was whether or not to create a united church. Reverend Hugh Munroe arrived in Cornwall in 1914, just in time to guide the congregation through the confusing church union debate. This was a national movement aimed at merging the memberships of the Methodist, Congregational, and Presbyterian denominations. Munroe, who was opposed to the proposal, was a strong supporter of keeping the Presbyterian Church a separate organization. The majority of the members of the St. John's congregation agreed with Munroe's opinion and voted against unity several times over the next decade. It remained a separate church, attracting 125 new members, many of whom were searching to retain some old-fashioned values at a time of increasing industrialization and immigration.[33]

The members of the Knox congregation, established in 1846 as an alternative to St. John's, permanently severed ties with the original church after the conclusion of the church union debate. Unlike the St. John's Presbyterians, the majority of Knox members supported the unification proposal and voted in favor of the resolution in 1911 and 1915.[34] Over the next decade a majority of elders and communicants continually voiced their approval of the merger. Following the passage of the Church Union Act in 1924 by the Canadian Parliament, Knox worshipers became members of the United Church of Canada. Approximately one-third of the congregation disagreed with the new affiliation and returned to St. John's. Despite the loss of numerous members, the Knox congregation grew steadily, and a number of renovation projects were undertaken in the decades prior to the St. Lawrence Seaway Project.

Even though the two Presbyterian congregations split over ideological and affiliation issues, women's charitable work remained united during the first two decades of the twentieth century. They, therefore, divided the proceeds from their numerous fund-raising events equally between the treasuries of St. John's and Knox. The most notable of these organizations were the two Women's Missionary Societies that financially supported relief work in Canada and overseas. In 1883 Mrs. Jacob Pringle held the initial meeting of the Women's Foreign Missionary at her home. Subsequently, the group met monthly at either church. In 1904 a chapter of the Women's Home Missionary Society was founded in Cornwall. The group provided clothing and other essentials to workers and their families in the newly settled areas of western Canada. In 1914 the Foreign and Home Missionary societies merged and added a Young Women's Auxiliary. When St. John's and Knox split over the issue of the United Church in 1925, the organization also splintered into two groups.[35] Both of these Presbyterian women's associations provided a personally fulfilling and uplifting social space for women outside the home.[36]

Regardless of the efforts of Presbyterian Church leaders to increase their membership and foster camaraderie among female members, Catholicism supplanted Presbyterianism as the dominant faith in Cornwall during the twentieth century. Father Corbet, the congregation's longtime leader, died in 1933, leaving behind the strongest denomination in Cornwall. Father John Foley succeeded Corbet in 1933 and during his eleven years at the congregation, he renovated church buildings and sponsored hockey and softball teams as a way for the parish leaders to become more involved in the social activities of young parishioners. He also emphasized the spiritual maintenance and growth of parishioners by conducting missions several times during his pastorship. Priests scheduled the one-week events separately for men and women, and missionaries preached four morning masses and evening benedictions to the participants. The missions were meant as a time for Catholics to reaffirm their faith and rededicate themselves to the objectives of the church doctrines.[37] Foley resigned in 1944 and was succeeded by Monsignor William Smith and Alexander Cameron. During the careers of these three pastors, diocesan leaders organized three new parishes: St. Francis de Sales, St. Felix de Valois, and St. John Bosco. These new houses of worship served French-Canadian factory workers and their families, who resided in the eastern, western, and northern ends of town. In 1951 Canadian census takers recorded 10,215 Cornwall Catholics compared to 3,274 in 1911.[38]

Unlike other area worshipers Catholic men organized their faith's first voluntary association, the Holy Name Society, in 1924. Pope Gregory X created the organization in 1274 to "spread and increase love for the sacred name of Jesus Christ." In the twentieth century, the mission of society members had expanded to include suppressing profanity and blasphemy, encouraging respect for civil and religious authority, and fostering the proper observance of the Sabbath. The members of the Cornwall Holy Name Society, led by mayor Dr. W. B. Cavanaugh, fulfilled their objectives by organizing fund-raising campaigns and bazaars in conjunction with the women's auxiliary, and by independently founding an Athletic Club in the 1930s and 1940s. The Athletic Club sponsored basketball, baseball, hockey, boxing, and lacrosse teams for teenage boys. The development of athletic activities for young Catholic men was seen as an integral part of the society's goal to promote Christian living.[39] The leadership of the Holy Name Society attracted members from the area's most prominent Catholics in the twentieth century, and remained an important part of the church's social component. According to Brian Clarke, "The development of these organizations gave male parishioners a more powerful religious identity."[40]

The female members of Cornwall's Catholic parishes organized a chapter of the Catholic Women's League (CWL) as a means of enhancing their charity work and furthering their spiritual knowledge. The first national CWL conference was held in 1920 in Toronto with more than 500 women in attendance, including members of the St. Columban's Auxiliary. The Cornwall delegation left the Toronto conference determined to establish an affiliate. The next year the local chapter reported seventy-nine members dedicated to promoting the involvement of female parishioners in fund-raising, educational seminars, and charity work. They supported the Cornwall orphanage through various annual events, purchased communion and confirmation clothes for poor children, and supplied books for the separate school library. From an educational standpoint the organization's members held annual conferences featuring speakers who addressed important religious and political issues.[41] Catholic women had traditionally played an important fund-raising role in local parishes. However, they were now being invited by Catholic bishops to keep abreast of church issues and voice opinions on important matters, a privilege previously reserved for male parishioners.

From 1900 to 1954 Cornwall's Anglicans struggled to preserve their administrative autonomy and faced financial and spiritual challenges from other denominations, whose ministers updated their services and social opportunities. After the turn of the century, the members of the Strachan Memorial Church struggled to retain control over their right to appoint ministers.

In 1906, when Reverend T. J. Stiles was designated by provincial church officials to lead the 440-member Cornwall congregation, local parishioners argued that diocesan officials employed their new pastor without consulting their opinion on his qualifications. Male congregants did not see the hiring of a new minister for the Strachan Memorial Church as the exclusive duty of the bishop. The vestry had historically recruited its own ministers and viewed the bishop's actions as another attempt by church leaders to take away its independence.

Reverend Stiles and his successors continued their predecessor's commitment to church organizations and enlarging the congregation. Like his Catholic counterparts, Stiles reestablished the Trinity Athletic Association, whose members competed against athletes from other local church groups. He also visited jails, factories, and homes seeking new believers and the return of those who had gone astray. During Reverend Harold Clark's 18-year tenure, he tried to increase the public awareness of the congregation's mission by starting a Sunday School radio show. All these efforts attracted new members and exhibited the dedication of current members to the faith.[42]

The leaders of the second Anglican congregation, the Church of the Good Shepherd, were at the center of the new social activist movement. They struggled to serve the increasing number of mill workers on a limited budget. Courtaulds' hiring preferences had increased the number of Cornwall residents of French origin. Social reformers believed that providing religious services and spiritual guidance for these new arrivals would make them more Canadian. As Marilyn Barber indicated, "This was part of a national trend to improve the social environment where immigrants lived as a way to transform their culture."[43] The Church of the Good Shepherd's dedicated ministers and parishioners were, therefore, determined to keep the congregation afloat even when worshipers' donations were not enough to pay the pastor's salary. The vestry undertook several measures to increase the church's income. In 1908 parishioners rented the church hall to the leaders of various community groups and organizations for their meetings and social events. Reverend S. Gower Poole also instituted an envelope system to encourage worshipers to bring a weekly contribution to Sunday service. However, these fund-raising efforts were unsuccessful since most members were factory workers with little discretionary income.

In 1917 the vestry discussed closing the church and rejoining the Trinity congregation. Church of the Good Shepherd's leaders, however, opted to remain a separate entity in order to serve the particular spiritual and linguistic needs of their worshipers. In 1925 they took out a $3,000 mortgage on their church, rectory, and several cottages. Four years later the vestry was only able to give Reverend David Floyde a $1,500 salary, the synod's minimum required allowance. Regardless of its financial dilemma, the vestry recorded a membership of 129 families and 500 individuals by the beginning of the

Seaway construction in 1954.[44] The congregation still gained members from the working-class neighborhoods and pursued its goal of assimilating French Canadians into the Protestant world.

The female parishioners of the Church of the Good Shepherd, unlike their Catholic and Presbyterian counterparts, created strong church associations, specifically to attract new adult and teenage worshipers. A. D. Floyde, the wife of the congregation's longtime rector, organized the Good Shepherd Guild in the early twentieth century. Mrs. Floyde and several female parishioners began visiting their colleagues' homes to promote the family values of the church and increase Sunday service attendance. The guild members compiled a list of all parish women who were visited monthly and encouraged to bring their families to Sunday service. Female congregants, who were not presently affiliated with the group, were asked to become members of the guild and attend monthly meetings. In the 1940s guild leaders created the Junior Auxiliary, comprised of teenage female parishioners, as a means of encouraging younger worshipers to become more involved in church affairs. This group was a further extension of ministers' efforts to modernize the church as well as stay competitive with the increasing number of evangelical Cornwall churches, particularly the Baptists.[45]

After the turn of the century, the Baptist Congregation, Cornwall's most prominent evangelical church, realized that the future success of their faith rested on their ability to extend their appeal to the young and immigrant populations. The eleven pastors who led the First Baptist worshipers from 1902 to 1951 guaranteed the permanence of the faith by making the congregation financially stable, by recruiting new members, and by constructing a more ornate building. Reverend S. Sheldon of Montreal oversaw the Cornwall Baptists from November 1902 to 1905 and again from 1907 to 1919. His main accomplishment was achieving the congregation's financial independence by canceling its Home Mission Board Grant and organizing annual fund-raisers to cover the church's expenses. Sheldon also revived the Baptist Young People's Society as a means of retaining teenage membership. The presence of a dedicated, full-time minister halted the exodus of worshipers, and the church membership leveled off at 100. Furthermore, the extension of the original structure in 1919 by Reverend H. A. Reid made the church more visibly appealing, and allowed a greater number of parishioners to comfortably attend services. The enlarged church housed services for the next two decades, and Baptists remained united in their efforts to improve their own spirituality while spreading the faith to other Cornwall residents. By mid-century, however, worshipers' dissatisfaction with church leadership and the content of weekly services caused several families to leave the First Baptist Church and form the Calvary Baptist Church in the west end.[46]

From 1900 to 1954 religion remained the central social and moral institution in Cornwall residents' lives, as it had for their ancestors in the nineteenth century. Members of all denominations, including many prominent citizens and local politicians, increasingly participated in voluntary associations. These organizations provided individuals with a new way to exercise their activism and leadership, attract new worshipers, and help the less fortunate.[47] The congregations' social welfare agendas spilled over into the public sector.

The financial and social success of Cornwall's religious voluntary associations encouraged other local residents to establish new fraternal and welfare organizations. According to Jeffrey Charles, "The need for fraternal organizations increased in the early twentieth century when corporate expansion altered local economic life and men sought opportunities for community service and an enriched social life."[48] In the nineteenth century, the first fraternal organizations established by Cornwall men were the Odd Fellows and the Masons. In the twentieth century these two groups were joined by a proliferation of associations that focused on providing community service opportunities and medical care for local residents. By 1918 Cornwall inhabitants had established thirty-four fraternal organizations, including the Knights of Columbus, the Kiwanis Club, and the Kinsmen.[49]

Local male Catholics formed a chapter of the Knights of Columbus to serve the financial and social welfare needs of members of their faith and the entire Cornwall community. In 1904 the forty-five initial recruits of Cornwall Council 755 were primarily drawn from the Catholic community, and included: William Donihee, the owner of the local meat market; Joseph Chevrier, the proprietor of the area's largest grocery store; and, Reverend William Corbet, the head of St. Columban's Church. As Neil Semple indicated, "These men were activists who reached beyond their local congregations and attempted a broader goal of reforming their communities."[50] The Cornwall Knights financially supported the widows and orphans of deceased members and organized annual fund-raisers to assist local charities. In terms of community service, the association used its membership dues and donations to buy school books and clothes for needy children and to make contributions to the maintenance of St. Paul's Nursing Home and the Nazareth Orphanage.[51]

The Kiwanis Club, created by the town's politicians and business owners, concentrated on serving the less fortunate members of the community, specifically sick and underprivileged children. The members of the Cornwall chapter received their charter from the Kiwanis Club of Ottawa on May 5, 1927. By the end of 1927, the thirty-two Kiwanis members included: the principal of Cornwall Collegiate, Alex Caldwell; local entrepreneur, Aaron Horovitz; and, the owner of a lacrosse stick factory, P. J. Lally. The group held weekly meetings to hear speeches on current events and plan its community and fund-raising activities. The Kiwanis' first community service project raised money to purchase a car for the Victorian Order of Nurses. The group's leaders also created an annual clinic for the area's crippled children, a summer camp for poor boys on Lake Francis, and distributed more than 100 Christmas baskets during the holiday season. Like other Kiwanis clubs, the members of the Cornwall affiliate purchased a swimming pool for Cornwall's Central Park, provided glasses for underprivileged kids, and drove sick children to the Shriner's Hospital in Montreal for medical care. Throughout the first five decades of the twentieth century, the membership of the Kiwanis remained fluid, based on the voluntary nature of affiliation. In 1940 the group recorded its highest membership of eighty-four, and appealed to community leaders who desired to assist the needy.[52]

The Kinsmen also became entrenched in the first fifty years of the twentieth century and solicited donations for several local causes. Captain Miller Donnelly and other members of the Kingston club established the 18-member Cornwall chapter in March 1933. Harry Rogers, the group's founder, was a World War I veteran. Upon his return to Toronto, he missed the support and companionship he had experienced in the trenches in France. He, therefore, created a fraternal association for men under the age of forty under the motto "Fellowship Through Service." Kinsmen were not required by the organization's bylaws to complete specific types of community service activities. Instead, the president of each affiliate identified particular fund-raising and service initiatives within his community that addressed the unique needs of the town's inhabitants.

The Cornwall Kinsmen organized many fund-raising projects to support local and national relief efforts. The "Give a Man a Job" campaign was the first project instigated by the local chapter. The organizers of the program found 3,200 unemployed men odd jobs with local merchants and other residents during the Depression. However, the group's most challenging undertaking was providing assistance and relief for individuals and business owners who lost their homes and stores on August 7, 1933, when a fire destroyed every building on Pitt Street between Second and Third Streets. The Kinsmen raised $2,000 in private and corporate donations for the fire victims within two weeks and continually solicited donations until all the families were relocated.[53] Other programs organized by the Kinsmen included a fund-raising drive to finance the construction of two children's wards at the Cornwall General Hospital and the coordination of a Milk for Britain Campaign during World War II. This organization truly exemplified the ability of voluntary associations to provide both friendship and community service opportunities.[54]

The Victorian Order of Nurses (VONA) was the most successful service organization established by Cornwall women in the early years of the twentieth century. Its members, unlike those of the men's organizations, did not organize to meet new friends, but to provide in-home healthcare. In 1883 Lady Aberdeen, the wife of the governor-general, initially proposed the creation of a local chapter of the VONA after she noticed a lack of local healthcare and convalescent facilities in Cornwall. Mrs. A. F. Cameron established the association two decades later in 1913 and remained the agency's president until 1918. Initially, the VONA was funded by individual donations and the contributions of other service organizations, like the Kinsmen. The nurses provided medical care and assistance for new mothers and newborns in the weeks following delivery. The Cornwall VONA began with one paid nurse, Alma Thompson, who cared for 290 patients. Besides her daily house call duties, Ms. Thompson worked at the local schools dealing with truancy and children's health problems. By 1925 the association's leaders hired three other nurses and accepted a car purchased by the Kinsmen for use on rounds. Over the next decade their duties expanded to include training family members to care for homebound patients and conducting public health education programs at local schools and at the town hall to promote the prevention of diseases.[55]

The fraternal and social welfare associations organized by Cornwall men and women exhibited the collective orientation and the concern for the quality of life and prosperity of all members of the community that had existed since settlement. As Jeffrey Charles suggested, "Whether used for altruism or community concern . . . the service clubs can trace their roots to the sociable, religious, and civic-minded organizations dating from the colonial area."[56] During the early years of settlement, the loyalists cooperatively built homes and harvested crops. Once Cornwall men and women moved away from their farms, these new organizations allowed them to continue their community service and self-help activities and improve the area's social life and healthcare facilities. Local citizens did not refrain from volunteering their time and donating their money to these causes because they expected government programs to solve their local problems.

The social, economic, and religious lives of Cornwall residents greatly changed from 1900 to 1954 as the town became a provincial manufacturing center. Unlike the neighboring town of Alexandria, Ontario, the area's economy was driven by the owners of factories. The French men and women who operated the machinery at these facilities challenged Cornwall residents to deal with neighbors who spoke a foreign language and worshiped at the Catholic Church. Cornwall residents created fraternal and social welfare organizations to combat the social and economic problems related to industrialization. They replaced the social bonds associated with agricultural living with the camaraderie achieved through group community service. The economic and social lives of Cornwall residents, therefore, resembled those of their Massena neighbors. As Robert Bothwell noted, "In this respect as in so many others, its [Canada's] residents resembled the Americans with whom they have such close connections."[57]

Massena

Between 1900 and 1954 Massena became the financial and retail center of St. Lawrence County. In 1902 the industrialization of Massena was stimulated by the completion of the canal project and its companion powerhouse. The owners of the Pittsburgh Reduction Company established a plant on the St. Lawrence River and hired many of the area's nonagricultural and former canal laborers. Local government leaders anticipated the shift of the town's economy from agricultural to industrial, and funded the improvement of telegraph and telephone lines, the installment of a sewer system, and the paving of roads.[58] Over the next several decades, other industrialists opened several small factories around town. By 1950 scholars described Massena as "a completely manufacturing town with approximately 60 percent of employed people in manufacturing . . . 94 percent at Alcoa."[59]

Massena's population and social life changed with the influx of foreigners to work at Alcoa. The town's population quadrupled and diversified with the arrival of European immigrants. The majority of these new arrivals were Catholic. Therefore, priests, similar to their Cornwall neighbors, constructed three new churches to meet the spiritual needs of new residents. The town's evolving spirituality was also illustrated by the establishment of a synagogue and a Pilgrim Holiness Church. Religion still remained the basis of a moral community. Socially, Massena men and women established several community service organizations that offered fraternity to their members and financial assistance to the sick and the poor. From 1900 to 1954 the changing social and economic lives of Massena residents resembled those of their Cornwall neighbors. It was the establishment of an Alcoa processing plant that transformed Massena from an agricultural to a manufacturing center.

The abundance of inexpensive power created by the Massena canal project in 1902 caught the attention of the directors of the Pittsburgh Reduction Company, later known as the Aluminum Company of America (Alcoa). In 1888 Charles Hall, the inventor of a new low-cost way of producing aluminum, and investors Alfred Hunt and R. B. Mellon, founded the Pittsburgh Reduction Company, America's first aluminum processing enterprise.[60] For almost a decade Hunt and the other Pittsburgh Reduction Company officials resisted expansion, concentrated on improving their Pittsburgh operations, and found customers for their aluminum. But aluminum production required large amounts of power. In *The Billion Dollar Story*, Nick Podgurski indicated that it took ten kilowatt hours of electricity to produce one pound of aluminum, the equivalent of the amount required to burn a 40-watt bulb constantly for ten days.[61] Pittsburgh's high electricity costs encouraged Alcoa executives to seek alternative manufacturing sites. In 1895 Pittsburgh Reduction's first subsidiary facility was erected in Niagara Falls, New York.

Seven years later Alcoa came to Massena. As George Smith noted, "from that time on, the availability of inexpensive power became the major determinant in the siting of Alcoa smelts."[62]

Following a May 15, 1902 visit to Massena by company executives Arthur Davis, Charles Hall, and E. S. Fickes, Pittsburgh Reduction purchased 100 acres of land east of the canal. Two months later contractors began construction of a $1 million facility that included five 550-feet long production buildings, a storage yard, and company-owned railroad tracks. Alcoa officials also purchased the entire annual output of the newly finished powerhouse from the owners of the St. Lawrence Power Company.[63] Davis, Hall, and Fickes expected their new Massena factory to eventually become Pittsburgh Reduction's main processing plant. They also forecasted the annual employment of 500 to 600 men and boys.[64]

Like Cornwall industrialists, from 1900 to 1954 Alcoa officials expanded their facilities and developed new products. At the inception of production on August 24, 1903, Pittsburgh Reduction's Massena managers hired sixty-seven men to manufacture aluminum wire, cable, and cooking utensils.[65] Within three years company executives approved the construction of a new reduction facility and enlarged the original wire department, thereby doubling the factory's production capacity and increasing the number of workers to 581.[66] Alcoa employees also deepened the Massena Canal, updated the generators and turbines in the powerhouse, and constructed another potroom, rolling mill, and a larger wire mill. By 1910, 171 men and boys were employed in the reduction division, 59 in the carbon plant, 140 in the fabricating plant, and 269 in the power division.[67] In 1920 the company's executives and stockholders illustrated their innovative, risk-taking mentality by constructing a $3 million structural shapes mill in Massena. While no market currently existed for such a product, company salesmen believed that they could compete with their counterparts in the steel industry if they could convince contractors that aluminum material was cheaper and stronger than the traditional metals they used to construct bridges and skyscrapers.[68] The Massena plant had proven to be a profitable investment.

For the first two decades of the twentieth century, Alcoa officials maintained their national monopoly of the aluminum market and they were confident that their economic prosperity would continue. However, the optimism of company executives and investors disappeared in 1929, as the Great Depression hit and aluminum sales and profits declined. From 1929 to 1934 the number of Massena workers dropped from 2,444 to 1,224. The remaining employees worked three 6-hour shifts a week for a $12 paycheck.[69] In 1932, following four straight years of staff cuts, the local workforce accepted a 10 percent pay cut, thus preventing further layoffs.[70] Comparable to other U.S. businesses, it would take the government orders for munitions and other military supplies during World War II to revive Alcoa's production levels.

During World War II Alcoa produced materials for the defense industry and operated an adjacent government-funded facility.[71] Workers made airplane rotors and rod and wire used by the defense industry in the new $15 million blooming mill and melting department. They also produced additional aluminum products at the federal installation from June 1942 to 1944. This factory had been built by the Truman Committee during the early stages of World War II when the existing Alcoa production facilities could not meet the federal government's demands. Between 1941 and 1943 twenty new facilities were built in eleven states. These plants were operated by Alcoa officials according to government criteria and produced materials exclusively for United States combat forces. Alcoa was also financially vested in these facilities. The company was renting the plants from the federal government under a multi-year lease plan, and also investing $474,000 of the company's own capital in these ventures. In 1944 Alcoa ran 91 percent of the aluminum and 96 percent of the alumina processing facilities in the country.[72] However, even with Alcoa's financial stake in the factories and the lending of the expertise of their employees, company officials were blocked from purchasing the plants when war production ceased. The sole plant they acquired was the one in Massena.

After the conclusion of World War II, Alcoa's production and employment levels declined, reflecting the impact of forced competition. In 1946 the War Surplus Board sold eight of the wartime plants to Kaiser Permanente and Reynolds for 10 cents on the dollar, well below the market value. While Reynolds had built two smelting and sheet mills in Washington and Alabama in 1939 with a loan from Reconstruction Finance Corporation, Kaiser was new to the United States aluminum production market.[73] As George David Smith noted, "World War I had been a stimulus to the aluminum industry, while World War II transformed it. . . . A temporary agency of the federal government established competition in an industry where free market and the federal courts had failed."[74] By 1950, because of Alcoa's lower production, many Massena workers were fired. This threatened the economic stability of the municipality, as Alcoa was the town's main employer and paid half of the annual property taxes. Other industries in town established in the last five decades also closed and increased local unemployment levels.

While Alcoa was the largest employer in Massena for over half a century, an insulating company, a silk mill, and a lingerie factory also began production prior to 1954. The owners of these businesses provided jobs for the wives and daughters of aluminum workers and local female residents who wanted to supplement their family's income. Officials of the Mica Company, a Canadian insulation manufacturing firm, purchased the former Diamond Creamery plant from local investors in 1923. The company's supervisors initially employed twenty-eight workers at their Massena plant, who manufactured insulation for electrical equipment and appliances. By

1942, 100 women were employed at the facility. However, Mica officials closed their Massena plant in the 1950s based on a significant decline in the demand for their product.[75]

Cedar Silk Mill officials also located a plant in the area in 1933. It employed 175 female workers, mostly the wives and daughters of Alcoa workers. These women operated 100 looms, and wove satin, crepe slippers, and liners for men's clothing, while sharing an annual payroll of $150,000.[76] In 1934 the silk mill ranked second only to Alcoa in terms of manufacturing jobs. The Massena mill's early success led corporate executives to consider expanding their facility to accommodate fifty more looms and hiring a larger workforce. However, there were not enough skilled weavers in Massena to operate more looms, and company recruiters could not entice workers from other towns to move to the area.[77] Therefore, the silk mill closed in the early 1940s.

In 1950 Warner Brothers' executives took over the silk mill building. They initially employed 265 workers to sew bras. Five years later local supervisors reported a workforce of 250 women with an annual payroll of $600,000.[78] However, Warner Brothers also shut its Massena facility in 1960 and relocated operations to South Carolina, where nonunion workers accepted lower wages. Company officials had faced increasing pressure from workers who threatened to unionize as their counterparts had at Alcoa.

During the first three decades of the twentieth century, Alcoa officials, unlike Cornwall industrialists, retained absolute control over their workers' lives through the successful use of various paternalistic and welfare capitalist initiatives. The company provided recreational activities and healthcare on the plant grounds for workers and their families. They also constructed housing around Massena, which they leased or sold to employees at a fair price.[79] According to one former worker, labor-management relations at Alcoa's plants were best described as a master-servant relationship.[80]

Alcoa managers lost their overall influence over workers' actions as the twentieth century progressed, and operatives turned to union leaders to protect their interests. Like their Cornwall counterparts, Massena's Alcoa employees used collective action to gain better wages and working conditions between 1900 and 1954. In 1915 company officials experienced their first strike at their Massena facility. While the walkout by pot room employees did not lead to the formal organization of a union, it served notice to Alcoa managers of the collective power and mentality of their workforce. According to George Smith, "Workers at Alcoa were no longer confident in the company's ability to look after their interests and formed industrial unions."[81]

In the 1930s Massena's Alcoa employees walked the picket line in support of their brothers at other company facilities and formed a permanent local union. National staff members of the Aluminum Workers Union, an affiliate of the International Council of Aluminum Workers, organized 450

Massena workers into Local 19256 in February 1934. In August 1934, after years of wage reductions, Alcoa workers staged their first company-wide strike, closing six plants including the Massena facility. However, Aluminum Workers' union officials were unable to get their entire list of conditions met. Instead, Alcoa negotiators agreed to implement a previous offer that created a workers' council, froze wages at their current levels, and established a grievance procedure controlled by management. The first effort to create a permanent union by the aluminum workers was largely a failure.[82] It did, however, lay the foundation for future success.

In 1941 Massena Local 19256 negotiated its first agreement with Alcoa management after a month-long strike. The inaugural contract improved working conditions by guaranteeing all employees paid vacations and a shorter work week. For the next several decades, management and union representatives at the Massena facility renewed their contract every four years. The success of this local affiliate was surprising, based on the ethnic diversity of the workforce.

Accompanying Massena's economic prosperity was a quadrupling and ethnic diversification of the town's population. These immigrants, initially consisting of Italians and Jews from New York City and later of recent arrivals from Eastern Europe, Central America, and Scandinavia, were employed predominantly in the most menial jobs at Alcoa, and as laborers on local farms and various road and bridge projects. Between 1910 and 1940 the Massena population increased from 2,951 to 11,328. By 1950, 28 percent of Massena's population was foreign born, compared with 9 percent in 1905. Four years later the citizenship of Massena had representatives from forty countries.[83]

With these workers came new cultures and religious traditions that taxed the patience of local residents and stressed the available housing market. The transformation that took place in the first half of the twentieth century pressured this small town to come to terms with its new identity as an industrial center and with the difficulties of dealing with a diverse population. According to Joan Dobbie, "Massena's Anglo-Saxon Protestants feared that their homogeneous community, its standards and values were undermined by Catholics, Greeks and other aliens."[84] To combat local residents' uneasiness, Pittsburgh Reduction officials constructed separate housing for workers and managers in previously undeveloped areas of town. Throughout the next several decades, Alcoa officials also enrolled their immigrant workers in company-sponsored Americanization programs, in which instructors taught new families the English language and the basic elements of American history. On a municipal level town councilors approved funding for a larger police force and the construction of more schools to accommodate the increasing number of school-age children. However, the implementation of these initiatives did not erase the intolerance community members held for outsiders and their unfamiliar customs.

For a community previously dominated by individuals who could trace their lineage back to the original settlers from Canada and New England, the arrival of workers from more than forty countries unearthed the fear of the unknown. Initially, Massena residents speculated that new inhabitants would erode community unity and harmony and result in an increase in crime and a collapse of the moral fabric of society. Accounts from metropolitan areas supported their apprehension, and Massena residents were prepared for the worst. Consequently, when the town's crime rate skyrocketed between 1900 and 1920, many argued that their suspicions of the unethical behavior and criminal tendency of foreigners were vindicated.[85]

Beginning with the arrival of Italian workers in Massena in the late nineteenth century, the front page of the *Massena Observer* was filled with the sordid details of crimes committed by new and unwanted immigrants. The charges ranged from the killing of songbirds to the assault of fellow Italians. Although most of these transgressions resulted in a fine or a minimal jail sentence, they garnered more press coverage than more serious offenses committed by "white" natives at the time.[86] Each article utilized a different stereotypical image in the text as a means of portraying the foreigners as drunks with a proclivity for unlawful behavior. This mirrored the popular national view at the turn of the century that classified Italian Americans as "volatile, unstable, undesirable and largely composed of the most vicious, ignorant, degraded paupers with something more than an admixture of the criminal element."[87] The community's intolerance for outsiders and their strange religious customs was exemplified by the massive hysteria caused in 1928 by the disappearance of a young girl.

Massena residents illustrated their ignorance of foreigners' religious practices when they mistakenly accused the Jewish community of kidnapping and sacrificing a local girl. On a Friday afternoon in September 1928, a 7-year-old girl failed to return home from school. Police initially treated the incident as a typical missing person case. However, a local woman circulated a rumor that it was a long tradition in Europe for Jews to sacrifice a gentile as part of a ritual associated with the celebration of Yom Kippur.[88] After the police exhausted all their leads, they turned toward the kidnapping and sacrifice theory and questioned prominent members of the Jewish community, including Rabbi Berel Brenglass. Law enforcement officials also ransacked all Jewish homes and businesses in Massena searching for possible clues. Representatives from the New York City Jewish Leadership Association traveled to the area to smooth relations between the police and Rabbi Brenglass, and to dispel the misconception surrounding the blood libel myth. However, the damage to local Jewish citizens' reputations and their relationship with other Massena residents had already occurred, and even when the girl wandered out of the woods unharmed two days later, the townspeople still tormented Jews en route to Yom Kippur ceremonies. After this incident, many Jewish families left the area.

As Massena's anti-semitic incident indicated, the arrival of men and women to work at Alcoa altered the religious makeup of Massena. Most workers and their families attended services at the First Congregational Church and the Sacred Heart Catholic parish. Massena church leaders, like their Cornwall brethren, discussed the construction of additional houses of worship to accommodate the evolving spiritual needs of longtime residents and new citizens. Between 1901 and 1953 the number of churches in Massena rose from seven to eleven, including the addition of two new Catholic parishes, a synagogue, and a Pilgrim Holiness congregation.[89] Massena's congregations also formed voluntary associations whose members held annual fund-raisers to cover church expenses and frequently performed other civic charitable duties at local orphanages, homes for the aged, and hospitals. According to Winthrop Hudson and John Corrigan, these groups illustrated the "development of a new frontier of social concern for the poor and working class."[90] These new organizations also filled the social void left by the demise of the agricultural lifestyle. Women no longer gathered to spin yarn or sew clothes. Instead they found companionship and personal satisfaction in church fund-raising and charity work. [91]

The membership of Massena's First Congregational Church soared with the arrival of Alcoa workers. Based on its emphasis on individual spirituality and worshipers' participation in all church administrative decisions, the faith appealed to both old and new residents. As the pews became increasingly crowded, members began discussing plans for constructing a new church. However, they did not own enough land to accommodate a new building, and no wealthy congregant offered to purchase more property. Regardless of these obstacles, Reverend E. D. Hardin appointed a building committee headed by J. J. Taylor in 1911. The group contacted architects regarding the possible design and expense of a new building. When the bids submitted by several firms proved too costly, the enlargement plans were put on hold for eight years.

In 1919 the congregation resurrected its construction plans and illustrated American worshipers' new commitment to fund-raising. As Dr. S. B. Fraser noted, "No longer is it considered to be the duty of the minister alone to prod the congregation in the matter of financial support."[92] Male and female members solicited funds for their new building through a variety of methods. Initially, they sold two lots on the edge of the current church property to cover contractors' building material costs and to supply them with a small downpayment.[93] Subsequently, female members of the parish established a 6-year fund-raising campaign. They collected $32,150 and partially financed the current construction project and future building maintenance costs. The men volunteered their time to assist local contractor, William

Cryderman, in erecting the new facility, and local building suppliers, including W. L. Pratt, sold the church minister construction materials at cost. To bankroll the remainder of the project, the financial committee, led by Hiriam Smith, sold the old church building to the Adath Israel Association. In 1926 contractors completed the new 350-seat church. Soon afterwards teachers commenced Sunday School classes in a 150-desk room, and the congregation officially changed its name to Emmanuel Congregational.[94]

The Congregational Church leaders acknowledged the importance of voluntary associations for the financial well-being of the congregation and the strengthening of the social cohesion of its members. In 1899 the women of the Emmanuel Congregational Church established the Ladies' Aid Society. Each year the members of the society conducted socials and bazaars. With the proceeds they purchased kitchen appliances, a sanctuary floor, and other materials needed for church maintenance. The group performed these necessary tasks for four decades before disbanding and becoming part of the Friendly Bible Society, a group which combined women's education and fund-raising efforts. The society began as a Sunday School class and later branched out into raising money for the building fund, mortgage payments, and missionary work. The officers of the Friendly Bible Society also influenced younger female parishioners to start the Congregation Guild, whose members not only followed the fund-raising examples of their elders, but also participated in local Red Cross relief work during both world wars.[95]

In the first five decades of the twentieth century, Alcoa workers also filled the pews of the First United Methodist Church and encouraged leaders to modernize and expand their facilities. The faith's leaders, who once preached damnation if members gave into sin, now were more lenient and began to appeal to men and women of all social classes.[96] In 1901 Massena's Methodists renovated their 30-year-old structure by adding a new auditorium ceiling, electric lights, carpet, and paint. Thirteen years later the remodelers doubled the church's seating and added a larger Sunday School room.

In 1920 the Methodist minister began conducting services specifically for Alcoa workers and their families in Pine Grove, the working-class section of town. For several years Alcoa provided a building where the worshipers gathered. In September 1923 Mr. and Mrs. Albert Fulton donated their store at the corner of Ober and Franklin Streets as a permanent location for the Pine Grove Mission. Methodists renovated the facility by adding several classrooms and an assembly room. Provincial church officials blessed the new building in 1925. Ministers continued to hold services at the mission until the 1950s, when the members of the First Methodist Church constructed a new social hall, chapel, and seven classrooms. The larger building allowed Methodists to hold services for all adherents under one roof.[97] In 1942 an area reporter classified the Methodist congregation as one of the "best examples of normal growth from pioneer days to the present."[98]

While the Congregationalists and Methodists attracted many new members after 1900, the Catholic Church attracted the most new parishioners and erected two additional churches. As Roger Finke and Rodney Stark noted, "In the U.S. the Roman Catholic Church was a very successful and competitive institution in a free market religious economy. The parish provided a secure haven for ethnic subcultures in which immigrant groups could retain an aspect of their native culture, while they were adapting to their new nation."[99] The majority of workers recruited by company officials to work in the plant's potrooms were European, single, and Catholic. Initially these new arrivals attended mass at Sacred Heart under the direction of Father Dennis Nolan. When Father Timothy Holland was assigned to Sacred Heart in 1914, he inherited a parish of 600 families. He, therefore, initiated services at the Pine Grove Mission near Alcoa for workers and their families.[100]

In 1919 the Pine Grove Mission was recognized by diocese leaders as Massena's second Catholic parish, St. Mary's, and awarded a full-time priest, Father John Bellamy. Members appointed a committee to manage their finances and approved plans to construct their own 635-seat church with classroom space for 350.[101] The St. Mary's congregation held its first service in its new building on Christmas Eve in 1920.[102] In that same year the parish recorded 2,000 communicants from twenty-six nationalities. Father John Bellamy supported the idea that the church was a good vehicle to help immigrants adapt to American life and values. Bellamy noted, "Those of foreign birth can be Americanized through the church more quickly and thoroughly than by other means."[103] He also championed the importance of Catholic education to instill lifelong Christian values. Therefore, in 1923 the St. Mary's congregation started the area's first Catholic school on the second floor of its church.

In 1947 another group of worshipers split from Sacred Heart and formed St. Joseph's, Massena's third and final Catholic Church. The parish was created on October 1, 1947 by Reverend Bryan McEngtegart, the bishop of Ogdensburg. The congregants, led by Father Harold Skelly, constructed a church building and worked on attracting new members in the seven years leading up to the Seaway. Father Skelly preached his first mass to worshipers on October 5, 1947 in the Project Community Hall. Services continued to be held there for the next year while the church building was completed on the corner of Bayley Road and Malby Avenue. Worshipers conducted their inaugural mass at St. Joseph's on Christmas Day, 1948.[104] The ethnic makeup of Massena's new worshipers made the Catholic faith the largest in the area.

Like the women of the Congregationalist Church, Catholic women developed voluntary organizations for their own social benefit and to financially support the church. On November 6, 1908, twenty-six women gathered at Forester Hall to meet with Bessie Matthews, the president of the national Ladies Catholic Benevolent Association (LCBA), who recognized them as branch #1100 of the association. The women appointed Ann Phillips O'Brien as the group's first president and named their chapter, St. Thomas, in honor of Father Thomas Fitzgerald. The LCBA members met monthly to pray and offer each other spiritual support and guidance. During World War I the members of the LCBA along with the local chapter of the Knights of Columbus solicited funds for care packages for local boys in the armed forces. The women also organized sewing circles to make clothes for the Red Cross. To attract new members the LCBA officers held social events for junior and senior high school girls. The attempt to get teenagers more involved in church work was a national campaign in the twentieth century. As Herbert Wallace Schneider noted, "If there was anything distinctive in the American pattern early in the century, it was the concentration of the religious on the period of adolescence."[105] By 1942, the LCBA chapter leaders recorded 190 members and a junior branch comprised of 29 girls under the age of 16.[106]

From 1900 to 1954 the leaders of St. John's Episcopal Church, one of Massena's more traditional congregations, recruited new members and fostered the inception of voluntary associations. The St. John's vestry also continually searched for ways to solve the church's financial problems. In 1903 the congregation's treasurer still relied on an annual grant from the Diocese Board of Missions to pay the pastor's $800 salary.[107] Members decided that the best way to improve their economic situation was to attract more worshipers by holding social functions. In 1916 they organized their first annual picnic. In attendance were current members and several new ones. Three years later the increased donations of these new worshipers allowed the vestry to cancel the parish's stipend from the missionary board. Sunday School teachers also reported a 50 percent increase in students.[108]

Episcopal leaders also improved St. John's financial maintenance and community service agenda. In 1925 the vestry hired Reverend N. Lascilles Ward, who was a skilled church administrator. Ward developed an accounting system for the parish and also outlined a decision-making framework for the vestry. In 1940 Ward's successor, Reverend Norman Godfrey, expanded the church's social activities by creating a theater group and initiating art classes and classical concerts for all town residents. These efforts resulted in St. John's becoming a more financially stable parish by 1954, as well as a more visible presence in the town's cultural and social arena.[109]

After 1900 the ladies of St. John's congregation played major roles in garnering funds for church renovation projects and encouraging the creation of women's and youth social groups. Marg Snaith and Mrs. H. H. Warren created the parish's first voluntary charitable organization, the Women's Visiting

Association. The group welcomed new members, made house visits, and focused on getting many of the old parishioners back in the pews for weekly service. They were joined in their efforts by the Ladies' Aid Association, the Daughters of the King, and the Ladies' Auxiliary. The latter group also contributed to the layman's knowledge of the town's past by publishing a brief history of Massena in 1900. By 1955 three organizations, the Ladies' Auxiliary, St. Monica's Guild, and the Young People's Fellowship still existed. Jointly, the more than 200 members of these groups raised $1,600 annually to support the national mission work of the Episcopal church, St. John's various renovation projects, and the annual Christmas gift distribution to the poor.[110] According to Herbert Schneider, the leaders of various religious women's organizations were trying to extend their charitable efforts outside the parish community. "Associations organized for fellowship, recreation, religious education, and missionary activities have expanded religious work beyond the church."[111]

The establishment of a Jewish synagogue in the twentieth century illustrated the ethnic diversification of Massena's population. While the first two Jewish residents, Ben Cohen and J. J. Kauffman, arrived in Massena in 1898, a visiting rabbi only periodically held services for area worshipers over the next three decades. In the interim Cohen, Kauffman, and their fellow merchants held their own services in buildings around town, including the town hall. They also established a Young Men's Hebrew Association that served as a social group for the many single Jewish men in Massena. In 1919 the group purchased the Congregational Church building and established a corporation on September 11, 1919 under the name Adath Israel, meaning the "community of Israel." The men elected an administrative committee led by Nathan Nadler, Alex Rosoff, and Nathan Cohen. The Jews moved into their new synagogue in 1920 and held an official dedication ceremony on Hanukkah.[112] That same year the Adath Israel membership unanimously elected Bren Brenglass, the former leader of the Tupper Lake synagogue, as their rabbi and offered him a salary of $23 per week. Brenglass remained in Massena until 1942, when he became too ill to continue his duties. During his career he played a major role in the resolution of the blood libel situation and expanded the synagogue's membership. Brenglass was described by historian Joan Dobbie as "the driving force in the religious life of Massena Jews, unyielding in his demands for adherence to tradition and orthodoxy."[113]

The Pilgrim Holiness fellowship established in 1931 represented a modernization of local religion. According to Brian Clarke, "This religion offered worshippers a new, richer, more fulfilling spiritual life based on social and moral reform."[114] It was an attempt by worshipers to return to old-time Methodist enthusiasm.[115] The Holiness movement was founded on John Wesley's argument that through time and effort, and with the help of the Holy

Spirit, worshipers could attain perfection. The adherents to this argument initially remained members of the Methodist Church and met at revival meetings or on Sunday afternoon, in an attempt to attain holiness. However, many who attended these meetings were not affiliated with a church and began to see these informal gatherings as their faith. By 1880 many Methodists ministers also started to neglect the Holiness doctrines. Therefore, Holiness congregations sprang up around the United States, and by 1922, became known as the Pilgrim Holiness Church.[116]

Massena's Pilgrim Holiness congregation followed the loose format of its creators. The group did not construct a church until 1954. However, believers began to meet in 1931, when Reverend William Shoemaker and his wife moved to the area, specifically to organize a congregation. The Shoemakers first held services at the Union Church in Massena Springs, and later moved their meetings to a house on Tamarack Street. Two years later the Shoemakers purchased an old building at 2 River Street, converted the first floor into a meeting room, and turned the upstairs into an apartment. The couple oversaw the expansion of the congregation over the next few years. William Shoemaker remained the group's leader until 1940, a year after his wife died. By 1941, only a decade after its first meeting, the congregation was incorporated as the Pilgrim Holiness Church of Massena.[117] In 1954 the Pilgrim Holiness congregation opened the doors of its new church on the corner of East Orvis and River Streets. The faith exhibited Massena's residents continual attraction to evangelical faiths.

Massena residents, like their Cornwall neighbors, formed fraternal associations concerned with performing community service and increasing the education level of their membership and the general public.[118] Jeffrey Charles argued, "The establishment of clubs and societies was the most important development in the social life of a twentieth century American town."[119] After the Industrial Revolution Americans redefined their personal lives and reshaped communities stripped of mutual aid and the artisan ideal. Cornwall and Massena residents saw these new associations as "new vehicles of community spirit and camaraderie as well as mechanisms for self-improvement and keeping the community loyal and orderly."[120] They offered men and women social opportunities, new sources of friendship, and a way to promote a sense of community among all social classes. According to Robert and Helen Merrell Lynd, "Organized clubs became more important than neighborhoods or churches as bases for association."[121]

Massena women were the first to change the focus of their associations from friendship to community reform. Mrs. Victor Doerschuk conducted the first gathering of the local chapter of the College Club at her home on March 16, 1928. The fifty-one meeting attendees elected officers and applied for affiliation with the American Association of University Women. Initially, this organization strove to improve the education levels of local women. Until mid-century the College Club members met in study groups and discussed current events, new books, and travel. They also promoted musical programs by local artists and lectures by area professors on topics such as child welfare and world poverty. The College Club soon expanded its duties beyond its original plans and organized several local fund-raising events. With the proceeds the women purchased educational material for Massena's library and schools, and set up a loan fund for local college students. To recruit new members the club held an annual tea for the female portion of the high school's graduating class to inform them of the group's goals and responsibilities.[122]

A decade later Massena women organized the Veterans of Foreign Wars (VFW) Auxiliary to promote patriotism and historical knowledge among citizens, and to assist male post members in fostering true allegiance to the United States government and constitution. Hazel Manville established the 19-member local affiliate and served as the auxiliary's first president. In December 1937 the group was admitted to the St. Lawrence County Council of the VFW. The members of the auxiliary sent food baskets and flowers to the sick and shut-ins, visited hospitalized veterans, assisted VFW members in their preparations for the Decoration and Armistice Day celebrations, and made financial contributions to the local chapters of the Red Cross and the Boy Scouts. The auxiliary funded its work with the profits from its annual poppy sale. Politically, the group employed a legislative chairwoman who kept abreast of legislation concerning veterans, and who sent letters to Massena's senator and congressman voicing the organization's approval or disapproval of pending laws. On a social level members attended card parties, birthday celebrations, and social evenings.[123]

The last prominent service organization created by Massena women was the Red Cross. According to John Hutchinson, founders of this association were considered the first champions of the cause of charity toward the sick and wounded.[124] In contrast to other charitable groups, the leaders of the Red Cross soon welcomed both male and female members. On April 26, 1917 Mrs. Judson Hyde organized the original members of the Red Cross into a branch of the National League of Women's Services and served as the association's first chairwoman. Within months of the group's establishment, Hyde and her fellow officers decided that relief efforts would be more effective if they involved men as well as women. On July 13, 1917 Professor R. W. Moore of Colgate University spoke to an audience at the Massena town hall about the virtues of the Red Cross and the success of the organization in other parts of the state. Andrew Hammer, a Massena lawyer, was elected the temporary chairman of the fledgling group, and the meeting attendees signed a petition to develop a Red Cross affiliate. A month later Hammer signed up 146 residents to help him recruit additional members and solicit financial contributions to fund the organization's community service programs. When its campaign ended in 1918, 2,035 Massena citizens had joined the Red Cross and had donated $3,548 to the organization.

From its office above the firehouse, Massena's Red Cross conducted several community service and relief projects. During World War I the group supplied sweaters, scarves, and socks to departing soldiers, and sent them Christmas packages when they were overseas. The men and women of the Red Cross also assisted local doctors during the October 1918 influenza epidemic by collecting and delivering milk, eggs, and other food to those confined to their homes. In 1927 the remaining 1,200 members became involved in national relief work by sending aid and supplies to the victims of a Midwest drought and a California earthquake. The effort of Massena's Red Cross leaders to prevent domestic disease and suffering during peacetime was part of a national campaign.[125]

The most significant community association established by Massena men was American Legion Post 79. Members of the American Expeditionary Forces created the national organization at a Paris Conference in March 1919. Meeting participants wanted to develop an international association that helped returning war veterans readjust to civilian life. Similar to the Kinsmen in Cornwall, the goal of the American Legion members was to extend the camaraderie formed between men on the battlefield into their peacetime existence. Dr. E. C. Elkins, a Massena resident, called a meeting of the town's veterans at the police station on July 25, 1919 to form an American Legion chapter. The twenty-nine men who attended the first meeting elected F. A. W. Davis as their president. In its inaugural year the Massena American Legion members sent a financial donation to a program that decorated veterans' graves in France on Memorial Day. Locally, the legion sponsored minstrel shows at the town hall, performed color guard displays at various town events, and held an annual Halloween party to keep local kids off the streets. Members also spoke to school children about their war experiences on Armistice Day as a way to infuse loyalty and patriotism in young people, one of the original legion tenets. In fulfillment of its founders' wishes, the Massena American Legion also cared for the town's veterans. Members provided food, shelter, clothing, and funding for veterans' hospital stays as a means of keeping them off welfare.[126]

The fraternal and community service associations created by Massena men and women after the turn of the century showed residents' collective orientation. Local residents were concerned with the prosperity and well-being of all members of the community. Massena inhabitants' affiliation with these new community service organizations provided them with the mutual aid and camaraderie their ancestors had extended to their neighbors through a bartering and cooperative work system. The Red Cross and other organizations, according to Jeffrey Charles, "exhibited cooperative individualism, community spirit, and good neighbor relations."[127] The cooperative mentality, which had allowed their forefathers to survive the harsh conditions associated with frontier living, also helped Massena residents in the twentieth century deal with poverty, disease, and other social issues related to an industrial society. The town's fraternal and community service association members, like their Cornwall counterparts, strove to increase the community's responsibility for those less fortunate, and to create an ideal living environment for all residents. The organizations' leaders on both sides of the border met the social, educational, and healthcare needs of area residents prior to the development of a national welfare system, and were joined by a large number of local residents.[128]

In 1954 Massena was a different community than the one founded by Amable Foucher. Throughout its 150-year history, the area underwent a myriad of economic and social changes, transforming it from an isolated farming town into a manufacturing center. After the establishment of an Alcoa plant in 1902, the economic development of Massena was more similar to Cornwall's than to that of neighboring New York State towns. While many local residents depended on these new corporations for jobs, the municipal government counted on their tax payments to finance local infrastructure improvements. Many immigrants were also employed in the area's new factories. The arrival of these foreign workers and their families forced Massena residents to deal with outsiders sooner than their neighbors. Local residents documented their ignorance of immigrants' cultures on the front page of the *Massena Observer*. Religiously, Massena congregations, specifically the Methodists, exhibited their lack of desire to worship alongside foreigners. The faith's minister instituted separate services for Alcoa workers and their families, a practice later followed by the area's Catholic priests. Finally, men and women formed fraternal and community service organizations to replace the social bonds and mutual aid previously associated with their agricultural society. These groups dealt with the social problems caused by industrialization, including poverty and disease. Their formation also exhibited Massena residents' continuing community orientation. The industrialization of Massena created a regional manufacturing center and fostered a feeling of differentness from neighboring towns.

In summary, from 1900 to 1954, Cornwall and Massena's location near hydropower made them ethnically and economically different from their more homogeneous agrarian neighbors. The turning point for Cornwall and Massena was the completion of canal and powerhouse projects. The available power and water supply encouraged the owners of the leading American producer of aluminum, the Pittsburgh Reduction Company (Alcoa), to locate a plant in Massena. On the other side of the border, Courtaulds constructed a plant in Cornwall for similar reasons. Alcoa officials, comparable to Courtaulds and Howard Smith Paper Mill executives, continually expanded their product lines and increased their workforce to remain competitive. They also funded research and development programs, and purchased the latest machinery. The success of these companies encouraged other manufacturers to locate facilities in Cornwall and Massena. Cornwall and Massena became factory towns with the majority of their male and female residents employed as factory operatives.

A quadrupling and ethnic diversification of Cornwall and Massena's populations accompanied this new found economic prosperity. Cornwall and Massena were more ethnically and religiously diverse than their neighbors. Industrialists in both areas recruited outside workers that caused an escalation in the population and an increase in ethnic groups that were foreign to the area. Cornwall manufacturers hired French-Canadian workers, while Massena companies recruited recent European immigrants. The criminal behavior of these new arrivals caused them to be classified as sinners who needed to be controlled by law enforcement and religious officials. Therefore, several new Catholic parishes were established in the expanding townships. These separate congregations allowed immigrants to preserve their ethnic identity, while allowing priests to introduce nationally held morals and values.

While both areas struggled to deal with new residents and their different religious customs, they still retained similar business, religious, and social values. The economies of both towns were driven by industrialists, who were ambitious and innovative and invested their profits in new facilities, equipment, and the development of new products. The efforts of John Barber, C. Howard Smith, and Charles Hall made their products marketable on a national and international level. Contractors in both towns constructed working-class neighborhoods and churches because of Massena and Cornwall residents' dislike of living near or worshiping with foreigners. Residents' aversion to immigrants and their strange customs refuted Seymour Lipset's argument that "one of Canadians most important self-images is that their society is a mosaic, one that gives diverse ethnic groups the right to cultural survival."[129] Religiously, the leaders of all of Cornwall's and Massena's congregations witnessed an increase in worshipers, particularly at Catholic masses. While churches on both sides of the border became more hierarchically administered, Cornwall and Massena residents retained their financial control over church affairs by forming voluntary associations charged with fund-raising efforts. Finally, residents of both towns formed fraternal and community service organizations to replace the social bonds and mutual aid previously associated with their agricultural society. These groups dealt with the social problems caused by industrialization, including poverty and disease. The formation of these groups by Cornwall and Massena residents exhibited their continued community orientation. In 1954 Cornwall and Massena residents retained the same values as those of their ancestors and continued along similar economic paths. The selection of these two towns as the headquarters for the St. Lawrence Seaway Project continued them on the same social and economic trajectory.

CHAPTER FOUR

The St. Lawrence Seaway Project and Its Short-Term Social Impact on Cornwall and Massena, 1954–1958

The St. Lawrence Seaway Project is fittingly referred to as one of the "greatest construction shows on earth."[1] Consisting of seven locks, the widening of various canals, and the taming of rapids between Alexandria Bay, New York and Montreal, Canada, the Seaway was the culmination of a century-long dream to link the Great Lakes interior industrial hubs in the United States to the Atlantic Ocean. Previously, ocean-going vessels were halted at the entrance to Lake Ontario, where their freight was unloaded onto train cars and transported by rail to waiting ships in the port of Montreal. Rivaling the great dam and waterway projects of the 1920s, the Seaway also introduced new state-of-the-art equipment, employed a large and diverse workforce, and required the cooperation of numerous contractors. At the time of its completion in 1959, the total cost for the construction of the 342-mile waterway was more than $1 billion, a financial burden shared equally by the national governments of the United States, Canada, and the provincial and state administrations of Ontario and New York.

Local politicians on both sides of the border predicted that the abundance of cheap power and accessible water transportation offered by the project would lure new industrial investors to Cornwall and Massena and transform them into annual tourist destinations. Mayor Aaron Horovitz, a longtime businessman and politician in Cornwall, stated in 1955, "The eyes of industrialists are on the St. Lawrence Seaway and power project and authorities predict a heavy concentration of industry in this area. . . . Cornwall is the envy of every city in Canada."[2] Conversely many scholars and economists were less optimistic. In two studies conducted by faculty and students at Syracuse University, the authors cautioned that there was no guarantee that the economies of Cornwall and Massena would experience permanent change.[3]

Canadian and American officials in the 1950s clearly viewed Cornwall and Massena as strategic construction centers for the Seaway, not as keys to the future of their nations. Even the pessimists conceded that the project would temporarily increase the areas' populations.

During the duration of construction, Massena and Cornwall experienced population expansion and religious diversification. The men who constructed the Seaway were from various regions of Canada and the United States. Most were transient workers who moved from one project to another. Cornwall and Massena residents mutually disliked their towns being invaded by these outsiders. They found the rowdy lifestyle of Seaway workers to be unacceptable and tried to curb their behavior. Town residents saw religion as a way to instill morals and spirituality in Seaway workers and retain traditional social bonds. Clerics built new churches near workers' houses and increased the number of Sunday services to coincide with workers' shifts and relieve pew overcrowding. According to Ron Cummings, "The construction of the St. Lawrence Seaway and Hydro Power Project had brought thousands of people to Cornwall, causing unprecedented social upheaval."[4]

The St. Lawrence Seaway Project had similar short-term social and economic impacts on Cornwall and Massena. For four years residents on both sides of the border encountered individuals from various regions of the country who harbored different religious and social values. The towns were also the center of national media attention and became tourist attractions. Merchants increased their sales by providing goods and services for workers and other visitors. Town officials hired new policemen to deal with increasing traffic and crime and enlarged schools to accommodate the large number of school-age children. The shared experience of Cornwall and Massena residents from 1954 to 1959 strengthened their regional identity and reinforced their differences with their more homogeneous rural neighbors.

Between 1895 and 1951 neither American nor Canadian officials viewed the St. Lawrence Seaway Project as a top priority. U.S. senators and presidents introduced two treaties, an executive order, several riders to river and transport bills, and more than a dozen individual bills seeking the approval of the St. Lawrence Seaway and Power Project. Each of their efforts met with outright rejection or strong opposition. In Canada, prior to World War II, prime ministers and members of Parliament saw no immediate need for the Seaway. Canadian engineers continually upgraded the nation's canal system and rail service to handle public and private transportation needs. The operators of government-owned hydro and coal plants also produced enough electricity for all of the country's industries and homes.

After World War II attitudes about the waterway changed on both sides of the border. In the 1940s, after Quebec and Ontario manufacturers experienced power shortages, the Seaway project became an increasingly important component of provincial officials' industrial expansion plans. Between 1945 and 1951 Ontario Hydro administrators opened fourteen new hydrodams and increased their annual output of electricity from 1,852,000 to 4,229,100 kilowatts.[5] The International Rapids section of the St. Lawrence River remained the country's last untapped power source by the 1950s. American supporters of the Seaway, including Vermont Senator George Aiken, Secretary of Commerce N. R. Danielian, and Secretary of State Dean Acheson, resurrected President Franklin Roosevelt's powerful national defense arguments for the project. The main elements of this strategy portrayed the Seaway as an important component of the nation's new role as a global trade and military leader. The power dam would supply electricity for America's expanding production of munitions and airplanes, and the deep waterway would allow the extension of trade with devastated European nations. Both would prevent countries from instituting communist regimes as a means of regaining their economic and social stability. Following fifty years of apprehension and apathy, the Canadian Parliament passed the Seaway bill in 1951. Three years later American congressmen approved the Wiley-Dondero bill when they realized that Canadian officials would make good on their threat to make the Seaway an exclusively Canadian waterway.

The construction of the St. Lawrence Seaway Project was overseen by two federal agencies. On December 21, 1951 the 3-member St. Lawrence Seaway Authority was created by Chapter 24 of the Acts of the Fifth Session of the Twenty-first Parliament of Canada. The Authority was given the power to acquire land, and to construct, maintain, and operate all deep waterway projects between the port of Montreal and Lake Erie.[6] The Dominion and Ontario government officials also signed an agreement to finance the construction of the power dam in the international rapids section. On the American side, the Wiley-Dondero Act authorized the St. Lawrence Seaway Development Corporation to complete the U.S. portion. The leaders of this new organization were also charged with making arrangements with the Canadian St. Lawrence Seaway Authority for construction, maintenance, and control of the waterway. The entire project was composed of four dams in the 46-mile International Rapids section, seven new locks, and four canals on the Canadian side to replace the existing 14-foot ones above Montreal.[7] Once the national administrative structure was finalized, the actual construction of the Seaway and power dam commenced in 1954.

The central part of the power project, the jointly built international power dam, involved several navigational and water-control structures within a 20-mile radius of Cornwall and Massena. These included a control dam to regulate the water level and maintain constant flow for the locks and canals, a power pool, two locks, a bypass channel, and a power dam with two powerhouses. Five contractors under the supervision of B. Perini and Sons of

Massachusetts constructed the U.S. half of the $600 million, 3,230-feet long, 167-feet high hydrodam. Seven Canadian builders, overseen by Iroquois Constructors Limited, completed the structure on the Canadian side. The two sections were equal in size, each containing sixteen turbines, with a combined annual power generation capacity of 2.2 million horsepower. Workers constructed the dam with 1,890,000 cubic yards of concrete, 116 million pounds of reinforced steel, and 15 million pounds of structural steel.[8] When the project was completed in 1959, Seaway contractors reported that there was a "deployment of an estimated $75 million in on-site equipment, the placing of more than six million cubic yards of concrete, and the dredging and excavation of 360 million tons of materials costing in excess of one billion dollars."[9]

Between 1954 and 1958 the arrival of more than 22,000 carpenters, laborers, and machine operators in Cornwall and Massena to complete the Seaway Project significantly altered the towns' demographics and cultures, and resurrected residents' dislike for outsiders. These new inhabitants and their families, similar to canal workers and factory operatives, challenged Cornwall and Massena residents to deal with men and women with different social values. The men who completed the navigational and power sections of the Seaway project near Cornwall and Massena were mostly from outside the area. Comparable to the workforce on the Hoover Dam Project, "They flocked in here from all parts of the United States. They picked up whatever they had, loaded it into a truck and drove here, and had hopes of getting a job."[10] The management structure and classification of workers who constructed the power dam were also similar to those on the Hoover Dam.[11] The intricate hierarchical framework guaranteed that concrete pouring and dirt removal were done on time and in an efficient manner.

A managerial chain of command oversaw the large and diverse workforce on the Seaway. The project manager was on the top of the ladder and was in charge of the entire undertaking. Directly under him was the general superintendent, who assisted the project manager with his day-to-day duties and handled on-site security and worker safety. The general superintendent also commanded six assistants who supervised the progress of contractors and their workers 24-hours-a-day. The heads of various departments were next in line and made up the bulk of the management personnel. These men administered the carpentry shops, excavating units, and electrical departments. Lowell Fitzsimmons, a dragline operator, stated, "You could tell the difference between a manager and a worker by the color of his hard hat. The managers always had on shiny silver hats that looked like they had never been worn. The workers, on the other hand, wore yellow hats that looked well worn."[12]

The majority of supervisors on the power dam project were from all over the United States and Canada. Most had worked on similar domestic and international waterway projects. Comparable to the companies that completed the Hoover Dam, the Seaway contractors retained a core group of experienced managers on all their job sites. Therefore, supervisors did not have to train new workers at the beginning of every project. As Jerry Richards, a machine repairer and operator, indicated, "If it hadn't been for the expertise of experienced supervisors from the South, who had previously worked for the Tennessee Valley Authority and other major water projects, the Seaway would have never been completed. We would have been lost."[13]

Most contractors transported their skilled work force and their families to Cornwall and Massena. Thirty-eight percent of skilled workers on the Canadian side were from outside the area, while 50 percent of all workers on the U.S. side were from elsewhere. Many were from as far away as California, Texas, North Dakota, the Maritimes, and Alberta. These men were drawn to the project by the considerable amount of labor needed, as well as by the good pay offered by contractors of at least $500 a month.[14] The bricklayers, cement finishers, and stone masons were the upper class of the Seaway workers. They were at the top of the contractors' pay scales, earning $3.35 an hour, or $135 for a 40-hour-week.

Some local workers managed to get skilled jobs on the project by lying about their experience. After 1955 the pool of workers was so limited on the project that anyone could pick up a hammer and say he was a carpenter. According to Carleton Mabee, "By the fall of 1955 there was a shortage of carpenters and masons, and contractors sent recruiters to the South and the Midwest."[15] In the meantime the available local workforce filled these positions. As Sam Agati, the head of Laborers' Local 322 stated, "I sent a lot of laborers out to be carpenters and iron workers. It was bull work. They did not require you to do anything too fancy."[16]

Although most of the managerial and skilled staff were outsiders, a majority of the laborers and machine operators were from New York State or from around the Cornwall and Massena area. The typical laborers, therefore, were local residents, though few had previous work experience. Some commuted from as far away as Watertown, Plattsburgh, and Prescott to take advantage of the steady, high-paying jobs.[17] Laborers performed a variety of tasks on the project, including carrying bags of concrete, shoveling dirt, and servicing equipment. These men were paid an average of $.90 to $2.30 an hour by contractors based on the complexity of the work they performed. Those who mastered new skills through advanced training easily moved up the laborers' pay scale or acquired jobs as skilled workers. The contractors also hired local farm boys as machine operators because they had previous experience driving tractors and other farm machinery. Jimmy Oakes, a bulldozer operator, indicated, "I started running machinery when I was fourteen on my father's farm. The Corps of Engineers hired me as a machinery operator when I was only twenty."[18] The various power equipment operators, who made $3.20 an hour, included the drivers of draglines, backhoes, concrete mixers, concrete pavers, and pile drivers. Lowell Fitzsimmons noted, "I made $3.10 an hour as a dragline operator. It was good pay for the time."[19]

Indians comprised a smaller portion of the worker population in the United States and Canada. They filled iron workers' positions and fused iron beams and support structures at the pinnacle of the power dam. As Sam Agati noted, "There were 800 Indians who worked on the Seaway project as iron workers, most of whom commuted from the St. Regis Reservation in Hogansburg or the Caughnawa reservations."[20] In the past conflicts had arisen between immigrant workers and Indians. During the Massena canal project, a fight broke out between Indians and Italian workers, resulting in multiple injuries and several arrests. However, on the Seaway project, Indians performed risky tasks that most workers willingly relinquished. Some Indians were believed to be less afraid of heights and better at balancing on high beams than other workers. One Indian countered, "We're the same as anybody. You just have to learn to deal with it."[21]

During the summer months contractors hired college students as laborers and machine operators on both sides of the border. In the United States students from several educational institutions shoveled dirt and drove backhoes. A roll call of Uhl, Hall, and Rich, the main U.S. contractor, revealed they employed students from twenty-five colleges, including Harvard, Princeton, Dartmouth, Columbia, and Cornell. Ross Violi remembered, "I went to Ithaca College, but I came back to my hometown of Massena to work on the project for three summers. It was the best paying summer job I could get. I made $1.80 an hour and I didn't have to pay rent. I just lived at home."[22] On the Canadian side, Iroquois Contractors Limited hired men from Queen's University and McGill. These students earned up to $1,000 for three months' work.[23] Both Indians and college students filled specialized and temporary positions that other workers could not satisfy.

The St. Lawrence Seaway provided valuable work experience for many men and was the largest waterway project jointly undertaken by the American and Canadian governments. Most of the workers on the St. Lawrence Seaway Project never forgot the time they spent on the job. For Jimmy Oakes, an equipment operator, the Seaway was just the beginning of a long, successful, and happy construction career. "Out of all of the forty years I have spent in the construction business, I have never learned as much as I did on the Seaway Project. I had the chance to work with so many experienced supervisors and workers."[24] The project also illustrated the triumph of contractors on both sides of the border to work together for a common goal. The Canadian and American managers and supervisors not only coordinated work between their own workers, but also cooperated with their counterparts on the other side of the border. Furthermore, workers from various parts of the country put aside their differences and worked together for a common goal. The American and Canadian Seaway workers and contractors, therefore, shared a similar work ethic.

The influx of Seaway workers and their families had a similar social impact on Cornwall and Massena. Between 1901 and 1958 the more than 20 percent increase in the populations of the two towns taxed their infrastructures and social service agencies, resulting in overcrowded schools and an increase in petty crime.[25] Town officials were financially responsible for funding all roadway and sanitation improvements. In 1956 Massena town councilmen were informed by New York State Commerce Commissioner, Edward Dickinson, that they would not be given any special financial assistance to fund their new water and sewer systems, to pay the salaries of additional policemen, or to construct additional housing and schools.[26] According to Massena Town Supervisor, F. Lloyd Hosmer, "The Seaway contractors' work is poorly planned and seemingly asinine. They began building without the preparation of proper access roads and bridges or the construction of housing, educational, and medical facilities."[27]

Workers and their families strained the financial resources of local unemployment and social services personnel, especially in Cornwall. In 1954 unemployed men flocked to the area in search of work. However, many contractors had brought their own workers and, therefore, fewer jobs were available than previously predicted. Contractors on both sides of the border also laid off a substantial portion of their workforce in the winter months when the temperatures became too cold to pour concrete, and the ground too hard to dredge. These men were put on the towns' unemployment rolls for several months. In February 1955 the manager of the Cornwall Unemployment Insurance Office reported 3,100 residents on relief.[28]

The children of Seaway workers overcrowded Massena schools and forced the superintendent to integrate facility administration, to construct new buildings, and to split the school day into two sessions. In June 1955 the Massena Central School Board members formed a central district, merging the supervision of the area's twenty-six rural districts under the guidance of one governing body. In that year the town had five elementary schools and one junior/senior high school. However, these facilities proved inadequate to accommodate all of the area's students. From 1954 to 1959 the Massena School Board financed the renovation of current school buildings and added extra class sessions. In 1955 the Jefferson Elementary School's library, auditorium, and gym were converted into classrooms. With an increase of 500 students aged thirteen to eighteen, the principal of Massena High School also implemented two sessions for students in grades seven to twelve. The first ran from 8:30 A.M. to 12:30 P.M., while the second was scheduled from 1:00 P.M. to 5:30 P.M. Even with these changes classrooms remained crowded. Therefore, in 1956 Massena voters approved a proposition to erect four new elementary schools and a new high school. Construction began on these projects the following year. However, contractors completed the facilities in 1959 after the number of school-age children returned to pre-Seaway levels.

In Cornwall, the board of education expanded its schools to accommodate the children of Seaway workers. In 1955 principals opened four new schools and discussed plans to renovate existing buildings. The following year the local school board approved more than $2 million to construct a new, separate school and purchase several mobile classroom buildings to house the children of Seaway workers.[29] Catholic school administrators also solicited funds to enlarge their facilities and construct a new high school. By 1961 there were more than 15,000 school-age children in Cornwall.

Massena law enforcement officials addressed the issue of crime prevention prior to the commencement of the Seaway construction by hiring more policemen and expanding their jail. Akin to local leaders in Las Vegas, who prepared for the worst before the inception of the Hoover Dam Project, both American and Canadian officials expected the number of offenses to increase over the next four years, and hired additional policemen.[30] According to Sam Agati, "I was approached by the New York State Department of Criminal Investigations before the project even began, because they expected forty homicides to be committed before the project was completed, as well as for the town to be filled with prostitutes. These statistics were based on the crime rates, which had been recorded during similar projects on the Hoover and Horseshoe Dams."[31] The Massena police chief employed four new patrolmen, ordered several pieces of new equipment [including a patrol wagon for transporting disorderly and intoxicated persons] and constructed nine additional cells in the village jail.[32] In December 1954 seven state troopers were added to the Massena substation.[33] Two years later, the town planning commission ordered New York Telephone employees to install alarm boxes on the corners of local streets and added four plainclothes policemen to the local force. By 1958 the Massena Town Board employed twenty-nine police officers compared to nineteen in 1955.[34]

The pessimistic predictions of Seaway workers' criminal behavior never materialized. In October 1957 Chief Thomas O'Neil stated that except for parking violations and traffic jams, crime in Massena remained close to its pre-Seaway level. "The Massena police force, which doubled in size in anticipation of a king-size increase in trouble, finds itself with fewer arrests than there were two years ago."[35] The reason for the lack of crime, according to Walter Gorrow, a union steward for Local 322, was that "In those days men solved their problems with their fists, not with knives or guns. Men would get bruises and black eyes, but no one ever got killed."[36] Most of the men were hardworking and married. There may have been an increase in drinking and driving and maybe a few more barroom brawls, but the majority of workers were too tired to make serious trouble.[37] The men also had worked on projects like this before and they had learned how to deal with the difficulties and problems of moving into a new area and having to get along with often hostile town inhabitants. Stories in the Potsdam, New York newspaper, the *Courier and Freeman*, that Massena had become a hotbed of prostitution were also unfounded. As Bill Massey, a local resident, stated, "It was free. Why should anyone want to pay for it."[38] Sam Agati concurred. "There were a lot of gals around, who wanted to fool around. Their husbands worked long shifts at the factory and they were lonely."[39]

In contrast, Cornwall police and court officials recorded an increase in crime, despite adding members to their police force and implementing other crime prevention measures. In 1955 the Cornwall city police commission asked for assistance from the Ontario government or Ontario Hydro officials to pay the salaries of five more policemen to deal with the escalation of petty crime. The group also wanted to brighten street lights as a theft deterrent.[40] Even with all these precautions, the number of total offenses addressed by the police in 1955 equaled 221, an increase of 15 percent over the previous year. These crimes included thirty-six traffic accidents and a growing number of robberies and violations of the Liquor Control Act.[41]

The incidents of juvenile delinquency also rose in Cornwall during the Seaway construction, as many workers brought their teenagers with them and often left them unsupervised for long periods of time. Magistrate P. C. Bergeron's 1957 annual court report indicated that the number of crimes committed by individuals under the age of twenty-one had not decreased, despite the implementation of a 9 P.M. curfew for teenagers.[42] According to his data, 80 percent of those charged with indictable offenses were between the ages of sixteen and twenty-one.[43] Local residents attributed the growth of juvenile crime to teenagers' increasing tendency to question the decisions of authority figures, and their additional free time based on shorter school days. Many children spent hours alone while their parents worked on the Seaway or in the town's factories. This lack of supervision and respect for authority was a sign of the times according to town residents. As Dr. S. B. Fraser, the St. John's Presbyterian historian, noted, "Great difficulties were experienced in these days when questioning [by teenagers] was the order of the day. All too often permissive behavior became the popular trend."[44]

Long-term Cornwall residents feared their community life would become disjointed and crime-ridden with the arrival of transient workers. This stable, close-knit society already showed signs of its lack of tolerance for people with different cultures. Geographically, Cornwall was divided into four very defined neighborhoods. Each area was predominantly populated by either French- or English-speaking citizens. In a 1957 study, local residents expressed their feelings about French workers and the Seaway men. One resident stated, "I don't like Cornwall because of so many French people. Their way of living is different from what I like."[45] Local residents had no problems with newcomers if they followed the rules and didn't interfere with social or work life. However, the increased number of drunks on the street convinced Cornwall citizens that Seaway workers were no different than the Irish canal or French mill workers of earlier times. One man stated, "Get rid of all those foreign men on the street. They are scaring the women. They are always drunk on the street."[46] Many Cornwall men were also angered by the small pool of local citizens employed on the project and blamed Seaway workers for their increasing rent payments.[47]

On the American side, Massena residents were more welcoming of the new arrivals. Initially, Massena inhabitants, like their Cornwall neighbors, were upset that local workers might not be hired on the project. According to Sam Agati, "Someone started a rumor in a barroom somewhere that they were going to bring in 600 Puerto Ricans to work on the project, and the locals got all fired up. However, this never occurred and a splendid relationship was maintained between our hardworking construction crews and engineers and the permanent residents of the area."[48] Walter Newtown, an air tamper operator, indicated that once this rumor passed, locals and transients worked together side by side. "The locals accepted the workers, because there was enough work to go around. We weren't taking work away from anyone."[49]

Massena storeowners, restaurateurs, and bar owners also embraced the Seaway employees. Like the Massena canal workers and factory operatives, these men and their families purchased goods and services from local merchants. From 1954 to 1958 the town's retail sales increased from $18,407,000 to $27,238,000.[50] According to Sam Agati, "Local businessmen welcomed the workers because the increase in population meant an increase in consumers, which led to an increase in profits."[51]

Local women were also very hospitable to Seaway workers. As Bill Massey noted, "I think the locals accepted the workers with open arms, especially the women. Their husbands worked at Alcoa all day and so they hung out in the saloons."[52] A lot of single Massena women also ended up marrying Seaway workers. Many were overwhelmed by the Southern accents of some of the workers. Jimmy Oakes, stated, "My sister married a man from South Carolina and after the project was over, she moved to Illinois, where he worked on the canal project there."[53] However, the fascination wore off after the women had experienced the migrant lifestyles for a few years.

The final issue Massena officials dealt with during the Seaway project was the shortage of housing for contractors and their workers. These conditions, however, were better than those on the Hoover Dam Project where, according to Andrew Dunar and Dennis McBride, workers slept in tents and poorly constructed dormitories.[54] In the past Massena manufacturers constructed accommodations for their operatives either on plant grounds or in new neighborhoods. Initially, in the 1940s when President Franklin Roosevelt signed the first Seaway agreement, the U.S. government had planned on building temporary housing for workers, along with a hospital and several schools. By 1954, however, they abandoned their initial plans and instead ordered Power Authority of the State of New York (PASNY) administrators to get recommendations from city planners on dealing with housing, schools, medical care, and other social problems. While the PASNY built 133 houses for its engineers, other workers and their families relied on local real estate agents to find accommodations. The creation of trailer parks seemed to Massena officials to be the best solution to the area's temporary housing shortage, especially since most of the workers were not planning to stay in the area permanently. In November 1957, at the height of the project's employment, there were 603 individuals and families living in trailers.[55]

The lack of worker housing in Cornwall raised rents and caused animosity between old and new residents. Neither town nor Ontario Hydro officials wanted to construct a large number of temporary houses. Instead, Ontario Hydro administrators built barracks for some of their workers, while the remainder were left to find their own lodging.[56] In Cornwall, many groups, like the Family Welfare Bureau, asked town councilmen to fund the construction of low-cost accommodations and implement a system of rent control. However, no action was taken, as Cornwall's town leaders were apprehensive about building too much housing that would not be used after the Seaway was completed. Living arrangements, therefore, remained a major problem for workers. According to a local reporter, "Housing is at a premium. New building has not kept pace with the influx and, as a result, there is a shortage of accommodations. Prices for rooms in many places have skyrocketed."[57] From January 1955 to January 1957, Cornwall apartment and homeowners raised their rents by 30 percent. In 1955 real estate agents leased apartments for $90 a month that a year earlier were priced at $65.[58] These rate increases caused hardship for both old people on fixed incomes and transient Seaway workers and their families. Under these conditions longtime Cornwall residents struggled to maintain social harmony and cohesion.

From 1954 to 1958 Cornwall church leaders and their congregants saw religion as their best option to curb the immoral behavior of their children and to tame the wild, criminal tendencies of Seaway workers. They believed that true Christianity could rehabilitate even the most depraved person and bring him back to God.[59] As Brian Clarke noted, "There was a renewed commitment to religion resulting in the growth of church membership and a sharp rise in the construction of new churches."[60] Cornwall's reverends and priests constructed new chapels near worker housing and added extra services to coincide with Seaway workers' schedules. Worshipers financed these renovation and expansion projects with generous donations. Many congregants also renewed their commitment to increasing membership by holding annual rallies and beautified their houses of worship as a way to make Sunday services more appealing.[61] Young parents, who wanted to instill Christian values in their children, sent them to Sunday School, thereby overcrowding church classrooms. Many pastors offered morning and afternoon Sunday Schools to accommodate these new students. Through all these social changes, Cornwall congregations and their leaders promoted morality and an ethical lifestyle for old residents and new arrivals and remained the town's only stable social institutions.

During the Seaway era Reverend W. L. MacLellan, the leader of St. John's, Cornwall's original Presbyterian parish, dealt with the challenges of physically accommodating an increasing number of worshipers at Sunday services and addressing the differing expectations of congregants from varying religious backgrounds. Longtime Cornwall residents were seeking more than just spiritual guidance from their minister. They wanted Sunday sermons to suggest ways to cope with their bewilderment over their changing political, economic, and social surroundings. According to church historians, "The gospel of the Good News of Jesus Christ as preached by Reverend MacLellan proved to be of great assistance in bringing confused minds back to the genuine standards of church living."[62] With his flamboyant style and sermons on ethical living and spirituality, MacLellan reached people from all walks of life and all age groups. He achieved the most successful pastorship in St. John's history by retaining the allegiance of current members and also attracting Seaway workers and their families to weekly services. From 1954 to 1958 as many as 500 worshipers attended mass at St. John's and exceeded the facility's seating capacity. To deal with the overcrowding, Reverend MacLellan headed a campaign to construct a new church hall. In 1959 builders completed the Caldwell Hall, which housed a gym and a new kitchen. By this time, however, the majority of Seaway workers and their families had moved on to the next project and the new building found few users.

Membership in the Knox congregation, the city's other Presbyterian church, also grew steadily during the Seaway era as many supervisors, contractors, and their families attended services. According to church historians, the relocation of many families to the area, beginning in 1954, and the effects of the postwar baby boom taxed the church and Sunday school facilities. Consequently, church leaders undertook a major building expansion project and scheduled additional services. Initially, in 1955 remodelers redecorated the church's interior by installing new stained glass windows and an elaborate pulpit. In 1956 Reverend P. C. Lewis added a third service at 9 A.M. to accommodate the increasing number of worshipers attending mass.

The following year the vestry raised the issue of constructing a new 2-story education building as the number of Sunday School pupils rose. In 1958 contractors finished the new Christian Education building containing classrooms and a large assembly room.[63] However, by the 1960s the leaders of the Knox congregation, like those of St. John's, saw their membership return to pre-Seaway levels.

During the Seaway years the Catholic Church remained Cornwall's predominant denomination. In 1951 Canadian census takers recorded 10,215 Catholics in Cornwall. A decade later the number equaled 31,153, or 71 percent of the town's population. The majority of new worshipers were French Canadians who arrived to construct the power dam. Father R. J. MacDonald led St. Columban's parishioners through the Seaway years, and sustained the spiritual and construction work of his predecessors. During his tenure from 1951 to 1968, he organized annual faith rallies, often drawing crowds in excess of 10,000. The first such gathering was held in 1949 and was seen by Catholics as a way to publicly display their faith. The inaugural event was aimed at preventing parishioners from being drawn to communism. More than 15,000 men, women, and children marched in a procession ending at the Cornwall Athletic Grounds. The participants heard speeches by Bishop Bordeur, Lionel Chevrier, and other leaders outlining the dangers of communism.[64] MacDonald also completed the earthquake restoration project by installing new stained glass windows and by redecorating the church's interior.

Cornwall Catholics remained active participants in the congregation's voluntary associations, including the Holy Name Society and the St. Columban's auxiliary. The leaders of both groups offered social cohesion for their members and held annual fund-raising bazaars and weekly bingo to cover church expenses. They were instrumental in soliciting funds to construct St. John Bosco's Parish in 1955 to serve Seaway workers and their families. The parish's priest said two Sunday masses during the Seaway project and ministered to more than 250 families. The Auxiliary officers also hosted summer socials and concerts to enhance the cultural lives of all Cornwall citizens. These events brought together Seaway workers and old residents in an attempt to break down some of the local stereotypes and insecurities. As Brian Clarke noted, "In practical terms, providing social activities offered Christians an opportunity to reach people who might otherwise have little or no contact with organized religion."[65]

From 1954 to 1958 the Baptists remained Cornwall's most successful evangelical congregation. Like other area faiths, they expanded their facilities to accommodate new worshipers and instituted new services. For more than a decade, the leaders of the First Baptist Church had discussed either constructing a new Sunday School hall at their current site or relocating the entire church building. At the annual 1955 meeting of deacons, Donald Dick and Freeman Elliott argued that a committee should be appointed to study the congregation's options. Reverend Donald Trimpany, who was hired as the congregation's new minister in 1956, favored the construction of a completely new facility. A year after his appointment, the pews became so overcrowded that Reverend Trimpany instituted a 9 A.M. service in addition to the traditional 11 A.M. assembly. He also organized a choir and purchased a new organ to make services more entertaining. As Brian Clarke noted, "As church buildings grew in size, congregations sought to beautify their interiors. Perhaps the most visible innovation was the introduction of the organ."[66] In September 1957 worshipers hired the Wells Church Fundraising Organization to review the church's financial situation and solicit funds for the new building. The congregation held a loyalty dinner in 1958 and raised $80,000 for the new structure and an additional $16,000 for its maintenance. However, two years later, when the new house of worship was completed, Cornwall town leaders recorded a 22 percent unemployment rate, and the Baptist congregation found few new worshipers to fill the extra pew space.[67]

The Calvary Baptist Church, which had split from the regular Baptist Church in 1951, gained many members because of its conservative outlook. For several years worshipers met at the house of Lorne Williams to discuss their plans for a new congregation. These men and women were not pleased with the liberal and modernist tendencies that had crept into their faith. As Brian Clarke indicated, "In the twentieth century the vast majority [of Baptists] came to accept Bible criticism because it offered an intellectually respectable rationale for a form of piety that updated, but did not repudiate, evangelical traditions."[68] Cornwall's newest congregation desired to conserve what they thought to be the central ideals of old-time religion. They wanted to start a parish that remained true to the Bible.

During the 1950s the new Baptist congregation gained popularity among Seaway workers and its membership searched for permanent worshiping facilities. Many Seaway workers were Southern Baptists, who rejected many of the faith's modern tendencies. In June 1951 Harry Read, one of the fellowship's inaugural members, donated a small building he owned to serve as a permanent meeting place for the new Baptist association. The male members of the congregation renovated the old bakery into a meetinghouse and on November 4 held their first service in their new building. On May 4, 1952 the twenty-five congregants hired William Stanley as their first full-time minister, and selected five deacons to administer congregation affairs. In 1957 the congregants purchased a lot on Brookdale Street to house a larger church. Another worshiper worked as a house mover for Ontario Hydro. He was hired to dismantle and dispose of the Milles Roche United Church Hall. Instead, he donated the structure to the Calvary Baptist congregation and moved the building to its new Cornwall location free of charge.[69] However, like the leaders of their sister church, the Calvary parish leaders witnessed a decline in membership after 1958. The two congregations recorded a combined membership of 627.[70]

The Anglicans expanded their membership during the Seaway years, adding more than 1,600 new members. Most of these new worshipers were supervisors, skilled workers, and contractors. During the 1950s Reverend Harold Clarke witnessed the number of new homes in Trinity Memorial congregation increase from 458 to 885, and believed the prosperity Cornwall businesses experienced during the project would continue.[71] He, therefore, initiated a fund-raising campaign to finance an addition to the church. The donations from new members covered the completion costs of the Trinity Parish Hall, which housed a new auditorium and classroom. However, once the workers left and parishioners' contributions declined, the vestry set aside further expansion plans.[72]

Like their Catholic brethren, Anglicans remained members of voluntary associations to solicit donations for the reverend's salary and various church construction projects. In May 1954 the Parochial Guild celebrated its sixtieth anniversary. Over the past three years, the group had raised $5,000 annually to pay off the remaining $10,000 debt for the new church hall, and purchased new roofs for the rectory and the church. The parish members also began a canvas of all congregants to collect donations for church renovations, and sold several of the lots they owned around town. The campaign raised more than $200,000 in individual bequests and capital gains. With these proceeds the vestry redecorated the church with new pews, an altar, and wooden flooring.[73] As Brian Clarke noted, "Parish life depended in large part on the efforts of lay people in a wide variety of voluntary associations."[74]

The arrival of Seaway workers in Cornwall in 1954 led to significant growth in the membership of local churches. The leaders of most denominations recorded increased attendance at church services and Sunday School classes. Ministers and priests also struggled against the new enticements of consumer society, which developed fully during postwar prosperity. Many changed their preaching style to attract more members and relaxed some of their stringent theological guidelines. There was a backlash against these efforts, particularly among members of the First Baptist Church, who left to form a more traditional congregation. Voluntary associations also remained an integral part of the social and financial framework of Cornwall parishes. The work of the male and female members of these organizations enhanced the social cohesion of parishioners and improved the community's cultural activities. Cornwall worshipers, similar to their Massena neighbors, still viewed religion as an integral part of their lives.

During the Seaway era Massena residents attended religious services in record numbers as a means of dealing with their evolving community.

Comparable to Canadians, Americans were also living in a changing society filled with new consumer goods and an international military threat. According to Douglas Miller and Marion Nowak, "Men and women turned to religion to provide them with a sense of control and security."[75] Longtime congregants were joined in the pews by Seaway workers and their families struggling to settle into a new area. Unlike previous eras of religious popularity that only enticed members of certain social classes back into church pews, the 1950s attracted rich, poor, urban, and rural residents to Sunday services. Worshipers were all searching for an enduring set of consensual values to guide their lives and a sense of belonging. As William McLoughlin indicated, "During this age of anxiety, Americans became uncertain of their future and frightened over their ability to cope with a world so complex and unpredictable."[76] Religion, therefore, changed from a vehicle of social reform to one that stressed common moral values and the achievement of peace of mind.[77]

To meet the needs of their growing number of worshipers, all Massena congregations either constructed new churches, expanded their current facilities, or held extra services. The influx of Seaway workers from the southern and western United States also encouraged ministers from two unrepresented religions, the Assembly of God and the Church of Christ, to come to Massena to establish congregations. Both of these new faiths appealed to the workers' transient lifestyles. Adherents fostered a personal relationship with God that allowed them to maintain their spirituality in the absence of a formal church structure. As one reporter stated in 1957, "Truly Massena's progress has gone hand in hand with God."[78]

During the Seaway years the members of Massena's St. John's Episcopal Church reached out to new arrivals and invited them to weekly services. Reverend Charles Bowen Persell and a group of church women visited trailer parks and worker housing in search of fellow worshipers. According to the bimonthly vestry meeting minutes, "Thanks to Mrs. Norma Burns, many new families and individuals have received a suitable welcome and quite a number of the new people have taken an active part in the affairs of the parish."[79] As pews became increasingly overcrowded at all three Sunday services, Persell resurrected the parish's decade-old expansion plans. Congregation members bought into the general belief that the Seaway project was going to foster long-term economic and social growth in the area, and the vestry wanted to be prepared for the permanent increase in Sunday worshipers and Sunday School students. Women led the fund-raising effort for the construction project. The 73-member women's auxiliary raised $594 by organizing a series of monthly suppers. The St. Monica's Guild also collected $981 at its annual Christmas sale. Many local worshipers and engineers from the project donated their time and money to double the seating capacity of the church, and to erect an additional classroom and chapel. When the renovations to St.

John's were finally completed in 1958, however, the number of parishioners had already begun to decline and by 1960 membership registration returned to pre-Seaway levels.[80]

Many Seaway workers and old residents were attracted to the Congregational faith because of its evangelical values. The church witnessed an increase in the number of worshipers at Sunday services, forcing the minister to preach two services and temporarily hold Sunday School classes in the church's kitchen. The membership initially alleviated the Sunday School overcrowding by converting the old rectory into a youth activities center. In 1956 a building committee was formed and approved a $50,000 expansion plan including alterations to the church's worship and social facilities. Two years later the education building was added, the sanctuary was remodeled, and the social hall was enlarged. In 1961 church leaders recorded a membership of 900 with a Sunday School attendance of 325.[81] The difficulties encountered by the Congregationalists were described by a local reporter as being typical of the problems faced by the people of Massena and all congregations during this era of expansion.[82] Many church leaders witnessed the church membership outgrowing their current worship and Sunday School facilities and were confronted with the decision of whether to renovate their building immediately or delay construction until 1960 to determine if the population growth associated with the Seaway was permanent.

Akin to Cornwall, during the 1950s Massena's Catholic parishes remained the area's largest congregations, as many workers were adherents to this faith. Priests at both Sacred Heart and St. Mary's recorded an increase in mass attendees during the Seaway. Comparable to other Massena congregations, in 1953 St. Mary's members began discussing plans to construct a larger church, rectory, and convent in anticipation of more worshipers during the project. Architects designed what was considered one of the most elaborate church building projects in the North Country. The new structure contained a larger pew capacity, several ornate altars, and numerous stained glass windows. Parishioners of all ages solicited donations to cover some of the costs of the construction. School-age children initially raised money to buy bricks for the church's exterior and later collected $2,000 to buy stained glass windows. The men of the Holy Names Society donated $3,500 for a statue and altar. The women of the League of Sacred Heart matched this contribution. Church historians viewed parishioners' financial offerings as extraordinary, since most members were working class, not professionals. Besides having little discretionary income, most members of St. Mary's had little free time to devote to fund-raising.

During the Seaway construction, Massena worshipers, workers, and itinerant preachers founded the Bethel Assembly of God. The spiritual association was a Pentecostal faith that grew out of the Holiness movement.

Members of Protestant denominations were trying to revive some of the spiritual practices that had attracted members during the Second Great Awakening in the nineteenth century. According to Winthrop Hudson and John Corrigan, "They emphasized baptism in the Holy Spirit and regarded sanctification as a gradual process, rather than an instantaneous work of grace."[83] This philosophy meant that anyone could join the congregation, even if he or she hadn't already been saved.

Massena's Bethel Assembly of God Church was spawned from the missionary efforts of Bill and Irene Riddle. The couple graduated from the Central Bible Institute in Springfield, Missouri in the early 1950s, and they wanted to start a new congregation in northern New York. Upon consulting the New York District Superintendent for the Assembly of God Church, they were informed that a Massena resident, Mrs. James Bean, had been waiting for an Assembly church for several decades. The Riddles traveled to Massena, found jobs at Alcoa, and after several months saved enough money to purchase a vacant store to serve as the congregation's first meeting hall. They used the rest of their funds to paint the new building, advertise a tent meeting in 1952, and rent land where the spiritual gathering would be held. Within three weeks the congregation consisted of three families, began holding children's and adult Sunday Schools, and was granted air time on a local radio station to share its beliefs with listeners. By 1954 the Assembly of God congregation had raised enough money to purchase an old church in a nearby town, which they tore down and reconstructed on Maple Street in Massena.[84]

The Church of Christ was another congregation founded by Seaway workers between 1954 and 1958. The popularity of this fundamentalist faith mounted during the 1950s. The focus on one's individual relationship with God fit into the American evangelical tradition. As William McLoughlin indicated, "The new concern was over a direct personal encounter with God's spirit." When there seemed to be no specific religious guidelines or pastors who provided people with answers to their individual problems, worshipers opened their hearts to God. During times of social crisis, people needed to come to understand their own identity and their place in the world.[85] The social changes in Massena residents' lives attracted them to this new religion which offered them a sense of inner peace.

In 1956, John Buster, a transient laborer from Arkansas, placed an advertisement in the *Massena Observer* in an effort to find other area Church of Christ adherents. A local woman responded to his initial message and they began to pray together. Within a few months the two were joined by other Massena residents and project workers who shared their faith. The group grew to ninety members over the next several years and met in rented rooms for the duration of the Seaway project. The original adherents did not institute any building plans, however, since many were only in the area temporarily. Membership began to dwindle toward the conclusion of the project, as workers and their families, including Buster, moved on to the next job. However, in 1959, the remaining thirteen members and their new minister, Jamie Hemphill, still held services and began an aggressive fund-raising campaign to cover the cost of constructing their own building.[86]

Cornwall and Massena's religious congregations remained the town's central social and moral institutions. As Henry Wallace Schneider indicated, "The church building was physically the center of the community and the parish was the vital institution of religious activities."[87] Similar to their reaction to the social and economic impact of industrialization from 1900 to 1954, area residents turned to their faith as a way to retain their traditional values, maintain their social ties, and regulate the activities of new arrivals. While the denominational makeup of Cornwall and Massena churches varied, congregation leaders faced similar challenges of servicing worshipers with changing spiritual needs, and expanding their facilities to accommodate these new adherents. Besides the influx of Seaway workers, the social and economic lives of residents on both sides of the border were in flux. Both Cornwall and Massena residents turned to their ministers to assist them in dealing with their anxieties, and to provide them and their children with a sense of security and a consensus of values. As William McLoughlin stated, "The 1950s were a time when we Americans desperately sought to reaffirm our old values, to get back to God, and rid ourselves of subversives who were conspiring to destroy our way of life."[88] From 1954 to 1958 Cornwall and Massena inhabitants retained comparable religious values and financially supported their churches through the fund-raising efforts of voluntary associations.

In summary, the influx of Seaway workers and their families temporarily altered Cornwall and Massena's populations and social institutions, and enhanced residents' regional identity. The more than 22,000 new inhabitants on both sides of the border often spoke with foreign accents, committed crimes, and worshiped at evangelical churches. Many were transient workers who had moved from one project to another and developed a rowdy lifestyle. Their children overcrowded schools and were juvenile delinquents. Therefore, the towns' roles as the headquarters for the Seaway project exposed Cornwall and Massena residents to outsiders from various regions of the country with different social and religious values sooner than their more homogeneous rural neighbors. Local leaders also addressed the problems associated with rapid social expansion that their counterparts never faced. During the four years of the project, law enforcement and religious officials struggled to retain order and social harmony in their ever changing societies. This shared experience added to the regional identity of Cornwall and Massena residents that had existed since the settlement days. The feelings of differentness and separateness from their neighbors remained even during the modern era of mass transportation and communication.

From 1954 to 1958 citizens' reaction to outsiders and their religious lives reflected similar values. Local citizens' reactions to these outsiders on both sides of the border exposed their varying levels of accommodation of individuals who were not like themselves. While Massena residents seemed more welcoming to the Seaway workers and their families, most hoped that they would leave once the project was done. In Cornwall, the increase in crime and public drunkenness reinforced longtime residents' fears and anxieties that new groups would disintegrate the town's social fabric. Both still retained introverted small town mentalities and feared the encroachment of outsiders. As during the previous decades of industrialization, Cornwall and Massena citizens turned to religion as a way to maintain social cohesion, engender a sense of common morals, and control the behavior of Seaway workers and their families. They looked to their preachers to help them survive in their changing society. Both areas' congregations instituted services to fit workers' schedules and made a concerted effort to attract new arrivals to church services to temper their immoral behavior. During this project local residents remained spiritually devout, collectively oriented, and unaccepting of outsiders. The financial downturn that followed the completion of the Seaway challenged Cornwall and Massena citizens to again face the challenges of being neglected border towns.

CHAPTER FIVE

The Long-Term Economic Impact of the St. Lawrence Seaway and Power Project on Cornwall and Massena

Despite hype and promise, the completion of the St. Lawrence Seaway did not economically revitalize Cornwall and Massena. Prior to 1958 journalists confidently expected that new industry would spring up along the path of the Seaway, and that the area would attract tourists, vacationers, and sightseers to enjoy the new beaches and recreation areas as well as to observe the functioning locks and power dam. According to an article in the *New York State Commerce Review*, the potential for growth in Massena was great, as it was one of the least industrialized parts of the state.[1] However, this recreational and manufacturing growth depended on several factors including improved water and land transportation and the availability of cheap power. In a 1954 speech at Queen's University, Lionel Chevrier indicated that the keys to the area recruiting new industry was getting a block of power set aside specifically to supply cheap power to factory owners and constructing a new deep water port.[2] While Cornwall's industrial commissioner enticed several small business owners to establish facilities in the area, and Massena officials signed power and land agreements with two manufacturing firms, none of these companies made up for the jobs lost during the plant closures and downsizing that occurred on both sides of the border prior to 1958. By the late 1950s both towns slipped into depressed financial states.

Scholars and local residents offer many observations as to why Cornwall and Massena never witnessed increased industrialization following the completion of the Seaway project. According to a Waterhouse report published in 1971, three factors contributed to this shared economic decline: the termination of the Seaway construction, layoffs by current plant owners, and the impact of foreign competition on the production levels of local facilities.[3] In addition both were far from major metropolitan markets. Cornwall lay eighty miles west of Montreal, while Massena was more than 200 miles from Syracuse, New York, the closest American city. As Leonard Yaseen noted, "Plant owners no longer located new production facilities based on intuition. Industrialists and their consultants now compared wage rates, holidays, fringe benefits, cost of power, transport and taxes, labor availability and skill level, and the general character of the area."[4] Therefore, once the bulldozers left town, promises of economic grandeur for Cornwall and Massena fell by the wayside. According to Clive and Frances Marin, "The St. Lawrence project went through with little positive impact on Massena or Cornwall."[5]

After 1970 Cornwall and Massena's industrial bases were weakened by the phasing out of their main manufacturing operations by national corporations, and town officials struggled to meet their financial obligations. Both towns were victims of the deindustrialization trend as large companies shut down their northern plants and moved to industrial areas in the South and overseas with more favorable business climates. The outdated equipment in the areas' factories made them obsolete and susceptible to phase out. The high corporate and income taxes imposed in New York State also convinced industrialists not to update their facilities. Besides the loss of thousands of jobs, Cornwall and Massena officials depended on tax payments from workers and factory owners for supporting police and fire protection, schools, and parks. This story of economic downturn was not unique. According to Daniel Creamer, between 1958 and 1963 many industrial cities lost employment as industries decreased their production.[6] Cornwall and Massena were no longer major regional manufacturing and retail centers. Instead, they were poor, isolated, and neglected areas with high unemployment rates. Both towns could not compete with the low wages and cheap operating costs offered by southern states.

Neither Cornwall nor Massena witnessed the prosperity analysts predicted prior to the completion of the Seaway. National and local circumstances hindered the economic development of the two towns. Their peripheral location resulted in high transportation costs that prevented manufacturing from locating new plants in the region and encouraged existing facilities to downsize. Unfortunately, both Cornwall and Massena were early leaders in the deindustrialization trend that continues to plague the former industrial cities of the Northeast.

Immediately following the completion of the Seaway, Cornwall officials reported high levels of unemployment and indicated they had not located any corporate executives who wanted to construct new factories in the area. According to Chris Jermyn, "In the first five or six years after the Seaway construction there was an industrial drought in Cornwall."[7] In 1959 Canadian contractors released 2,000 workers, many of whom remained temporarily in Cornwall. Local welfare payments reached $569,000 in that year, up from

$319,000 in 1958.[8] This was part of a larger national recession from 1959 to 1961 caused by a decline in consumer spending. Based on increasing unemployment rates, national officials designated Cornwall a depressed area. In an effort to revive the town's economy, federal and provincial government leaders offered tax exemptions and cash grants to the owners of existing plants and those industrialists willing to establish new factories in the area. As Robert Bothwell noted, "In December 1960 and thereafter, the conservative government had provided tax concessions for firms which might be established in designated high unemployment areas."[9]

In September 1959 Cornwall's industrial commissioner, Edgar May, and several local merchants started Cornwall Industrial Developments Limited (CIDL) to try to alleviate the town's financial dilemma. The leaders of this organization purchased available land and buildings suitable for manufacturing, and marketed and sold them to interested buyers. May initially obtained property from Ontario Hydro with the proceeds from a sale of 10,000 shares of stock to local investors for $25 a piece. The CIDL officials also convinced the supervisor of Cornwall's Public Works Department to extend his current water and sewer lines to their parcels. By 1960 May sold all these lots to manufacturers, who were also offered federal tax exemptions and start-up capital. Iroquois Chemicals, one of TCF's chemical suppliers and a subsidiary of Courtaulds, made furniture lacquer for the national market and was the most successful new Cornwall company.

CIDL investors also bought the vacant Canadian Cotton Mill buildings and sold or leased all the available spaces to business owners by 1965.[10] The officials of Dominion Tape bought one of the mill buildings in 1960, converted it into a facility to manufacture pressure sensitive tape, and employed 300 workers throughout the 1960s. Other CIDL tenants were Vanguard Glove, which manufactured leather gloves between 1962 and 1972; Reach Plastics and Chemicals, which made pipe coverings using material from Courtaulds; and, Sovereign Seat Covers, which assembled car seat covers.[11] These new facilities illustrated a shift in Cornwall's industrial sector from large-scale manufacturing operations to small enterprises that employed under 100 workers and made one specific product. However, the owners of most of these facilities closed their operations in the 1970s, when the federal government discontinued their financial assistance programs.

Simultaneously, Courtaulds and Domtar Paper Mill researchers created new product lines to keep pace with changing consumer demands. In the late 1950s and early 1960s, Courtaulds' executives diversified their product lines to try to regain some of their market share. In 1959 the company's investors bought a styrolite plant from the owners of the Guardian Chemical and Equipment company. They moved the insulation manufacturing operation to mill number four at their Cornwall facility. However, Courtaulds' salesmen could not sell this product to building suppliers and contractors, and company officials closed down production after only a few years. The next venture Courtaulds' executives attempted in an effort to revive the Cornwall plant's profits was the fabrication of carpets. In 1962 they created Courtaulds Carpet Limited and employed workers to weave rayon fibers into rugs. Two years later West Point Pepperell investors purchased this division and began to produce nylon and acrylic remnants. Even with the failure of these first two endeavors, Courtaulds' researchers continually searched for new products.[12]

The most important postwar developments at Courtaulds were the discovery by scientists of the extraction of sodium sulfate from the wastewater created by the processing of viscose and the establishment of nylon yarn production. The marketing department sold sodium sulfate to detergent producers and it became the company's main product. According to George Holland, a Courtaulds' historian, the profits from the sale of sodium sulfate allowed officials to keep the Cornwall plant in operation for three more decades.[13] Workers also produced nylon yarn after a disagreement between Courtaulds and a longtime business partner. For the past twenty years, employees at the British Nylon Spinners facility, a joint venture between the I.C.I. Chemical Company and Courtaulds, had manufactured this material. However, in 1962 I.C.I. investors attempted a hostile takeover of Courtaulds and, therefore, executives no longer felt comfortable cooperatively operating that facility. Courtaulds' officials transferred the nylon production equipment to mill number one at their Cornwall plant.

The production of sodium sulfate and nylon yarn could not replace the profits lost when Courtaulds closed down its tire yarn and continuous textile divisions in 1966. Since the 1920s both materials had been the company's most successful products. By the 1960s, however, Asian and Latin American manufacturers fabricated cheaper cotton tire yarn and nylon material and became Canadian tire and clothing producers' main suppliers. Courtaulds investors, like the financial backers of other Canadian companies, were unwilling to spend their money on new equipment to modernize their facility to meet this new foreign competition. After 1966 the Cornwall personnel officer laid off hundreds of his employees. In 1970 Courtaulds employed 899 men and women, down from 1,891 in 1951.[14]

In the 1960s Howard Smith Paper Mill remained one of Cornwall's leading industries. As Edgar McInnis indicated, "The pulp and paper industry rose to the rank of a major industry in the 1920s, and its growth was linked with a parallel expansion in the development of hydroelectric power."[15] After 1952 the owners of these facilities led all others in terms of profits and supplied one-half of the world's newsprint. Unlike the owners of Courtaulds, the paper mill's executives modernized their plant and increased their employment levels and customer base between 1960 and 1970. In 1957 the facility had become part of the Dominion Tar and Chemical Company (Domtar), when the latter's stockholders bought a controlling interest in the Cornwall operation. Domtar officials already owned plants in Sainte Catherine's and Beauharnois, Quebec and Don Valley, and Georgetown, Ontario. In 1960 and 1966 company executives purchased two paper machines and spent more than $11 million on additions to their Cornwall vanillin plant, wood yard, and finishing room. Three years later Domtar officials announced a $1.75 million two-floor expansion of their finishing and shipping rooms.[16]

The management of the Domtar Paper Corporation illustrated the national trend of company owners specializing their product lines as a way to remain competitive. The concentration of industrialists on the manufacturing of one specific material allowed them to eliminate the costs associated with producing a diversified product line, and to downsize their workforce. Domtar workers produced fine milled paper that was purchased by consumers because of its high quality, not its low price. Thus their market share and profits were not as affected by cheap imports as their Courtaulds' counterparts. As David Rayside noted, "Specialization has placed firms in better standing to compete in the highly pressured markets."[17] In 1970 Domtar employed 1,770 men and women, up from 1,622 in 1951.[18]

In the initial decade after the completion of the Seaway, Cornwall officials and investors recruited new industry to the area by offering entrepreneurs attractive plant locations. Edgar May and his associates realized that the only way that the town's economy would expand was through their own financial contributions and marketing efforts. Unfortunately, the managers at these new companies did not hire enough workers to absorb those laid off by Courtaulds' personnel department and the Seaway contractors, and little land remained for the CIDL to acquire. Between 1945 and 1970, 3,950 textile workers lost their jobs and only 2,150 found employment at other area businesses.[19] In 1971 only ninety-three acres of land suitable for industry remained in the hands of local owners willing to sell their property to Cornwall's industrial commissioner. Absentee owners from Montreal, Ottawa, and New York City held the deeds on other parcels of property. They purchased them on speculation during the Seaway project and were not enthusiastic about parting with their plots, since most were convenient tax write-offs. As J. E. Clubb noted, "Absentee owners are less concerned with community welfare than with their own profits."[20] Therefore, Cornwall residents and government officials entered the 1970s with a high unemployment rate. According to Mayor Edward Lumley, "After almost 15 years of frustration, all we have to show is a net gain of 1.9 percent in persons employed in industries."[21]

In the 1970s Courtaulds' profits continued to diminish, while industrialists established several new high-tech firms in the area. C-Tech, a sonar production firm, was one of the most successful new companies. These small, specialized firms replaced the town's giant factories. Domtar Paper Mill also diversified its product line and hired more workers. By 1980 only 2,730 Cornwall residents were employed in the clothing and textile industry, a decline of 50 percent since 1949.[22] Canadian national officials also tried to assist floundering factory owners, particularly those who operated textile plants, by resurrecting their protectionist policies from the Great Depression, including the "buy at home" campaign and the placement of import quotas on clothing from Asia and Japan.[23] These measures came too late for Courtaulds' supervisors, who had already phased out many of their divisions that had historically served the Canadian market.

Courtaulds' executives struggled financially in the 1970s as their domestic market share dwindled. In 1974 the plant's workers produced stable fiber and sodium sulfate, exclusively for the American and British markets. As Edgar McInnis indicated, "The domestic market was often too small for some profitable ventures in highly specialized products. To remain competitive, these companies had to find customers abroad."[24] The Cornwall facility's supervisor derived some additional income from renting his empty mills to other manufacturers. From 1973 to 1979 he leased space in mill number four to the owners of Cornwall Appliances and Best Form Brassiere.

In 1990 the Courtaulds' sales department lost its foreign customer base, ultimately leading to the plant's closure. As Courtaulds' historian Doug Heuer noted, "The North American recession and the increasing imports of cheap textiles from the Far East caused a decline in American consumers' demand for rayon."[25] New cost-cutting measures were considered by Courtaulds' executives to avoid a further decrease in profits, but they feared that a loss in product quality would damage the company's reputation. Instead, in 1992 Courtaulds' officials closed their entire Cornwall plant.[26] According to Courtaulds' manager, William Cowling, "The free trade policies of the federal government have been responsible for the steady decline of the textile industry in Canada."[27] The shutting down of the Courtaulds' facility also reflected a practice of foreign companies closing their overseas branch plants before downsizing their central operations. As Maurice Yeates indicated, "When parent companies do not perform as well as other competitors, then foreign branch plants are the first to reduce output."[28]

After 1970 the efforts of Domtar company owners to make their Cornwall factory profitable and competitive were more successful than Courtaulds'. While the plant managers closed down their vanillin and sulfate mills, they started the production of fire-resistant insulation for pipes and ceiling tiles. In 1977 they were awarded a provincial and federal grant of $15 million for plant modernization. Corporate investors also earmarked $112 million of the company's assets to retool their five Canadian plants over the next five years, particularly their Cornwall operation.[29] In the 1990s Cornwall researchers developed the world's first cardboard recycling plant, turning the former into fine paper. By 1997 Domtar's executives had invested more than $150 million in new equipment and employed 1,000 workers at their Cornwall facility. The paper mill remained the area's only surviving large factory, and became the main employer of town residents. Like the company's founder, John Barber, Domtar executives were innovative risk-takers who reinvested their profits into their operations and continued to create new product lines.

With the decline of several of the traditional industries in Cornwall, small high-tech operations became the key to the area's financial survival. The most successful firm was C-Tech, whose owners were given federal grants to build their facility in 1973. Scientists at the locally owned electronics firm discovered new ways to improve underwater surveillance equipment. During the next thirty years C-Tech employees became known as worldwide experts in analog and digital electronics, as well as electromechanical and underwater acoustics. Initially, researchers developed a sonar system for commercial fishermen in Norway, Japan, Denmark, Canada, and the United States. The device assisted these men in locating larger schools of fish, enabling them to increase their daily catch. C-Tech scientists then adapted this technology to serve many of the world's navies. They created sensitive sonar systems, which helped seamen detect mines, assisted them in mapping the ocean floor, and enhanced their harbor surveillance techniques. C-Tech's customers included the Australian, Swedish, Belgian, Canadian, and U.S. navies. The company's president, Dennis Derouin, stated, "The reason the firm has been so successful is that we understand the need for equipment which can meet the many diverse requirements of the modern navy." In 1997 the company employed eighty workers and researchers and represented the future of Cornwall industry.[30]

The decades following the completion of the St. Lawrence Seaway, while economically devastating for Canadian corporations, were seen by historians, including Charles Lipton, as a watershed for Canadian unions. At the beginning of the 1960s, Canadian union officials were worried that they were not organizing enough new workers into their locals. With the high levels of unemployment in the traditional union strongholds of textiles and auto manufacturing, few new affiliates were being created. However, with the revival of the economy in the 1970s, and changes in workplace management techniques, labor union membership rose to 3,042,000 by the end of the decade, double the number of rank and file in 1962.[31] Workers also began to stage an increasing number of protests to protect their wages and regulate their working conditions. According to Robert Bothwell, "By the end of the decade [1960s], plenty of old-fashioned strikes over wages, working conditions, and fringe benefits were staged."[32]

The issue of the escalating workloads of operatives in certain factories became the subject of many grievances and strikes. As foreign competition intensified, many factory managers reduced their workforces and installed increasingly advanced equipment. This resulted in the speeding up of many assembly lines and an increase in daily quotas. Company owners said that these changes came under management's prerogative to improve their facility's efficiency, and were therefore, not subject to negotiation. In 1957 the workers at the Dominion Textile Company in Sherbrooke, Quebec staged a strike to protest a 25 percent increase in their workload that had not been accompanied by a pay increase. Many workers would follow this example and make workloads part of their contract negotiations with management. According to David Rayside, "Unionization is thought to have generated a substantial improvement in wages and benefit packages and to have significantly narrowed the room for arbitrary styles of management."[33]

From 1960 to 1980 Cornwall union members, like their predecessors, staged protests to increase their wages and limit management's alteration of the production process. Workers at Domtar Paper Mill walked out of the plant three times in the 1960s over unfair work schedules and unequal duties. As one worker stated, "It is hard work and often numbingly routine with almost unending pressure to keep up with production levels."[34] In each case company officials hired efficiency experts to evaluate the production process over several days to determine whether the strain on workers was equally shared and within their capabilities. According to Charles Lipton, many union officials viewed these short-term evaluations as an inadequate way to properly measure the actual strain on workers. Most negotiations over this issue were hard-fought and prolonged.[35] However, Domtar workers were able to reach an agreement with company officials on each of these occasions, reducing production quotas and more evenly dividing the workload. The situation was not so easily resolved in September 1975, when the mill workers began a 188-day strike. The operatives were angered over the rumor that the company was about to randomly lay off more than 100 workers. The union members wanted Domtar officials to abide by the seniority clause in their current contract and ensure that their jobs were secure. The 1,300 strikers initially refused the management's wage increase offer in January 1976. Three months later the union members agreed to a contract which included a cost of living increase, but managers still refused to discuss the seniority issue. This proved a fatal mistake on the part of union negotiators when 1,000 workers were temporarily laid off in November of 1976.[36]

The aftermath of a strike staged by the employees of MCA Record Company in 1976 illustrated the proclivity of industrialists to relocate their operations when workers were unwilling to accept wage cuts and longer hours. The company was established in 1969 with a development grant from the Ontario provincial government. The 400 employees manufactured blank records for the American recording industry. After seven years the members of the International Union of Electrical, Radio, and Machine Workers realized they were being paid well below the rate of their counterparts at an American facility. MCA workers, therefore, staged a 194-day walkout in 1976. This was part of what Edgar McInnis called an upswing of labor restlessness as they tried to attain the same wage levels as their American counterparts.[37] MCA workers rejected management's offer of a 45 percent pay increase in February 1976, and the plant was subsequently closed down. The company's vice president, Richard Bibby, insisted that his product could be made cheaper in another country.

The attitude of MCA's executives reflected a dominant management mentality that the high wages demanded by Canadian workers were unreasonable when the same work could be performed more cheaply by operatives in another part of the world. Economist Harold Vatter indicated that the rise in competition from western Europe and Japan meant manufacturers were increasingly concerned with their production costs. This encouraged many to move their plants to areas with lower wages, an unorganized labor force, and no right to work laws.[38] The fact that 80 percent of Cornwall's workforce was unionized by 1971 and its volatile history have given the town the reputation of a tough union town. While no prospective manufacturers have cited the labor conditions as a reason for not locating a plant in the area, the absence of the construction of any large facility since 1924 seems to support this assessment.

From 1970 to 2001 the entire industrial makeup of Cornwall underwent a significant transformation. For half a century the town's residents had depended on the owners of the area's three large mills for their livelihood. With the initial phase down and eventual closure of the Courtaulds' plant in 1994, workers, who had been employed for several decades at the facility, found themselves standing in line to collect unemployment checks. Most of these men and women were considered unskilled and were, therefore, unemployable by the area's new high-tech firms. The owners of Domtar and C-Tech, with their innovative products and commitment to research and development, represented a new direction for Cornwall industry. The human resource managers at these firms, however, never employed as many residents as the area's former industrial giants. Therefore, after the completion of the St. Lawrence Seaway Project in 1958, Cornwall residents and politicians never experienced the economic prosperity that Seaway promoters had predicted. According to the authors of a Cornwall planning report, "Industrial growth in the St. Lawrence area has proceeded slowly in recent years in comparison to the remainder of southern Ontario. The navigation and power generating facilities constructed as part of the St. Lawrence Seaway have not attracted new manufacturing plants to the extent originally anticipated."[39] Nonetheless, in the year 2001, many Cornwall political leaders continued to predict that the full social and economic benefits of the Seaway will materialize over the next several decades.

Massena

Massena residents and politicians, similar to their Cornwall counterparts, expected the cheap power provided by the new hydrodam to attract new industry to the area. In 1955 geographer Harold Wood stated, "The completion of the Seaway will introduce an era of prosperity that will surpass anything previously experienced."[40] Initially, the industrial sector in Massena appeared to be faring better than Cornwall's due to the addition of two new manufacturing plants. Before the completion of the power project, executives from Reynolds Metals and General Motors announced plans to construct an aluminum processing and complementary fabricating plant in Massena. In 1957 both companies' contractors broke ground on adjacent plots along the St. Lawrence River, and corporate officials signed multi-year power contracts with PASNY. However, over the next three decades, Alcoa laid off half its workforce and the employment levels at the two new companies never surpassed 1,200. Massena town leaders, contrary to their counterparts in Cornwall, did not attract any additional industrialists to locate small, specialized plants in the area. Therefore, Massena ended the century as one of the most underdeveloped areas in the Northeast.

Economists John H. Thompson, James M. Jennings, Sidney C. Sufrin, and Edward E. Palmer of Syracuse University blamed Massena's industrial stagnation on poor roads, the lack of suitable industrial land, and the absence of surplus electricity. Even after the highway era of the 1960s, Massena remained seventy-two miles away from Route 81, the closest four-lane interstate highway. After 1958 no kilowatts of electricity or industrially zoned property remained available for interested industrialists to purchase from either PASNY or Massena realtors. Alcoa, Reynolds, and General Motors executives not only contracted the entire PASNY industrial allotment, but also owned more than 1,000 acres of riverfront land. In the 1960s Massena officials also lost potential industries to southern and western states, whose economic developers offered factory owners municipal bonds to fund plant construction, long-term tax exemptions, and favorable lease terms. According to Michael French, "The most striking feature of the U.S. economy since 1945 has been the increase in importance of western and southern states in terms of manufacturing."[41] The better climate, abundant land, and cheap labor made these new areas more appealing to industrialists than the old industrial regions of the Northeast. Massena plant managers, like their Cornwall counterparts, experienced both financial prosperity and failure.

During the 1960s Alcoa, Reynolds, and General Motors supervisors all increased their production and employment levels. However, after 1969 the industrial world entered unpredictable times. By the end of the decade, according to Robert Sobel, "The power, self-confidence, and reputation of American big business that had prevailed in the mid-1960s was replaced with uncertainty and deep soul searching."[42] From 1970 to 1997 Alcoa, Reynolds, and General Motors executives downsized their plants and streamlined their products to remain competitive. The local operations managers struggled to retain their workforces and keep their plants operating, as corporate executives implemented cost-cutting measures and moved some of their production overseas. The expensive transportation costs of getting raw materials to the northern New York plants and shipping out finished products caused executives to cut production at their Massena outlets first. While local supervisors were goal-oriented, innovative, and driven by success, their isolated location prevented them from benefiting from the financial prosperity of the 1990s. Neither General Motors nor Reynolds ever reached their projected levels of employment, and no other major industry located in Massena offered jobs to the increasing number of unemployed factory workers. Thus, while the waterway prospered in the decades following the completion of the St. Lawrence Seaway, Massena did not.[43] As E. G. Faludi stated, "Unfortunately these immense projects of national and international importance were never conceived or coordinated within a long-range regional plan encompassing the future development of the new city and its region."[44]

By 1958 Alcoa was Massena's largest employer, but it struggled to retain its market share against Kaiser Permanente and Reynolds, the nation's other two leading aluminum producers. Unlike Courtaulds' executives who competed for customers against foreign manufacturers, Alcoa leaders debated how to combat their domestic competitors who were developing innovative aluminum products and gaining name recognition among consumers. As George Smith indicated, "There was no great Japanese threat in the integrated production of aluminum [power was much too expensive for that to happen]."[45] Alcoa's 50-year monopoly ended after World War II, when the members of the Surplus Production Board sold government-owned alumina and aluminum plants to Kaiser and Reynolds investors. Within a decade the owners of these two companies jointly claimed 50 percent of the national and global market share. By 1960 Alcoa's market share dropped to an all-time low of 34 percent. The once monopolistic market had turned into a competitive oligarchy.[46] Alcoa executives barely sustained their efficiency and product quality in an era of declining demand for traditional alloy products, rising costs, and increasing uncertainty.[47]

Over the next three decades, Alcoa's CEOs and Massena managers tried to increase the company's profits by retooling their plants and improving the strength of their aluminum. Their accountants and scientists also investigated cost-cutting measures and undertook efficiency studies as a means of regaining their former competitive edge. Initially, these initiatives led to the expansion of Alcoa's North American plants.[48] In 1957 Massena managers implemented a $25 million modernization and expansion program that included the construction of two new potlines, the reactivation of two product lines, and the upgrading of their cable, wire, rod, and structural shapes assembly processes.[49] When the renovations were completed, town tax assessors placed the value of the facility [including twenty-two miles of railroad and twenty-five miles of highway] at $80 million.[50] These projects temporarily improved the financial situation of the Massena facility and gave workers short-term job security.

In 1963 Alcoa followed the lead of other American manufacturers by forming a partnership with a foreign company to diversify its production activities. National officials reached an agreement with Lockheed and Japanese manufacturer Furukawa Electric to form Furalco, a producer of aluminum aircraft parts. Workers at the Massena facility fashioned new aluminum sheets that were then sent to employees at other Alcoa subsidiaries for assembly into various airplane components.[51] According to Michael French, "U.S. firms began to make great use of coalitions with other firms in the form of joint ventures between 1970 and 1982, as they sought to improve their access to technological expertise."[52] But even with the addition of a new product and increased efficiency, Alcoa's Massena human resource manager laid off 2,000 workers from 1958 to 1970. National officials also closed down fabricating plants in Pennsylvania and Texas, as well as refining operations in Alabama. They cited high American wages and utility costs as reasons for expanding their overseas production facilities and downsizng their North American plants.[53] As economists Barry Bluestone and Bennett Harrison indicated, one of the main characteristics of deindustrialization was the tendency of company executives to move their plants out of old industrial areas, where labor costs and unionization levels were high compared to overseas locations where conditions were more favorable. "Capital's second strategy for coping with the crisis was to relocate facilities to different areas of the globe."[54]

After 1975 Alcoa came under the leadership of several CEOs who focused on researching new high-tech uses for aluminum and more effective management structures. As Michael French suggested, this was part of a national trend of executives searching for a managerial strategy to cope with more uncertain times. Company executives tried to reduce the size and complexity of their administrative hierarchy to imitate the successful practices of the owners of smaller firms, who thrived on rapid product development and decentralized operations.[55] While Alcoa's senior executives in Pittsburgh still dictated the company's national marketing and production plans, they delegated the responsibility for day-to-day decisions to local plant managers and business unit leaders. The elimination of middle managers resembled the early days of the company, when each supervisor was in charge of his own production and employment policies. At the Massena plant the operations manager was responsible for overseeing the smelting and fabricating plant. He was also the business unit manager for the Wire, Rod, and Bar Department and took part in the corporate-wide planning and marketing strategy for the entire division.[56]

Even though Massena managers became more involved in national policy making, in 1983 the production level at their facility was threatened when Alcoa's Senior Management Policy Committee unveiled a new corporate mission statement that de-emphasized alumina and ingot production in favor of additional high-tech products. Executives wanted to reduce the company's dependence on metal and diversify into more innovative flat-rolled products. From 1983 to 1997 Massena's human resource department trimmed its workforce from 1,654 to 1,102, as the smelting operations were further phased out. Unlike other Alcoa plants, the Massena facility's equipment was never updated or converted to produce any of the company's new products. According to Barry Bluestone, "It was a practice of company executives to increase their profits by diversifying their product lines and using their earnings to acquire competitors' plants as a means of increasing their production capacity versus upgrading their current facilities."[57] The only investment Alcoa's executives authorized for their Massena facility in the last decade of the twentieth century was funding for the remediation projects ordered by the EPA to clean up contaminated soil on the plant site and to improve the operation's air emissions system.[58] As Joel Garreau stated, "The U.S. slowed down revitalization by forcing corporations to invest billions in environmental equipment to clean the water and air that should have been spent increasing productivity."[59]

Presently, the Massena plant faces closure because of its outdated equipment and increasing energy costs. According to Edward Renshaw, "Firms in long-standing, capital intensive industries have little incentive to modernize their plants and can be expected to abandon their New York-based facilities when they deteriorate to the point of not yielding a profit."[60] Alcoa spokesman, Michael Cooper, indicated at the turn of the twenty-first century that company officials continued to phase out certain product lines to meet changing markets and customers' demands. Massena supervisors closed their facility's cable assembly line when orders from utility companies declined. Once overhead transmission lines were installed, the demand for cable ceased. A recent occurrence threatening the jobs of the remaining 1,250 employees at the Massena facility was the May 3, 2000 completion of the merger between Alcoa and Reynolds Metals. Massena was the only American town with plants operated by both companies. This may mean the elimination of redundant workers at each facility, or the complete closure of one entire plant. In addition Alcoa's electrical contract with PASNY expires in 2013. In the past company executives closed facilities in areas where their energy costs have increased. If a favorable contract is not renegotiated, Alcoa officials may phase out their Massena operation and move the few remaining product lines to another facility.[61]

Unlike their Cornwall counterparts, Alcoa workers did not respond to the reduction of the workforce or changes in production methods by walking the picket line. Instead, workers and managers developed a partnership in terms of contract negotiations and the support of local charities. To keep the factory operating smoothly, Alcoa human resource personnel and members of the Aluminum Brick and Glass Workers International Union negotiated successive 6-year contracts. As George David Smith noted, "Massena was considered one of the company's most placid sites, as the plant suffered no extended strikes after World War II."[62] Factory workers retained the collective-orientation of their predecessors and strove to gain the same standard of living and treatment for all operatives through the negotiation of union contracts. The local also continued its tradition of supporting local charity efforts. From 1970 to 1997 employees also contributed more than $100,000 to the United Way and 40,000 items to the annual food drive. Like their forefathers, they were community-oriented and were concerned more with saving jobs than with their own individual prosperity.

The managers of Massena's new General Motors Powertrain plant experienced both financial success and failure based on changing demands for domestic cars and the introduction of foreign cars into the American market. Like his neighbors at Alcoa, the supervisor's daily operation of his plant was affected by the decisions of national officials concerning overall company profitability. In 1959 the seventy employees at the 224-acre, $15 million plant began production of aluminum engine and transmission castings for the Chevrolet Corvair.[63] Company executives had previously negotiated a deal with Reynolds officials to use their aluminum in the manufacturing of these parts, thereby saving the transportation costs associated with using an out-of-town raw material supplier.[64] At the 1957 groundbreaking ceremony, E. N. Cole, general manager of the Chevrolet Division of General Motors, stated, "Chevrolet considers these original plans only a beginning. If the potential for aluminum in our industry expands, as we confidently believe it will, we will expect this installation to participate and share in that growth. Our plant is being designed so that additional expansions can easily be made as needs arise."[65] By 1978 the Massena General Motors Powertrain plant employed 1,100 workers.

After 1979 General Motors struggled to maintain its market share against Japanese manufacturers, and the Massena plant faced closure. National executives downsized their entire line of cars, eliminated second shifts at most of their plants, and closed assembly lines in others because of increasing foreign competition. Small imported front-wheel drive vehicles captured 20 percent of the American market by 1980 and proved more attractive to buyers than traditional large domestic rear-wheel drive models. As Robert Sobel noted, "Foreigners not only turned out more economical cars, but also designed and manufactured them with greater care and ability. American cars were plagued by recalls and defects."[66] In the 1980s, as this consumer trend continued, General Motors closed several of its plants and concentrated on lowering its transportation costs by locating parts and assembly plants near each other. According to Bryan Jones and Lynn Bachelor, "Since a single parts plant served several assembly facilities, the entire logic of the inventory control system dictated geographic concentration in the industry."[67] General Motors officials considered shutting down the Massena plant in 1986, but the innovative process used at the factory to manufacture engines allowed local supervisors to keep the factory running with a reduced staff until a new market was found for their remaining product line.

In the 1980s production at the Massena plant was reduced based on its worn out and obsolete equipment. On August 6, 1986, General Motors officials announced that two of the three Massena production lines would be phased out by the end of the 1988 model year. A recent study conducted by analysts at the company's national headquarters in Detroit had uncovered the excessive production of aluminum castings within its Central Foundry Division. As Michael French noted, "This reflected a new phase in corporate policies aimed at reducing or relocating employment from unnecessary facilities."[68] Massena officials subsequently fired 1,250 of their 1,500 employees and concentrated on a remaining assembly line that produced lost foam molds. Many locals believed this partial slowdown was a sign that national officials were progressing toward closing the plant entirely.

In the 1990s the Massena plant became an integral part of General Motors' revitalization program. On August 6, 1996 General Motors' executives informed Massena plant managers that they would begin manufacturing two new products. This was part of General Motors' overall plan to use its profits to refurbish its old parts plants instead of building new ones.[69] Company executives authorized a $100 million retooling of the Massena plant to equip the facility with the machines to produce four-cylinder aluminum engine blocks and cylinder heads for their new L61 global engine. Human resource personnel also hired 300 new workers to operate the new equipment. General Motors managers later added a 2.2 liter engine to the Massena production line, as well as drive sprockets for Cadillacs and Oldmobiles. In 1997 the 383 workers also began to fabricate new cylinder heads and blocks for the new midsize Saturn.[70] As plant manager Rick Sutton stated, "We have taken our technology to the competitive forefront and have laid a strong foundation for our future growth."[71]

Reynolds Metals' executives were the last industrialists to locate a production facility in Massena following the completion of the St. Lawrence Seaway. Company officials cited the area's cheap electricity as the central reason for constructing their reduction operation on the St. Lawrence River. A company brochure proclaimed, "Since electricity is a key requirement in the production of aluminum, Reynolds chose this plant location due to the abundant supply of competitively priced hydroelectric power available from the nearby St. Lawrence Power Project."[72] In 1959, 1,000 workers began production of aluminum ingot at the $88 million, 9-acre plant. The company's freight department shipped the ingot to automobile and steel manufacturers. Workers manned the facility's assembly line 24-hours-a-day, 7-days-a-week. The owners of the neighboring General Motors plant purchased one-third of the Reynolds facility's local annual output. However, they ended this deal in the 1960s, as they were able to purchase cheaper molten aluminum from a Canadian supplier. The Massena plant owners, however, signed national contracts with General Motors executives and other car manufacturers that are still in effect.

Massena government officials hoped that Reynolds would increase its employment levels and hire some of the workers who had been laid off by Alcoa. Unfortunately, over the last three decades, the facility's production level has remained unchanged. According to company spokesman Fred Wigginton, "All of the American Reynolds plants make one or two specific products. This corporate strategy of specialization has prevented any expansion of the Massena operation and its workforce."[73] By 1984, while plant officials had increased the facility's capacity to 126,000 tons of aluminum annually, they only employed 800 workers.

In 2003 the Massena reduction plant is one of only six remaining Reynolds facilities in the United States because of its unique product line and low energy costs. Since 1969 corporate executives have closed three other reduction plants in Alabama, Arkansas, and Texas because of alterations in their power contracts with local utilities. Massena plant employees fear that when corporate officials' contract expires with PASNY in 2013, their operations may also be phased out. Currently, the 683 workers still produce aluminum ingot and extrusion billets. The freight department ships half of the plant's total output to the managers of General Motors, Chrysler, and Mazda facilities, who remelt the metal and cast it onto wheels, cylinder heads, and other structural components. The owners of steel companies and other miscellaneous enterprises purchase the remaining 50 percent of the ingot [61,000 metric tons]. Massena plant workers also fashion extrusion billets, solid rods of aluminum used for highway guard rails, window and door frames, and automobile sunroofs. National officials, like their Alcoa and General Motors counterparts, invested $200 million in upgrading their pollution control equipment to meet the new stringent Environmental Protection Agency requirements.[74]

From 1960 to the present day, Massena's economic progress has been hindered by national industrial trends and its peripheral location. The Reynolds and General Motors plants were built in the 1960s, a time of revived employment and investment in large manufacturing firms. However, in the 1970s foreign competition, cost-cutting, and mergers made isolated plants more vulnerable to downsizing or closure. Massena's poor roads, lack of suitable land, and absence of surplus hydropower discouraged current plant owners from enlarging their plants and prevented other industrialists from locating facilities in the area. According to H. D. Watts, "New plants can only be established where there are adequate land or buildings of the right shape, and existing plants can only expand if adjacent land or buildings are available. . . . Transport costs also play a key role in industrial location decisions."[75]

Massena's industrial commissioner, unlike his Cornwall and New England counterparts, was not able to convince the owners of smaller, more specialized firms to locate facilities in an area that lacked a skilled work force. As Michael French noted, "New England residents were able to develop new cutting edge ventures staffed by engineers educated at the Massachusetts Institute of Technology."[76] However, in Massena there were no retraining programs to teach unemployed workers new trades, and college students who attended Clarkson University moved to larger cities once they completed their degrees. Therefore, Massena officials were not as capable as municipal leaders in other areas of the Northeast to meet the employment or spatial needs of the owners of the new high-tech and specialized industries that began to dominate the American economy. Many Massena officials agree with Frank Alguire, the Economic Development director, who believes that the full benefits of the Seaway have yet to be experienced. They continue to search for new employment avenues for residents. It remains to be seen whether the area's isolated location and inadequate transportation system can be overcome.

In summary, while both Massena and Cornwall witnessed social and economic growth during the construction phase of the St. Lawrence Seaway Project, the prosperity faded soon after the 1958 completion date based on several factors. The owners of Cornwall and Massena's mainstay industries faced mounting competition at the national and international level, and decreased their production and downsized their workforces to further cut their manufacturing costs. In the 1960s and 1970s, Cornwall officials recruited some high-tech firms, but the area lost the large manufacturing firms that had historically accounted for the town's economic stability and high levels of employment. Comparatively, General Motors and Reynolds executives chose

Massena as the location for their new production facilities in 1957. However, since human resource managers at both of these plants jointly hired fewer than the 2,000 employees at a time when Alcoa officials were cutting their workforce, this did not increase the number of men and women employed in the manufacturing sector.

The abundant, affordable electricity historically promoted by Cornwall and Massena's Board of Trade and Chamber of Commerce as a major benefit of the Seaway project was never made available for the owners of new industries to purchase, based on the policies adopted by the two regional power management organizations. On the American side, PASNY officials awarded multiyear contracts to Alcoa, General Motors, and Reynolds, splitting the American industrial quota, as well as all future reserve power, three ways. Comparably, the entire Canadian share of electricity from the hydrodam was transmitted to the southern Ontario provincial grid and distributed to locales according to need.[77] The power allotment schemes of PASNY and Ontario Hydro officials did not give Massena or Cornwall politicians the competitive edge they needed to make their towns more attractive to industrialists than other areas of the country.

Finally, the opening of the Seaway to commercial traffic in 1959 dovetailed with the beginning of an era of transition in national and international trade practices that affected plants on both sides of the border. Canadian and American policymakers relaxed their tariffs with the advent of the global economy, and subsequently cheap textile and aluminum goods saturated the nations' markets.[78] These circumstances pressured industrialists on both sides of the border to search for ways to lower their production costs. The high wages commanded by northeastern factory workers drove many entrepreneurs south and overseas in search of cheap labor, and caused others to cease operations altogether. Manufacturers in Cornwall and Massena were no exception, as Courtaulds' executives closed their Cornwall operation and Alcoa officials continued to cut their local workforce and transfer production to their foreign plants. Collectively, these local and national economic circumstances meant that the residents of neither town received any long-term financial benefits from the project. As the twenty-first century began, Cornwall and Massena government officials still argued that the full local advantages of the Seaway were yet to be realized.

Conclusion

Cornwall and Massena settlers faced the same obstacles as other borderlanders in their quest for social and economic survival based on their isolated and peripheral locations. The towns' distance from their nations' heartland forced residents to work collectively to stave off starvation, foster a comparable frontier mentality, and encourage the establishment of a shared regional identity. Early settlers had little contact with the outside world and created political, social, and religious organizations contrary to those in other areas of the country. Unlike their more homogeneous rural neighbors, Cornwall and Massena residents in the nineteenth and twentieth centuries experienced economic prosperity and ethnic diversification. Even before the construction of the St. Lawrence Seaway in the 1950s, the areas underwent industrialization that altered the size and makeup of their populations and caused fear and anxiety among permanent residents. The towns' factories also contrasted with the surrounding agricultural landscape. Cornwall residents developed a unique society and culture that mirrored those of their Massena neighbors. The histories of Cornwall and Massena, exceptional though they may be, cast doubt on Seymour Lipset's value-orientation theory and add a new dimension to borderland studies. These two communities within the same world system and situated in comparable space are more alike than different in all ways and hence no "continental divide" separates the United States and Canada in the most fundamental aspects of human behavior and beliefs.

The analysis of Cornwall and Massena from 1784 to 2001 identified a consistent pattern of common social, religious, and economic values and beliefs that refuted Seymour Lipset's central thesis. The residents of both areas desired democratic political organizations, created congregational religious organizations, and were financially ambitious and innovative. This challenges Lipset's argument that all sectors of Canadian and American society differ because of the countries' contrasting organizing principles that stem from the outcome of the American Revolution and historically influenced behavior and community structure on both sides of the border. Even though Cornwall and Massena were settled by the Loyalists and Patriots of the American Revolution, this did not guarantee that these individuals cherished contrasting religious, economic, and political ideologies. Both were former residents of the American colonies and desired similar democratic political institutions and congregational churches that often brought them into conflict with national leaders. After industrialization Cornwall and Massena businessmen were driven by a desire for financial success and developed innovative technology. Cornwall and Massena's parallel social and economic development call into question Seymour Lipset's assertion that "Canada and the U.S. continue to differ considerably. America and Canada are not the same, they are products of two different histories, two different situations."[1] The differences Cornwall and Massena residents had with their larger societies flowed from their relatively isolated borderland location.

The towns' comparable histories support Oscar Martinez's borderland milieu theory. Like other borderlanders around the globe, Cornwall and Massena residents lived in a unique human environment on the periphery of their nations and developed a set of values and beliefs that contrasted with that of their compatriots in the heartland. According to Martinez, borderlanders stand apart because of the singular world in which they live that is isolated, underdeveloped, and neglected. Historically, Cornwall and Massena had greater differences in race, religion, and level of economic development than other regions, which caused intergroup tension and social uneasiness. The towns' location near waterpower encouraged industrialists to erect plants in the area and employ foreign workers. Politically, residents also encountered conflicts with provincial and national government officials because of their desire for a democratic government. Their isolation from major population centers tended to dilute their national identity and fostered a regional identity shared with their American neighbors. Cornwall and Massena residents' ethnic diversity, industrial economy, and interaction with foreigners made them differ from their immediate neighbors, while their religious diversity and geographic location made their lives stand apart from the national norm.[2]

The founding fathers of Cornwall did not desire a strong paternalistic government and did not defer to authority, like most Canadians, as Seymour Lipset suggested.[3] From the early settlement of Cornwall and Massena, inhabitants built communities and survived on their own without government assistance. They did not see government as a benign presence whose help was needed in the struggle for survival against geography and climate.[4] Cornwall residents, unlike their counterparts in the neighboring towns of Alexandria and Kingston, never developed hierarchical political structures. Instead, Cornwall settlers, similar to Massena residents, demanded a democratic, popularly elected government. Loyalists attempted to establish the same participatory government structure they had in their former home towns. Residents wanted town meetings and local courts administered by officials who concerned themselves solely with the financial and legal administration of the towns, and who did not interfere with individuals' rights. While Cornwall loyalists initially failed in their efforts to gain a democratic local government, their protests exhibited their desire for the same political system that their American neighbors implemented after the Revolution. Like other frontiersmen, they insisted on a degree of political autonomy which set them apart from other Canadians and angered provincial government officials. After 1834 Cornwall residents, comparable to their Massena neighbors, were ruled by officials who staffed a democratically elected town government.

In the twentieth century Cornwall and Massena men and women still favored a popularly elected, democratic government staffed by men who were well-respected and upheld the consensual community values of equality and individualism. Voters in both towns elected local businessmen and merchants to public office, whom they thought were the right men for the job based on their success in the private sector. The admiration of inhabitants on both sides of the border for prosperous, self-made men challenged Seymour Lipset's statement that "Canadians find it [success] slightly in bad taste and are not as materialistic and achievement-oriented as Americans."[5] Cornwall's borderland location encouraged residents to adopt values and beliefs that were often contrary to the national standard. These unique values also spilled over into religious organizations.

The spiritual values of Cornwall and Massena inhabitants challenged Seymour Lipset's argument that "the differences between religion in Canada and the U.S. are large and clear cut."[6] Historically, churches have served as the focal point of Cornwall and Massena residents' social and cultural lives. During the many economic and social transitions that took place from 1784 to 2001, congregations have remained the areas' only stable institutions. The towns' men and women dealt with starvation, geographic isolation, the arrival of immigrants, and their own uncertainty about their financial futures by retaining their personal relationship with God and seeking the spiritual guidance of their fellow worshipers and ministers. The parallel social and economic developments of Cornwall and Massena encouraged residents to harbor similar religious values. Men and women on both sides of the border were searching for ways to create harmonious communities shaped by an enduring set of consensual values that guided the lives of both current and new residents. From the canal construction to the completion of the Seaway, religion remained the vehicle Cornwall and Massena worshipers used to control the behavior of new arrivals and to hold onto their own traditional values. Area residents retained the spiritual dedication of their ancestors and found solace in their individual relationships with God as a way to deal with the world around them. Cornwall and Massena inhabitants' similar levels of religious dedication challenged Seymour Lipset's argument that "Americans are more religious and more moralistic than Canadians."[7]

Worshipers in both towns formed evangelical associations and defied the central religious authority of other faiths by creating independent churches. This contrasted the strong Protestant and hierarchical institutions established in the heartland. During the frontier days, in the absence of ministers, Cornwall and Massena inhabitants took charge of their spiritual lives by organizing congregations and recruiting new worshipers as a way to create social bonds between members of scattered and often transient populations. Most faiths did not have enough ministers to serve their nations' expanding frontier population, and settlers were left on their own to maintain their spirituality. Members of all religions, including Catholics, conducted their own services, constructed churches and performed weddings and funerals. In the second half of the nineteenth and in the twentieth century, Cornwall and Massena worshipers retained their control over church financial affairs and sustained their personal relationships with God, even with the arrival of full-time ministers and the construction of permanent church buildings. Members of Massena's and Cornwall's congregations cherished the voluntary, populist, and egalitarian values and beliefs that Seymour Lipset noted were inherent in America.

Members of all denominations also participated in voluntary associations. These organizations represented individuals' new way to control their spirituality, exercise their activism, and foster new social bonds in an industrial society.[8] Men and women also found new forms of friendship and financial support to replace the bonds previously associated with agricultural life. The fund-raisers organized by the leaders of the denominations' various societies and guilds covered the cost of church construction and renovation projects. The work of the male and female members of these organizations, therefore, enhanced the social cohesion of parishioners, and improved the cultural activities for the greater community. The development of strong parish associations by both Cornwall and Massena residents contrasts with Seymour Lipset's statement that only "American ministers and laypeople recognized they had to foster a variety of voluntary associations both to maintain support for the church and to fulfill community needs."[9] The unique spiritual practices of foreigners, however, continued to trouble longtime residents.

During the completion of the Cornwall and Massena canals and the industrial era, Cornwall and Massena residents, like most borderlanders, dealt with ethnic diversification. In this respect, the two towns did not differ so much from the quite diverse nations and societies in which they were embedded, but from their more homogeneous rural neighbors. Following the inception of the canal projects on both sides of the border in 1834 and 1898, the number of French-Canadian and European immigrants increased. The reaction to both Irish and Italian laborers, while several decades apart, illustrated the desire of Cornwall and Massena residents for newcomers to assimilate into society and set aside their traditional religious and social values. The rowdy and criminal behavior of migrant workers reinforced local residents' images of the bloodthirsty and barbaric foreigner and contradicts Seymour Lipset's argument that "One of Canadians' most important self-images is their society is a mosaic, one that gives diverse groups the right to survive."[10]

The negative reaction of Cornwall and Massena residents to outsiders supported Martinez's statement that people of border regions are more likely to live in heterogeneous environments because of ethnic mixing. "In the case of relatively isolated villages, discord with other groups may arise out of fear and resentment."[11] To combat this ill-will, industrialists financed the construction of separate worker housing after the turn of the century, either on plant grounds or in previously unoccupied neighborhoods. Local parish leaders, particularly Catholic priests, also established new congregations for workers. Cornwall and Massena residents did not want to live next to, or share a pew during Sunday services, with these new arrivals. Worshipers, however, believed that if they improved the social and living environments of immigrants and encouraged their moral regeneration through religious worship, the immigrants would naturally alter their cultures to adhere to the dominant national values. Canadians and Americans still agreed that immigrants needed to be assimilated as a way to create a better society where harmony prevailed.[12] As Seymour Lipset noted, "American universalism—the desire to incorporate diverse groups into a culturally unified whole—is inherent in the country's founding ideology."[13]

At the beginning of the Seaway project in 1954, Cornwall and Massena residents still harbored a mutual aversion to men and women who held different spiritual beliefs or spoke a foreign language. Area inhabitants found the untamed lifestyle of Seaway workers to be unacceptable, and tried to curb their behavior with an increase in law enforcement and crime prevention initiatives. Local parish leaders also added Sunday services to accommodate workers' schedules. While Massena natives on the surface appeared more accepting of newcomers, they were happy to see them leave after the project's completion. With these workers came new cultures and religious traditions that taxed the patience of local residents. The social transformation that took place in the twentieth century pressured Cornwall and Massena residents to come to terms with their new identity as an industrial center, and with the difficulties of dealing with a diverse population. In the present day current residents still express hostility toward outsiders, and fully admit they like their homogeneous population.[14] Therefore, Cornwall and Massena residents held comparable beliefs with regard to foreigners and their right to cultural survival.

The ambition and innovation of Cornwall industrialists defied Seymour Lipset's description of the prudent and unimaginative businessman and illustrated their differences from their larger society and culture which flowed from their relatively isolated border location. The aggressive business strategies and investment policies of George Stephen, John Barber, and the owners of Courtaulds resembled those of their American neighbors. Canadian investors were willing to take the financial risk of building factories in Cornwall that they continued to expand and update over the next several decades. Stephens and his counterparts developed new technology and were innovative and aggressive in terms of business practices. In the nineteenth century Cornwall manufacturers marketed new products to meet changing consumer needs and retooled their factories to fashion these new materials. Courtaulds' and Toronto Paper Mill's executives followed suit in the twentieth century by reinvesting their capital in new buildings and equipment. They also funded research and development programs and risked their profits on new product lines that often had no established customers. The owners of these plants disprove Seymour Lipset's statement that "private enterprise in Canada has been a monumental failure in developing new technology and industry, and their involvement in research and development is low."[15] All these men were risk-takers who were innovative, motivated by profits, and respected by residents because of their financial success.

In Massena, John Polley, his fellow resort owners, and H. H. Warren and the canal promoters personified Seymour Lipset's characterization of American businessmen, who "worshipped success and were achievement oriented."[16] They were willing to invest their life savings in new ventures, akin to Cornwall entrepreneurs. All these men took advantage of Massena's natural assets and persevered regardless of the town's isolated location. In contrast to other regions of northern New York, Massena became a manufacturing town with the establishment of Alcoa in 1902. The success of the plant in this formerly neglected area encouraged other manufacturers to locate plants in the area. Industrialists on both sides of the border were committed to increasing their production and employment levels and augmenting their profits by creating new products. These entrepreneurs also became the town's new political leaders as they gained the respect of their fellow male citizens because of their financial prosperity. As David Rayside noted, "In this period of expansion . . . the local manufacturer occupied a position of unassailable prominence and virtue."[17]

In sum, my study supports the main aspects of Oscar Martinez's border milieu theory and calls into question Seymour Lipset's argument that all Americans and Canadians share the same nationally held social, economic, and political values. Cornwall and Massena's border location, parallel histories, settlement experience, and social development encouraged residents to adopt values and beliefs that were more similar to each other than to those of their compatriots on the same side of the border. Inhabitants of both towns, therefore, provided a perfect example of American and Canadian citizens who were the exception to Seymour Lipset's value-orientation theory and his concept of a "continental divide." Their experiences also add a new aspect to the study of borderlands that in the past have focused on the lives of residents on the U.S.–Mexican border.

Notes

Introduction

1. Seymour Martin Lipset, "The Value Patterns of Democracy: A Case Study in Comparative View," *American Sociological Review* 28 (August 1963): 515–531, "Canada and the U.S.: A Comparative View," *Canadian Review of Sociology and Anthropology* 1 (November 1964): 173–185, "Historical Traditions and National Characteristics: A Comparative Analysis of Canada and the United States," in *Canadian Journal of Sociology*, 11 (1986): 113–155, "Canada and the United States: The Cultural Dimension," in *Canada and the United States: Enduring Friendship, Persistent Stress,* eds. Charles Doran and John Sigler (Upper Saddle River: Prentice Hall, 1985), 108–160.

2. Seymour Lipset, *Continental Divide: The Values and Institutions of the United States and Canada* (New York: Routledge, Chapman, and Hall, 1990), 120–122.

3. Ibid., 44 and 45.

4. Ibid., 152–153.

5. Irving Horowitz, "The Hemispheric Connection: A Critique and Corrective to the Entrepreneurial Thesis of Development with Special Emphasis on the Canadian Case," *Queen's Quarterly* 80 (Autumn 1973): 346.

6. S. D. Clark, *Canadian Society in Historical Perspective* (Toronto: McGraw Hill, 1976), 53.

7. Craig Crawford and James Curtis, "English Canadian-American Differences in Value-Orientations: Survey Comparisons Bearing on Lipset's Theory," *Studies in Comparative International Development* (Fall–Winter 1979): 23–44, James Curtis, Ronald Lambert, Steven Brown, and Barry Kay, "Affiliating with Voluntary Associations: Canadian-American Comparisons," *Canadian Journal of Sociology* 14 (1989): 143–161, and Stephen Arnold and Douglas Tigert, "Canadians and Americans: A Comparative Analysis," *International Journal of Comparative Sociology* 15 (March–June 1974): 68–83.

8. Arnold and Tigert, 69.

9. Curtis, Lambert, et al., 143.

10. Oscar Martinez, *Border People: Life and Society in the U.S.–Mexico Borderland* (Tucson: University of Arizona Press, 1994), 10.

11. Hastings Donnan and Thomas M. Wilson, *Borders: Frontiers of Identity, Nation and State* (Oxford, England: Oxford International Printers, 1999), 13.

12. Louis Hartz, *The Founding of New Societies*, 1–48 cited by Seymour Lipset in *Continental Divide*.

Chapter One. The Early Settlement of Cornwall, Ontario and Massena, New York, 1784–1834

1. Elinor Kyte Senior, *From Royal Township to Industrial City: Cornwall 1784–1984* (Belleville, Ontario: Mika Publishing, 1983), 14.

2. J. F. Pringle, *Lunenburgh or the Old Eastern District* (Belleville, Ontario: Mika Publishing, 1980), 3.

3. *Cornwall Standard-Freeholder* (Cornwall) 29 June 1934, 3.

4. Also known as New Johnstown and later renamed Cornwall in the late 1780s in honor of the Prince of Wales, a.k.a. the Duke of Cornwall.

5. E. G. Faludi, *The Making of a New Cornwall, 1963–1983: An Urban Renewal Study*, 15.

6. Edgar McInnis, *Canada: A Political and Social History* (Toronto: Holt, Rinehart, and Winston of Canada, 1982), 203.

7. John Graham Harkness, *Stormont, Dundas and Glengarry: A History 1784–1945* (Oshawa, Ontario: Mundy-Goodfellow Printing Company, 1946), 45, McInnis, 184, Pringle, 101–102, and Senior, 23.

8. Harkness, 45, McInnis, 184, Pringle, 101–102, Senior, 23, and W. S. Herrington, *Pioneer Life Among Loyalists in Upper Canada* (Toronto: The Macmillan Company of Canada, 1915), 13.

9. Edwin Guillet, *Pioneer Days in Upper Canada* (Toronto: University of Toronto Press, 1933), 25 and 554.

10. Ibid.

11. *Cornwall Standard-Freeholder* (Cornwall) 29 June 1934, 3.

12. McInnis, 201.

13. Harkness, 46.

14. Ibid., McInnis, 184, William John Patterson, *Joyous Is Our Praise: Trinity (Bishop Strachan Memorial) Church 1784–1984* (Kingston: Brown and Martin, 1984), 7, *Cornwall Standard-Freeholder* (Cornwall) 29 June 1934, 33 and 3, and Pringle, 25–28 and 90–94.

15. M. A. Garland and J. J. Talman, "Pioneer Drinking Habits and the Rise of the Temperance Agitation in Upper Canada Prior to 1840," in *Aspects of Nineteenth Century Ontario*, ed. James J. Talman (Toronto: The University of Toronto Press, 1974), 175.

16. William Catermole, *The Advantages of Emigration to Canada* (London: Simpkin and Marshall, 1831), 173.

17. Herrington, 20, 27, 28, and 33, Catermole, 86, and Guillet, 2–7.

18. Catermole, 87.

19. Guillet, 28–29 and 41 and Herrington, 34, 87–88.

20. Harkness, 46, *Cornwall Standard-Freeholder* (Cornwall) 29 June 1934, 33, *Official Souvenir Booklet for the Stormont, Dundas, Glengarry Old Boy's Reunion, July 31 to August 7, 1926*, 3, and Herrington, 87–88.

21. Susanna Moodie, *Roughing It in the Bush* (New York: G. Putnam and Company, 1923), 305.

22. Thomas Need, *Six Years in the Bush* (Bobcaygeon, Ontario: Bobcaygeon Public Library Committee, 1838), 96.

23. Guillet, 171.

24. Gerald M. Craig, *Upper Canada, The Formative Years, 1784–1841* (London: Oxford University Press, 1963), 5.

25. A British vice admiralty judge refused to recognize these products as American exports, although the Essex had intentionally stopped at a U.S. port in order to make this claim.

26. Senior, 99–100 and Lieutenant Colonel W. Boss, *The Stormont, Dundas and Glengarry Highlanders, 1783–1951* (Ottawa: The Runge Press, 1952), 8–10.

27. *Official Souvenir Booklet for the Stormont, Dundas, Glengarry Old Boy's Reunion, July 31 to August 7, 1926*, 9 and *Official Souvenir Booklet for the Stormont, Dundas, Glengarry Old Boy's Reunion, August 11 to 15, 1906*, 5.

28. Senior, 99–111, Pringle, 76–80, *Cornwall Standard-Freeholder* (Cornwall) 29 June 1934, 46, and Boss, 8–21.

29. Senior, 102.

30. Ibid., 99–111, Pringle, 76–80, *Cornwall Standard-Freeholder* (Cornwall) 29 June 1934, 46, and Boss, 8–21.

31. Guillet, 14.

32. Catherine Traill, *The Backwoods of Canada* (London: C. Knight, 1836), 161.

33. Pringle, 144–145.

34. David Rayside, *A Small Town in Modern Times, Alexandria, Ontario* (Montreal: McGill University Press, 1991), 36.

35. Craig, 18.

36. S. D. Clark, *Church and Sect in Canada* (Toronto: Toronto University Press, 1948), 166.

37. Terrence Murphy and Roberto Persin, eds., *A Concise History of Christianity in Canada.* (Oxford: Oxford University Press, 1996), 108–109. See also Clark, 90–224.

38. Donald MacMillan, *The Kirk of Glengarry* 1984, 275 and Dr. S. B. Fraser et al., *St. John's Presbyterian Church: A History 1787–1975*, 1.

39. MacMillan, 276, Fraser et al., 2, and Pringle, 213.

40. MacMillan, 276.

41. Ibid., 279 and 280 and Fraser et al., 3–7.

42. Murphy, 162, 166, and 167.

43. *Upper Canada Returns of Population and Assessment, Volume I*, 574.

44. Sydney E. Ahlstrom, *A Religious History of the American People* (New Haven: Yale University Press, 1972), 532.

45. Rolland Clarence Fobert, *Faith Is Our Strength: The Story of St. Columban's Parish, 1829–1993*, 8 and Harkness, 166–120.

46. Fobert, 9 and Senior, 44.

47. Murphy, 120.

48. In 1801 a 25-year-old missionary from England, James Rudd, was assigned to the Cornwall parish with his family. Rudd resigned his post in 1803 and moved to Sorel, Quebec.

49. Patterson, 28.

50. Murphy, 121.

51. Patterson, xvi, Pringle, 227, and *Upper Canada Returns of Population and Assessment, Volume I,* 574.

52. Murphy, 131, Clark, 147–150 and 172, and McInnis, 242.

53. *Cornwall Standard-Freeholder* (Cornwall) 29 June 1934, 30 and *Upper Canada Returns of Population and Assessment, Volume I*, 574.

54. Ahlstrom, 348.

55. McInnis, 132.

56. Ibid., 187.

57. Report of Ten Inhabitants of Township #2 on Meeting of 12 January 1787 and Ensign Francis Mccarty Deposition, 12 January 1787.

58. Senior, 62.

59. McInnis, 187.

60. Pringle, 81, Senior, 79, and Harkness, 56.

61. Rayside, 36.

62. Murphy, 191 and H. H. Walsh, *The Christian Church in Canada* (Toronto: Ryerson Press, 1956), 5.

63. Craig, 111.

64. Leonard Prince, ed., *1802–1952: The Story of Massena* (Massena: Massena Chamber of Commerce, 1952), 2.

65. Richard Peer, Leonard Prince, and Nick Podgurski, eds., *The Billion Dollar Story* (Massena: Massena Chamber of Commerce, 1955), 4.

66. Prince, 3.

67. Sidney C. Sufrin and Edward E. Palmer, *The New St. Lawrence Frontier: A Survey of the Economic Potential of the St. Lawrence Area of New York State* (Syracuse, New York: Syracuse University Press, 1957), 8.

68. The treaty in 1796 referred to earlier was supposed to end territorial disputes between the Indians and new landowners. Instead, loopholes were discovered in the agreement soon after it was signed that necessitated subsequent land purchases by New York State over the next fifty years. However, during this lag time, Indians, in deference to the agreement, insisted they had rightful access to land along a 20-mile stretch of the Grasse and Raquette River and a right to destroy animals that strayed onto the reservation. Further details of this conflict are described in Peer et al.

69. Thomas MacKesey, *Massena Master Plan: A Report to the Town and Village of Massena* (Watertown: Sargent, Webster, Crenshaw and Folley Consultants, 1958), 6.

70. Peer et al., 9 and *Watertown Daily Times* (Watertown) 3 March 1952.

71. Eleanor L. Dumas and Nina E. Dumas, *History of Massena the Orphan Town* (Massena: 1977), 2.

72. Ladies Auxiliary, St. John's Church, *Town of Massena, N.Y.* (Camden: Moesius Phototype, 1900), 1.

73. The town was named after Andre Massena, a French hero of the Battle of Rivoli.

74. Prince, 8.

75. Nick Podgurski, Leonard Prince, and Richard Peer, eds., *The Massena Story*, 5 and Gates Curtis, ed., *Our County and Its People: A Memorial of St. Lawrence County, New York* (Syracuse, New York: D. Mason and Company, 1894), 405.

76. Percy Wells Bidwell and John Falconer, *History of Agriculture in the Northern United States* (New York: Peter Smith, 1941), 77–78.

77. Prince, 7.

78. Podgurski et al., 6, Orin Wheeler, *Early Days of Massena* (Massena: Massena Historical Association), 2, *Watertown Daily Times* (Watertown) 3 March 1952, 10, Bidwell and Falconer, 69, and Franklin Benjamin Hough, *History of St. Lawrence and Franklin Counties* (Baltimore: Regional Publishing Company, 1970), 275 and 334.

79. *Watertown Daily Times* (Watertown) 3 March 1952, 10 and Bidwell and Falconer, 69, 77–78, and 101.

80. Hough, xix and ix.

81. Besides being two of the earliest recorded families to settle in Massena, these pioneers illustrated the hardship of early life in the area. Three of the Denison's children died in 1802 and 1803, and Ichabod Robinson, father of Daniel, became ill and died during a visit to the area.

82. Diary of Cornelia McEwen Day, cited in Dumas and Dumas, 13 and supported by description in Hough, 309.

83. Dumas and Dumas, 6 and 82 and Bidwell and Falconer, 121.

84. Bidwell and Falconer, 82.

85. Ibid., 123.

86. Hough, 275 and 334.

87. *Phoebe Orvis Diary, 1820–1830.*

88. Bidwell and Falconer, 126.

89. Dumas and Dumas, 3–8, and 15 and Bidwell and Falconer, 127.

90. Dumas and Dumas, 32, Gates Curtis, 408–409, and Hough, 335, 352, and 357.

91. *Massena Gazeteer* (1873) listed twenty-eight tenants and Dumas, 36.

92. Podgurski et al., 7.

93. Hough, 475.

94. Ahlstrom, 470.

95. Dumas and Dumas, 105, *The Story of a Church: Congregationalism in Massena* (Waddington, New York: Northland Press), 1964, 1 and *Massena Observer* (Massena) 30 January 1942, 7–C.

96. *The Story of a Church*, 3.

97. As late as the early twentieth century, descendants still paused before meals to read the Bible and ask for the food to be blessed. Dumas and Dumas, 7.

98. Mary Ryan, *Cradle of the Middle Class: The Family in Oneida County, New York, 1790–1865* (New York: Cambridge University Press, 1994), 66.

99. Dumas and Dumas, 4 and Hough, 358.

100. *The Story of a Church*, 4 and L. H. Everts and J. M. Holcomb, *History of St. Lawrence County, New York* (Philadelphia: L. H. Everts and Company, 1878), 408.

101. Dumas and Dumas, 105.

102. *Massena Observer* (Massena) 30 January 1942, 6–C.

103. William McLoughlin, *Revivals, Awakenings and Reform: An Essay on Religion and Social Change in America, 1607–1977,* 86.

104. Paul Johnson, *A Shopkeeper's Millennium: Society and Revivals in Rochester, New York, 1815–1837* (New York: Hill and Wang, 1978), 121.

105. Nathan Hatch, *The Democratization of American Christianity* (New Haven: Yale University Press, 1989), 1–6, 7–16.

106. *Laws of New York xxvth Session,* 25.

107. Prince, 11.

108. Johnson, 73.

109. List compiled by a local reporter; no date appears on the article.

110. Peer et al., 7.

111. Dumas and Dumas, 54 and Hal Barron, *Mixed Harvest: The Second Great Transformation in the Rural North, 1870–1930* (Chapel Hill: The University of North Carolina Press, 1997), 21.

112. Barron, 21–22.

113. Everts and Holcomb, 402–404.

114. Prince, 11.

Chapter Two. The Canal Era and the First Manufacturing Boom in Cornwall and Massena, 1834–1900

1. Others included the Welland and Williamsburg canals, Jeremy Stein, "Industrializing Cornwall: Time, Space and the Pace of Change in a Nineteenth-Century Ontario Town" (Master's thesis, Queen's University, 1992), 52.

2. *Cornwall Standard-Freeholder* (Cornwall) 29 August 1939, 12 and W. T. Easterbrook and Hugh Aitken, *Canadian Economic History* (Toronto: Macmillan of Canada, 1958), 79.

3. Pringle, 163 and *Cornwall Standard-Freeholder* (Cornwall) 29 June 1934, 12 and 29 August 1889, 1.

4. *Cornwall Standard-Freeholder* (Cornwall) 29 August 1939, 1.

5. Ruth Elisabeth Bleasdale, "Irish Labourers on the Cornwall, Welland and Williamsburg Canals in the 1840s" (Master's thesis, University of Western Ontario, 1975), 1–2, 5, 11, 17–18, 20–27, 30, and 59.

6. *Cornwall Standard-Freeholder* (Cornwall) 29 June 1934, 13 and Pringle, 159.

7. Martinez, 17.

8. Fobert, 24 and *Cornwall Standard-Freeholder* (Cornwall) 29 June 1934, 13.

9. Pringle, 160.

10. *Cornwall Observer* (Cornwall) 23 December 1834, 1.

11. Fobert, 24, Pringle, 158, and Senior, 126.

12. *Trinity Church Records,* 5 February 1836, no page numbers indicated.

13. Senior, 147.

14. *Census Reports of the Canadas*, 1861, 74–77 and *Census of Canada*, 1881, 76 and 77.

15. Stein, 88.

16. Easterbrook and Aitken, 377 and 388 and William Marr and Donald Patterson, *Canada: An Economic History* (Toronto: Macmillan of Canada, 1980), 5–6.

17. Ian Drummond, *Progress Without Planning: The Economic History of Ontario from Confederation to the Second World War* (Toronto: University of Toronto Press, 1987), 107.

18. Senior, 227.

19. Ibid., 106.

20. Drummond, 179.

21. Senior, 225–226.

22. Ibid.

23. Ibid.

24. Stormont had to pay taxation on 40 percent of the assessed property value and in return the company agreed to spend at least $150,000 on new buildings and machinery and within five years employ at least 900 hands for nine months out of the year. *The Freeholder* (Cornwall) 17 February 1899, no page numbers indicated.

25. *The Freeholder* (Cornwall) 4 April 1887.

26. R. T. Naylor, *The History of Canadian Business, 1867–1914, Volume Two, Industrial Development* (Toronto: James Lorimer and Company Publishers, 1975), 192–193.

27. Senior, 227–228 and Pringle, 141.

28. Town Council Minutes 11 November 1878, 412–413.

29. Pringle, 294.

30. Naylor, 170.

31. Senior, 233, *Reporter and Eastern Counties Gazette* (Cornwall) 26 April and 10 May 1879, no page numbers indicated, Pringle, 294, *Saturday Globe* (Toronto) 18 November 1893, 7, and *Cornwall Standard-Freeholder* (Cornwall) 29 June 1934, 55.

32. Pringle, 295, Harkness, 236, Senior, 234, and *Saturday Globe* (Toronto) 18 November 1893, 7.

33. Pringle, 295 and Senior, 234.

34. Pringle, 295, Senior, 234, *Massena Observer* (Massena) 24 June 1967, 38C, and *Saturday Globe* (Toronto) 18 November 1893, no page numbers indicated.

35. *The Cornwall Mill Story*, a brochure published by Domtar Fine Papers, Limited, 2–6 and *Cornwall Standard-Freeholder* (Cornwall) 29 June 1934, 53.

36. Ibid.

37. *Souvenir of Stormont, Dundas and Glengarry Commemorating Old Boy's Reunion, August 11–15,1906*, no page numbers indicated.

38. Rudolph Villeneuve, *Catholic Education in Cornwall, Ontario: Yesterday, Today and Tomorrow* (Cornwall: The Stormont, Dundas and Glengarry County Separate School Board, 1971), 12.

39. *Census of Canada, 1941*, Table 10, 113, *First Report of the Board of Registration and Statistics on the Census of the Canadas for 1851–1852* (Quebec: John Lovell, 1858), 26, *Census of Canada, 1871*, Table 4, 274, and *Census of Canada, 1901*, Table 17, 459.

40. Terence Murphy, "The English Speaking Colonies to 1854," and Brian Clarke, "The English Speaking Colonies After 1854" in *A Concise History of Christianity in Canada,* eds., Murphy and Persin, 141, 151, 166, 188, and 274.

41. MacMillan, 280–281.

42. MacMillan, 286, Pringle, 225, and *St. John's Presbyterian Church, A History, 1787–1975*, 17.

43. Murphy, 151.

44. *History of Knox United Church, 1846–1975,* 5–6.

45. *Census of Canada, 1891*, Table 4, 258–259.

46. Fobert, 9.

47. Fobert, 24–25 and *Cornwall Standard-Freeholder* (Cornwall) 30 January 1942, 29.

48. Ibid.

49. Fobert, 29.

50. Ibid.

51. Clarke, 271.

52. *Census of Canada, 1891*, Table 4, 258–259 and *Census Reports of the Canadas*, 1861, 152–153.

53. Patterson, 77–81.

54. This was an affiliate of the Church Society that distributed Bibles, established and maintained schools, built churches, and solicited funds to support the widows of clergymen.

55. Patterson, 97–109.

56. Ibid., 116–145 and Senior, 293.

57. Patterson, 145.

58. Letter from treasurer, Jack Haworth to Claire Parham, September 11, 1998 and Roy Parmelee, *The Anglican Church of the Good Shepherd, Cornwall, Ontario, Celebrate the Light 100 Years, 1893–1993*, 4 and 10.

59. *Census of Canada, 1891*, Table 4, 258–259.

60. Senior, 297, Myrla Scott, *The Trail of the Past: The History of the First Baptist Church, Cornwall, Ontario, 1882–1982*, 2–11, and *Cornwall Standard-Freeholder* (Cornwall) 29 June 1934, 26.

61. Scott, 12–17.

62. Town Council Minutes, 1 May 1876, no page numbers indicated, *Reporter and Eastern Counties Gazette* (Cornwall), 15 September 1877, Senior, 257, Pringle, 137, and *Cornwall Standard-Freeholder* (Cornwall) 29 June 1934, 2.

63. Pringle, 140 and *Old Boy's Reunion, 1906*, 9.

64. Pringle, 140 and 210.

65. *1855 and 1875 New York State Census.*

66. David M. Ellis, James A. Frost, Harold C. Syrett, and Harry J. Carman, *A Short History of New York State* (Ithaca: Cornell University Press, 1967), 273.

67. *1845 New York State Census*, no page numbers indicated.
68. Ibid., 43–44 and *Massena Observer* (Massena) 7 October 1915, 1–5.
69. Prince, 17.
70. Ibid.
71. Podgurski et al., 11, Peer et al., 9, and Massena Mineral Springs Committee, *Massena Mineral Springs: A Great Natural Resource, Massena, New York*, 1936, 1.
72. *Massena Observer* (Massena) 10 January 1939, 1.
73. *Massena Observer* (Massena) 18 June 1903, 5.
74. Lipset, 45 and 127.
75. Prince, 28 and *Massena Observer* (Massena) 31 July 1902, 8.
76. Podgurski et al., 14, Prince, 28, *The Massena Alcoan* 21 January 1946, Volume 4, 2 and 9, *Massena Observer* (Massena) 18 July 1901, 1, and *Massena Observer* (Massena) 31 July 1902, 8.
77. Ibid.
78. *Laws of New York 1896,* Chapter 484, Prince, 29, and *Massena Observer* (Massena) 9 August 1954, 6.
79. Prince, 32.
80. Ibid., 29, *Massena Observer* (Massena) 6 November 1945, Ladies Auxiliary, 3, *Massena Observer* (Massena) 23 June 1952, and *The Massena Alcoan*, January 21, 1946, Volumes 4, 2, and 9.
81. *Massena Observer* (Massena) 21 October 1941 and 9 August 1954.
82. *Massena Observer* (Massena) 13 April 1961.
83. 1875 and 1905 New York State Census
84. *Canal to Company Town, Alcoa in Massena, N.Y.* (Canton: St. Lawrence County Historical Society, 1989), 4.
85. Winthrop S. Hudson and John Corrigan, *Religion in America: An Historical Account of the Development of American Religious Life* (New York: Macmillan Publishing Company, 1992), 129, 148, and 149.
86. Ibid., 208.
87. Everts and Holcomb, 408 and *The Story of a Church: Congregationalism in Massena* (Waddington, New York: Northland Press, 1964), 4.
88. *Massena Observer* (Massena) 30 January 1942, 6-C.
89. Everts and Holcomb, 408 and *Massena Observer* (Massena) 30 January 1942, 6-C.
90. *Massena Observer* (Massena) 30 January 1942, 8-C.
91. *The 165th Anniversary of the First Baptist Church, Massena, New York: A Celebration of Faithfulness to God's Word Since 1829*, 3 and Everts and Holcomb, 407–408.
92. Everts and Holcomb, 408.
93. Dumas and Dumas, 109–111, Everts, 409, and *Sacred Heart Church, 100 Years of Community in Faith, 1874–1974,* 3–5.
94. Everts and Holcomb, 409 and *Massena Observer* (Massena) 30 January 1942, 7–C.
95. Everts and Holcomb, 408 and *St. John's Church, Massena, New York, 1869–1969*, 7–8.

96. Everts and Holcomb, 408 and *St. John's Church, Massena, New York, 1869–1969*, 7–8.

97. *St. John's Church, Massena, New York, 1869–1969*, 13.

98. Ahlstrom, 480.

99. *Massena Observer* (Massena) 30 January 1942, 8-C.

100. Ibid.

101. Herbert Wallace Schneider, *Religion in 20th Century America* (Cambridge: Harvard University Press, 1952), 6.

102. List compiled by Robert Dansforth, Massena Historian, 1942.

103. Peer et al., 20.

Chapter Three. The Era of Large Corporations in Cornwall and Massena, 1900–1954

1. Peer et al., 16.

2. *The Freeholder* (Cornwall) 1 April 1887.

3. Senior, 351.

4. *Cornwall Standard-Freeholder* (Cornwall) 29 June 1934, 53, 22 February and 5 May 1933, 1, Town Council Minutes, 1907–1914, 13 April 1908, 123, Town Council Minutes, 1902–1907, 27 October 1905, 438, Town Council Minutes, 1907–1914, 14 November 1910, 331, *Official Souvenir Booklet for the Stormont, Dundas, and Glengarry Old Boy's Reunion, August 11 to 15*, 1906, 44 and 70, Harkness, 358–361, and Harlow Stiles, *The Official History of the Cornwall Cheese and Butter Board: A History, Biography and Descriptive Account of the Dairy Industry in the Cornwall District* (Cornwall: The Cheese and Butter Board, 1919), 236.

5. *Cornwall Standard-Freeholder* (Cornwall) 29 June 1934, 55, and 17 October 1944, 1, *Census of Canada,* 1891, iii, 120–377, and Harkness, 236.

6. Steve Dunwell, *The Run of the Mill* (Boston: David R. Godine Publishers, 1978), 144.

7. Harkness, 447.

8. Senior, 352 and *The Cornwall Mill Story*, a brochure published by Domtar Fine Papers, 2.

9. *Cornwall Standard-Freeholder* (Cornwall) 29 June 1934, 53, and *The Cornwall Mill Story*, 19.

10. Lipset, 121–122.

11. *The Souvenir Book of Courtauld's in Cornwall 1924–1992*, 15.

12. Ibid. and *Cornwall Standard-Freeholder* (Cornwall) 24 June 1967, 38C.

13. *The Souvenir Book of Courtauld's in Cornwall 1924–1992*, 15, *Cornwall Standard-Freeholder* (Cornwall) 24 June 1967, 38C, and Harkness, 358.

14. Harkness, 358.

15. McInnis, 570.

16. *The Souvenir Book of Courtaulds in Cornwall 1924–1992*, 44.

17. *Cornwall Standard-Freeholder* (Cornwall) 8 May 1954, 3.

18. Ibid. and *Cornwall Standard-Freeholder* (Cornwall) 1 September 1954, 3.

19. *The Souvenir Book of Courtaulds in Cornwall 1924–1992*, 28 and *Cornwall Standard-Freeholder* (Cornwall) 24 June 1967, 38C.

20. *Cornwall Standard-Freeholder* (Cornwall) 1 September 1954, 3.

21. *Cornwall Standard-Freeholder* (Cornwall) 12 August 1936, Memo by M. S. Campbell, Department of Labor Councillator, 31 August 1936, and *Final Report on Courtaulds Strike* 22 September 1936.

22. *Ottawa Evening Journal* (Ottawa) 31 August 1936, 1 and Ralph Ellis, "Labour and Politics in Cornwall, 1936–1939" (Master's thesis, Department of History, McGill University, Spring 1982), 4.

23. *Canada's Party of Socialism: A History of the Communist Party of Canada* (Toronto: Progress Books, 1982), 37, 70–83, 85, 100–112, and 117 and Ian Angus, *Canadian Bolsheviks: Early Years of the Communist Party of Canada* (Montreal: Vanguard Publications, 1981), 281–288.

24. *Ottawa Morning Journal* (Ottawa) 23 October 1936, 5, *Daily Clarin* (Toronto) 7 August 1936, 1, Ellis, 7. *Cornwall Standard-Freeholder* (Cornwall) 12 August 1936, 1 and 19 August 1936, 1 and 8, *Ottawa Evening Citizen* (Ottawa) 4 September 1936, 1 and 21 October 1936, 1, Courtaulds Report to Department of Labor, 13 August 1936, and *Souvenir Book of Courtaulds in Cornwall 1924–1992*, 27.

25. Ibid.

26. *Cornwall Standard-Freeholder* (Cornwall) 21 July 1937, 1, Royal Commission on Textile Industry, 1938, 286 and *Ottawa Morning Journal* (Ottawa) 23 October 1936, 5.

27. *Cornwall Standard-Freeholder* (Cornwall) 25 August 1936, 1.

28. *Cornwall Standard-Freeholder* (Cornwall) 15 September 1937, 1.

29. Senior, 401.

30. Canada Census 1851–1941.

31. Marilyn Fardig Whiteley, "Do Just About What They Please: Ladies' Aid in Ontario Methodism," *Ontario History* 82 (1990): 292 and Lynne Sorel Marks, "Ladies, Loafers, Knights, and Lasses: The Social Dimension of Religion and Leisure in a Late Nineteenth Century Small Ontario Town," (Ph.D. diss., York University, 1992), 177.

32. Fraser et al., 27.

33. Fraser et al., 30 and MacMillan, 287.

34. Fraser et al., 11 and Clarke, 341.

35. *History of Knox United Church, 1846–1975*, 49.

36. Clarke, 289.

37. Jay P. Dolan, *Catholic Revivalism: The American Experience, 1830–1900* (Notre Dame: Notre Dame University Press, 1978), 60 and Gilbert J. Garraghan, *The Jesuits of the Middle U.S.* (Chicago: Loyola University Press, 1984), 58.

38. *Fifth Census of Canada, 1911*, C. H. Parmelee, 1913, Volume II, Table II, 76, and *Ninth Census of Canada*,Volume I, Dominion Bureau of Statistics, Department of Trade and Commerce, Ottawa, 1953, Table 41, 41–57.

39. Fobert, 138–145.

40. Clarke, 282–283.

41. Fobert, 195–201.

42. Patterson, 208–240 and 247–257.

43. Marilyn Barber, "National, Nativism, and the Social Gospel: The Protestant Response to Foreign Immigrants in Western Canada, 1897–1914," in *The Social Gospel*

in Canada, ed. Richard Allen (Ottawa: National Museum of Man, 1975), 220–223 and Clarke, 331.

44. Letter from treasurer, Jack Haworth to Claire Parham, September 11, 1998; Parmelee, 4 and 10 and Clarke, 282.

45. Parmelee, 22–23.

46. Parmelee, 22–31 and *Cornwall Standard-Freeholder* (Cornwall) 29 June 1934, 26.

47. Clarke, 282.

48. Jeffrey Charles, *Service Clubs in American Society: Rotary, Kiwanis, and Lions* (Urbana: University of Illinois Press, 1993), 2.

49. *Cornwall Standard-Freeholder* (Cornwall) 7 February 1918, 1 and 29 June 1934, 37.

50. Neil Semple, "The Nurture and Admonition of the Lord: Nineteenth Century Methodism's Response to Childhood," *Social History* 14 (1981): 172 and 174.

51. *Cornwall Standard-Freeholder* (Cornwall) 26 June 1934, 37.

52. *Cornwall Standard-Freeholder* (Cornwall) 26 June 1934, 37 and *Old Home Week City of Cornwall and United Counties of Stormont, Dundas and Glengarry, August 3–10, 1946, Souvenir Book and Program,* 75.

53. *Cornwall Standard-Freeholder* (Cornwall) 9 August 1933, 1.

54. *Old Home Week, 1946*, 77–79.

55. *Report on Victorian Order of Nurses* (Cornwall, 1945), Mrs. Earl Malcolm, *History of Victorian Order of Nurses*, April 1973, and Town Council Meeting Minutes, 30 April 1897, 290–291.

56. Charles, 2.

57. Robert Bothwell, Ian Drummond, and John English, *Canada Since 1945: Power, Politics, and Provincialism* (Toronto: University of Toronto Press, 1981), 109.

58. Podgurski et al., 14 and *Massena Observer* (Massena) 27 June 1907, 1.

59. John H. Thompson and James M. Jennings, *Manufacturing in the St. Lawrence Area of New York State* (Syracuse: Syracuse University Press, 1958), 14 and Figure 4 and *Massena Observer* (Massena) 15 August 1901, 6.

60. The company later became known as the Aluminum Company of America (Alcoa).

61. Podgurski et al., 16.

62. George David Smith, *From Monopoly to Competition: The Transformations of Alcoa, 1888–1986* (Cambridge: Cambridge University Press, 1988), 94–95.

63. Peer et al., 33 and Charles Carr, *Alcoa: An American Enterprise* (New York: Rinehart and Company, 1952), 93.

64. *Massena Observer* (Massena) 15 May 1902, 1.

65. Podgurski et al., 16, Harry Landon, *History of the North Country: A History Embracing St. Lawrence, Oswego, Lewis and Franklin Counties* (Indianapolis: Historical Publishing Company, 1932), 504 and *Massena Observer* (Massena) 26 June 1952, 1.

66. Internal Alcoa document provided by Kevin Cooper, Public Information Officer for Alcoa Massena, with average number of employees from 1903 to 1937 and *Massena Alcoan, 50th Anniversary Issue*, June 1952, 7.

67. Internal Alcoa document.

68. Donald Wallace, *Market Control in the Aluminum Industry* (Cambridge, Mass.: Harvard University Press, 1937), 79.

69. *Canal to Company Town, Alcoa in Massena, N.Y.* (Canton: St. Lawrence County Historical Society, 1989), 6.

70. George David Smith, 178.

71. When the Alcoa production facilities could not meet the federal government's demands for aluminum during the early stages of World War II, the Truman Committee authorized the construction of new plants that were operated by Alcoa according to government critieria.

72. *International Directory of Company Histories, Volume V* (Chicago: St. James Press, 1991), 14–15 and Smith, 217–234.

73. Carr, 236.

74. George David Smith, 191 and 241.

75. *Massena Observer* (Massena) 7 February 1942, 2-E, Dumas and Dumas, 40–41, Peer et al., 9, and WCAD, Canton, New York Massena Broadcast transcript April 30, 1936, no page numbers indicated.

76. *Massena Observer* (Massena) 22 February 1934, 1 and 1 February 1934, 1 and 7.

77. *Massena Observer* (Massena) 1 February 1934, 1 and 7.

78. St. Lawrence Seaway and Power Project Facts, brochure.

79. George David Smith, 119 and 177.

80. George Smith, Notes from conversations with retired Alcoa Employees, Bauxite, Arkansas, 10 August 1983.

81. George David Smith, 138.

82. Ibid., 181–183.

83. WPA Writers Project, *New York: A Guide to the Empire State* (New York: Oxford University Press, 1938), 532 and Figure 2.

84. Joan Dobbie, Louis Greenblatt, and Blanche Levine, *Before Us: Studies of Early Jewish Families in St. Lawrence County, 1855–1920* (Ogdensburg: Ryan Press, 1981), 144.

85. *Massena Observer* (Massena) 29 January 1920, 1. Also, 477 arrests were recorded in 1923.

86. A careful reading of the *Massena Observer* between 1900–1930 showed that in almost every issue of the weekly newspaper an account of an immigrant crime graced the front page. The descriptions of crimes committed by native whites appeared in the local section of the paper, previously reserved for the announcement of weddings and comments on recent social events.

87. Rudolph Vecoli, "The Italian Americans," in *Uncertain Americans: Readings in Ethnic History*, edited by Leonard Dinnerstien and Frederic Cople Jaher (New York: Oxford University Press, 1977), 201.

88. This was the first accusation in the United States regarding a ritual murder or blood libel. In Europe it was rumored that such a sacrifice required the blood of a pure Christian child and was meant to recreate the passion of Christ at Easter. The practice is more fully explained by Saul Friedman in *Incident at Massena: The Blood Libel in America* (New York: Stein and Day, 1978), 99.

89. *Directory of Massena, New York, Volume I* (Ithaca, N.Y.: Interstate Directory Company, 1901), 12–13, and *Manning's Classified Business Directory* (New York: H. A. Manning Company, 1933 and 1957), 11.

90. Hudson and Corrigan, 299.

91. Schneider, 6, 21, and 25.

92. Fraser et al., 37 and Clarke, 282.

93. Marian O'Keefe and Theresa Sharp, *Massena Historic Sites, 1803–1995* (Massena, New York, Stubbs Printing, 1995), 9, C. I. Allen, *Historical Sketch of the Congregational Church of Massena*, 3, and *The Story of a Church*, 10.

94. *Massena Observer* (Massena) 20 May 1920, 1

95. *The Story of a Church*, 14–15.

96. Roger Finke and Rodney Stark, *The Churching of America, 1776–1990: Winners and Losers in Our Religious Economy* (New Brunswick, N.J.: Rutgers University Press, 1992), 163.

97. Dumas and Dumas, 114.

98. Ibid. and *Massena Observer* (Massena), 30 January 1942, 6-C.

99. Finke and Stark, 110 and 115.

100. The coverage area for the parish included residents of neighborhoods east of North Main Street and north of the Grasse River.

101. *Massena Observer* (Massena) 23 December 1920, 1.

102. Dumas and Dumas, 111–112, *Massena Observer* (Massena) 30 January 1942, 8-C.

103. *Massena Observer* (Massena) 23 December 1920, 1.

104. *Sacred Heart Church 100 Years of Community in Faith, 1874–1974*, 15.

105. Schneider, 60.

106. *Massena Observer* (Massena) 30 January 1942, 2-C.

107. *Sacred Heart Church 100 Years of Community in Faith, 1874–1974*, 19.

108. *St. John's Church, Massena, New York, 1869–1969*, 19–20.

109. Ibid., 20–23.

110. Ibid., 14.

111. Schneider, 25.

112. *Massena Observer* (Massena) 30 January 1942, 8-C and Dumas and Dumas, 140–142.

113. Dobbie, Greenblatt, and Levine, 197–199.

114. Clarke, 285.

115. Finke and Stark, 163.

116. Paul Conklin, *American Originals: Homemade Varieties of Christianity* (Chapel Hill: University of North Carolina Press, 1997), 277–287.

117. *Massena Observer* (Massena) 30 January 1942, 7-C.

118. The 1900 Massena directory listed seven associations, whereas *The Massena Story,* a 1957 local history, mentioned eighteen.

119. Charles, 2.

120. Ibid.

121. Robert S. and Helen Merrell Lynd, *Middletown: A Study of American Culture* (New York: Harcourt, Brace and Company, 1929), 276.

122. *Massena Observer* (Massena) 30 January 1942, 3-C and 4-C.

123. *Massena Observer* (Massena) 30 January 1942, 1-C and 3-C.

124. John Hutchinson, *Champions of Charity: War and the Rise of the Red Cross* (Colorado: Westview Press, 1996), 6.

125. *Massena Observer* (Massena) 30 January 1942, 5-C and Hutchinson, 283–284, 317, and 321.

126. *Massena Observer* (Massena) 30 January 1942, 6-C and Thomas Rumer, *The American Legion: An Official History, 1919–1989* (New York: M. Evans and Company, 1990), 3 and 26.

127. Charles, 7.

128. Ibid., 75–77.

129. Lipset, 173.

Chapter Four. The St. Lawrence Seaway Project and Its Short-Term Social Impact on Cornwall and Massena, 1954-1958

1. M. W. Oettershagen, "Saint Lawrence Seaway—Fact and Future," (Massena, N.Y.: Saint Lawrence Seaway Development Corporation, 1959), 1.

2. *Massena Observer* (Massena) 6 January 1955, 1.

3. Sufrin and Palmer and Business and Research Center, Syracuse University, *Impact of the St. Lawrence Seaway and Power Projects Upon Upstate New York Business and Industry: A Forum Discussion at the Student Faculty and Alumni Conference April 27, 1955.*

4. Ron Cummings, *The Trail of the Past: The History of the First Baptist Church, Cornwall, Ontario 1882–1982* (Cornwall: Centennial Committee, 1982), 27–28.

5. Ontario Hydro brochure, St. Lawrence Seaway Project, August 1956, 2.

6. R. Baxter ed., *Documents on the St. Lawrence Seaway* (New York: Frederick Praeger, 1961), 20–21.

7. Alexander Wiley, *St. Lawrence Seaway Manual: A Compilation of Documents on the Great Lakes Seaway Project and Correlated Power Development* (Washington: United States Government Printing Office, 1955), 195–199, Forrest Keesbury, "The Role of Dwight D. Eisenhower in the Development of the St. Lawrence Seaway," (Master's thesis, Bowling Green State University, 1965) 22, T. L. Hill, *The St. Lawrence Seaway* (New York: Frederick Praeger, 1959), 90, and Baxter, 3.

8. "St. Lawrence Power and Seaway Projects," 6, Ontario Hydro, brochure, St. Lawrence Power Project, August 1956, 7, "St. Lawrence Seaway Epoch Begins," *E-M Kayan*, November 1955, 5–6, Podgurski et al., 37, and *The St. Lawrence-FDR Power Project* (New York Power Authority, November 1995), 4.

9. M. W. Oettershagen, 2.

10. Andrew Dunar and Dennis McBride, *Building the Hoover Dam: An Oral History of the Great Depression* (New York: Twayne Publisher, 1993), 23.

11. Ibid., 87–91.

12. Lowell Fitzsimmons, dragline operator, interviewed by author, 25 February 1989, Alexandria Bay, N.Y. tape recording.

13. Jerry Richards, machine repairer and operator, interviewed by author, 4 March 1989, Massena, N.Y., telephone conversation.

14. Ibid.

15. Carleton Mabee, *The Seaway Story* (New York: Macmillan, 1961), 180.

16. Sam Agati, founder and longtime administrator of the Laborers' Union Local 322, interviewed by author, 8 March 1989, Massena, N.Y., tape recording.

17. Ibid.

18. Jimmy Oakes, machine operator, interviewed by author, 23 March 1989, telephone conversation.

19. Lowell Fitzsimmons interview.

20. Sam Agati interview.

21. *Watertown Daily Times* (Watertown) 29 July 1957, 3

22. Ross Violi, laborer, interviewed by author, 23 March 1989, telephone conversation.

23. *Watertown Daily Times* (Watertown) 29 July 1957, 3.

24. Jimmy Oakes interview.

25. Massena Chamber of Commerce Brief Massena Facts, July, 1958, *The New York State Department of Commerce Business Fact Book,* 1957, 12, Foster Business Services Limited, Ottawa, Report for the Eastern Ontario Development Association, January 3, 1955, and *Census of Canada*, Volume I, 1961, 66.

26. *Watertown Daily Times* (Watertown) 16 February 1956, 1.

27. Mabee, 241 and *Massena Observer* (Massena) 12 May 1955, 1.

28. *Montreal Star* (Montreal) 26 February 1955, 1.

29. Podgurski, 11, Nick Podgurski, Leonard Prince, and Richard Peer, eds., *The Massena Story*, 26, Clive Marin and Frances Marin, *Stormont, Dundas and Glengarry, 1945–1978* (Belleville, Ontario: Mika Publishing, 1982), 338 and Mabee, 241.

30. Dunar and McBride, 30.

31. Sam Agati interview.

32. *Massena Observer* (Massena) 22 October 1956, 1.

33. *Watertown Daily Times* (Watertown) 28 December 1954, 8.

34. *Massena Observer* (Massena) 22 October 1956, 1.

35. *Watertown Daily Times* (Watertown) 21 May 1956, 13.

36. Walter Gorrow, union steward for Local 322 during the Seaway construction, interviewed by author, 8 March 1989, Massena, N.Y., taped conversation.

37. Jerry Richards interview.

38. Bill Massey, Waddington resident and tug boat operator during the construction of the Seaway, interviewed by author, 24 February 1989, Waddington, N.Y., tape recording.

39. Sam Agati interview.

40. *Cornwall Standard-Freeholder* (Cornwall) 14 April 1955, 3.

41. *Cornwall Standard-Freeholder* (Cornwall) 23 June 1955, 1 and *Cornwall Standard-Freeholder* (Cornwall) 11 June 1955, 1.

42. *Cornwall Standard-Freeholder* (Cornwall) 2 October 1957, 1.

43. *Cornwall Standard-Freeholder* (Cornwall) 31 December 1957, 1.

44. Fraser et al., 39.

45. *Community Survey Report St. Lawrence Seaway Area* (Toronto: University of Toronto School of Social Work, 1957), 9.

46. Ibid., 15.

47. Ibid., 25.

48. Sam Agati interview.

49. Walter Newtown, air tamper operator on the Seaway for three months, interviewed by author, 4 March 1989, telephone conversation.

50. *Cornwall Standard-Freeholder* (Cornwall) 18 August, 1958, 1.

51. Sam Agati interview.

52. Bill Massey interview.

53. Jimmy Oakes interview.

54. Dunar and McBride, 34, 40, and 61.

55. MacKesey, 21.

56. Mabee, 242.

57. *Watertown Daily Times* (Watertown) 28 May 1955, 1.

58. Ibid.

59. Clarke, 329.

60. Ibid., 355–356.

61. Ibid., 355.

62. Fraser et al., 39–40.

63. *History of Knox United Church, 1846–1975*, 27.

64. Fobert, 83 and 88.

65. Clarke, 309.

66. Ibid., 273.

67. *The Trail of the Past: The History of First Baptist Church, Cornwall, Ontario, 1882–1982*, 22–31 and *Cornwall Standard-Freeholder* (Cornwall) 29 June 1934, 26.

68. Clarke, 322.

69. Letter from Reverend Earle Smith, Calvary Baptist Church, to Claire Parham, 6 October 1998.

70. Ibid.

71. Patterson, 257.

72. Ibid., 247–257.

73. Ibid., 253–260.

74. Clarke, 282.

75. Douglas T. Miller and Marion Nowak, *The Fifties: The Way We Really Were* (New York: Doubleday, 1977), 92.

76. McLoughlin, 184–185.

77. Ibid., 93 and 102.

78. *Massena Observer* (Massena) 28 October 1957, 7.

79. St. John's Episcopal Church Vestry Minutes, 21 March 1956, 1.

80. *St. John's Church, Massena, New York, 1869–1969*, 17, Dumas and Dumas, 111 and 112, and Annual Vestry Meeting minutes for St. John's 1955 and 1956.

81. Allen, 5.

82. *Massena Observer* (Massena) 22 February 1957, 1.

83. Hudson and Corrigan, 333.

84. Letter to Pastor Durst from Bill and Irene Riddle, 30 August 1977.

85. McLoughlin, 192–193 and 214.

86. *Massena Observer* (Massena) 9 June 1960, 1 and Ted La France, *History of Massena Church of Christ, Upstate New York is Calling*, 1.

87. Schneider, 6.

88. McLoughlin, 179.

Chapter Five. The Long-Term Economic Impact of the St. Lawrence Seaway and Power Project on Cornwall and Massena

1. "St. Lawrence Power and Seaway Projects," 1–13.

2. *Massena Observer* (Massena) 12 May 1955 and Address of Lionel Chevrier at Queen's University, 15 February 1954, 1.

3. J. E. Clubb, *Government of Canada Department of Regional Economic Expansion, Industrial Opportunity Study, Cornwall, Ontario*, June 1971, Waterhouse Associates, 1.

4. Leonard Yaseen, *Plant Location* (New York: American Research Council, 1960), 47.

5. Marin and Marin, 222.

6. Daniel Creamer, "Manufacturing Employment by Type of Location," *Studies in Business Economics*, Number 106, (New York: National Industrial Conference Board, 1969), 10.

7. Chris Jermyn, "Some St. Lawrence Seaway Communities, 1959–1969," *Canadian Geographical Journal* 79 (1969): 158.

8. *The Globe and Mail* (Toronto) 9 December 1959, 22.

9. Bothwell et al., 314.

10. *Ottawa Journal* (Ottawa) 7 June 1965, 10.

11. Marin and Marin, 227, *Statistics for Industrialists, City of Cornwall, Cornwall Industrial and Economic Commission,* 1970, 21–22 and Foster Business Services Limited, Ottawa, Report for Eastern Ontario Development, 3 January 1955, no page numbers indicated.

12. George Holland, "A Decade of Diversification, 1954–1963," *The Souvenir Book of Courtaulds in Cornwall, 1924–1992*, 67–74.

13. Ibid., 67.

14. *The Souvenir Book of Courtaulds in Cornwall, 1924–1992*, 7 and 67–74, Marin and Marin, 229, and *Scott's Industrial Directory of Ontario Manufacturing*, 1979, 2–91.

15. McInnis, 495.

16. Marin and Marin, 229 and *The Cornwall Mill Story*, 20 and 21.

17. Rayside, 81.

18. Foster Business Services Limited, Ottawa, Report for Eastern Ontario Development Association, 3 January 1955, no page numbers indicated and *Statistics for Industrialists* (Cornwall: Cornwall Industrial and Economic Commission, 1970), 22.

19. Faludi, 32 and *Cornwall Standard-Freeholder* (Cornwall) 7 June 1954, 3.

20. Clubb, 21 and 36.

21. City of Cornwall, Submission to the Minister of the Department of Regional Economic Expansion, the Honorable Mr. Donald Jamieson and the Minister of Industry and Tourism, the Honorable Claude Bennett, 1973, no page numbers.

22. Marin and Marin, 232.

23. McInnis, 669 and 674.

24. Ibid., 640.

25. Doug Heuer, "The Final Years, 1984–1992," *The Souvenir Book of Courtaulds in Cornwall, 1924–1992,* 102.

26. Ibid.

27. *Cornwall Standard-Freeholder* (Cornwall) 28 March 1978, 1.

28. Maurice Yeates, "The Industrial Heartland in Transition: Problems and Prospects of an Urbanized Region," in *A Geography of Canada: Heartland and Hinterland,* ed., L. D. McCann (Scarborough, Ontario: Prentice-Hall, 1982), 129.

29. *Cornwall Standard-Freeholder* (Cornwall) 20 December 1979, 1 and *Ottawa Citizen* (Ottawa) 19 November 1976, 5.

30. "C-Tech Travels the World's Oceans," *Cornwall Business Magazine* (1998): 22 and *Cornwall Industrial Directory*, Cornwall Industrial Development, 21.

31. McInnis, 680.

32. Bothwell, 316.

33. Rayside, 91.

34. Ibid., 83.

35. Charles Lipton, *The Trade Union Movement in Canada, 1827–1959* (Toronto: NC Press, 1973), 303 and 305.

36. *Ottawa Citizen* (Ottawa)19 November 1976.

37. McInnis, 639.

38. Harold Vatter, *The U.S. Economy in the 1950s* (New York: W.W. Norton and Company, 1963), 15.

39. Damus and Smith Limited, *City of Cornwall Traffic Planning Report 1962–1985*, no page numbers indicated.

40. Harold Wood, "The St. Lawrence Seaway and Urban Geography, Cornwall-Cardinal, Ontario," *The Geographical Review* (October 1955): 530.

41. Michael French, *U.S. Economic History Since 1945* (Manchester, England: Manchester University Press, 1997), 54.

42. Robert Sobel, *The Age of Giant Corporations: A Microeconomic History of American Business, 1914–1984* (Westport: Greenwood Press, 1984), 236.

43. Marin and Marin, 250.

44. Faludi, 15.

45. George David Smith, 376.

46. Ibid., 285.

47. Ibid., 372 and 385

48. Sobel, 309.

49. *The New York Times* (New York) 29 June 1958, Section SW, 1 and "A New Era for Massena," *North Country Life* (Winter 1959): 13.

50. John Brior, *Taming of the Sault* (1960), 57.

51. *International Directory of Company Histories, Volume V,* 15–16.

52. French, 145.

53. Smith, 385–394 and Internal Alcoa Memorandum from J. H. Park, April 4, 1990 Re: Workforce History.

54. Barry Bluestone and Bennett Harrison, *The Deindustrialization of America: Plant Closings, Community Abandonment, and the Dismantling of Basic Industry* (New York: Basic Books, 1982), 164.

55. French, 143 and 146.

56. Smith, 385–394 and Internal Alcoa Memorandum from J. H. Park, April 4, 1990 Re: Workforce History.

57. Bluestone and Harrison, 158 and 198.

58. Smith, 385–394, Internal Alcoa Memorandum from J. H. Park, April 4, 1990 Re: Workforce History, and Massena Alcoa Operations Annual Reports, 1985 to 1990.

59. Joel Garreau, *The Nine Nations of North America* (Boston: Houghton and Mifflin Company, 1981), 78.

60. Edward Renshaw, "Trends in Manufacturing Employment and Reflections on Infrastructure Investment, Tax and Expenditure Policy in New York State," in *Reindustrializing New York State: Strategies, Implications and Challenges,* eds. Morton Schoolman and Alvin Magid (Albany, N.Y.: State University of New York Press, 1986), 91.

61. Michael Cooper, Alcoa spokesman, interviewed by author, 4 May 2000, telephone conversation.

62. Ibid., 407.

63. Plant history provided by Tom Donovan, 12 April 2000 and Brior, 4.

64. *New York Times* (New York) 29 June 1958, Section SW, 1.

65. Plant history provided by Tom Donovan, 12 April 2000.

66. Sobel, 240.

67. Bryan D. Jones and Lynn W. Bachelor, *The Sustaining Hand: Community Leadership and Corporate Power* (Lawrence: University of Kansas Press, 1993), 75.

68. French, 72 and 146.

69. Jones and Bachelor, 89.

70. Plant history provided by Tom Donovan on April 12, 2000.

71. "General Motors to Add 160 to Staff A Massena," *Outlook* (January 1997): 1.

72. Informational brochure published by the Reynolds Metals Company Aluminum Reduction Plant in 1998.

73. Fred Wigginton, human resources specialist, interviewed by author, 26 April 2000, telephone conversation.

74. Wigginton interview and brochure published by the Reynolds Metals Company Aluminum Reduction Plant in 1997.

75. H. D. Watts, *Industrial Geography* (New York: John Wiley and Sons, 1987), 106 and 112.

76. French, 71.

77. Marin and Marin, 17, *Massena Observer* (Massena) 21 April 1955, 1, and *Watertown Times* (Watertown) 10 March 1955, 10.

78. *Cornwall Standard-Freeholder* (Cornwall) 18 October 1954, 3 and *Cornwall Standard-Freeholder* (Cornwall) 5 June 1954, 3.

Conclusion

1. Lipset, *Continental Divide,* 212.
2. Martinez, 3–20.
3. Lipset, 44 and 45.
4. Ibid., 21.
5. Ibid., 55 and 121.
6. Ibid., 88.
7. Ibid., 85.
8. Clarke, 282.
9. Lipset, 75.
10. Ibid., 172.
11. Martinez, 17.
12. Clarke, 331.
13. Lipset, 172.
14. Mark Schneider and Florence Pellegrino, Massena residents, interviewed by author, June 1998.
15. Lipset, 123.
16. Ibid., 45 and 127.
17. Rayside, 43.

Works Cited

Cornwall Town Council Meeting Minutes, 30 April 1897

Newspapers

The Massena Gazeteer

Massena Observer

Cornwall Standard-Freeholder

Watertown Daily Times

Ottawa Gazette

Syracuse Post Standard

The *New York Times*

Ottawa Citizen

Ottawa Journal

Globe and Mail

Montreal Gazette

Montreal Star

Reporter and Eastern Counties Gazette

Saturday Globe

The Freeholder

Daily Clarin

Published Sources

"A New Era for Massena." *North Country Life* (Winter 1959): 13–16.

Agati, Sam, founder and longtime administrator of the Laborers' Union Local 322. Interviewed by author, 8 March 1989, Massena, N.Y., tape recording.

Ahlstrom, Sydney F. *A Religious History of the American People*. New Haven: Yale University Press, 1972.

Allen, C. I. *Historical Sketch of the Congregational Church of Massena.*

Angus, Ian. *Canadian Bolsheviks: Early Years of the Communist Party of Canada.* Montreal: Vanguard Publications, 1981.

Arnold, Stephen and Douglas Tigert. "Canadians and Americans: A Comparative Analysis." *International Journal of Comparative Sociology* 15 (March–June 1974): 68–83.

Barber, Marilyn. "National, Nativism, and the Social Gospel: The Protestant Response to Foreign Immigrants in Western Canada, 1897–1914." In *The Social Gospel in Canada*, ed. Richard Allen. Ottawa: National Museum of Man, 1975.

Barron, Hal. *Mixed Harvest: The Second Great Transformation in the Rural North, 1870–1930.* Chapel Hill: University of North Carolina Press, 1997.

Baxter, R. R., ed. *Documents on the St. Lawrence Seaway*. New York: Frederick Praeger, 1961.

Bidwell, Percy Wells and John Falconer. *History of Agriculture in the Northern United States, 1620–1860*. New York: Peter Smith, 1941.

Bleasdale, Ruth Elisabeth. "Irish Labourers on the Cornwall, Welland and Williamsburg Canals in the 1840s." Master's thesis, University of Western Ontario, 1975.

Bluestone, Barry and Bennett Harrison. *The Deindustrialization of America: Plant Closings, Community Abandonment, and the Dismantling of Basic Industry.* New York: Basic Books, 1982.

Boss, Colonel W. *The Stormont, Dundas and Glengarry Highlanders, 1783–1951.* (Ottawa: The Runge Press, 1952).

Bothwell, Robert, Ian Drummond, and John English. *Canada Since 1945: Power, Politics, and Provincialism.* Toronto: University of Toronto Press, 1981.

Brior, John. *Taming of the Sault*. 1960.

Brochure published by Reynolds Metals Company Aluminum Reduction Plant in 1997.

Business and Research Center, Syracuse University. *Impact of the St. Lawrence Seaway and Power Projects Upon Upstate New York Business and Industry: A Forum Discussion at the Student Faculty and Alumni Conference April 27, 1955.*

"C-Tech Travels the World's Oceans." *Cornwall Business Magazine* (1998): 22.

Canada's Party of Socialism: A History of the Communist Party of Canada, 1921–1976. Toronto: Progress Books, 1982.

Canal to Company Town, Alcoa in Massena, N.Y. Canton: St. Lawrence County Historical Society, 1989.

Carr, Charles. *Alcoa: An American Enterprise*. New York: Rinehart and Company, 1952.

Catermole, William. *The Advantages of Emigration to Canada*. London: Simpkin and Marshall, 1831.

Census of Canada, 1850–1961.

Chandler, Alfred. *The Visible Hand: The Managerial Revolution in American Business.* Cambridge, Mass.: The Belknap Press of Harvard University Press, 1977.

Charles, Jeffrey. *Service Clubs in American Society: Rotary, Kiwanis, and Lions.* Urbana: University of Illinois Press, 1993.

Chevrier, Lionel. *The St. Lawrence Seaway*. Toronto: Macmillan Company of Canada Limited, 1959.

Chevrolet plant history provided by Tom Donovan, April 12, 2000.

Church of the Good Shepherd. *Cornwall, Ontario, Celebrate the Light 100 Years, 1893–1993*.

City of Cornwall Economic Development. *Community Profile: The City of Cornwall.* Cornwall: Cornwall Economic Development, 1998.

City of Cornwall, Submission to Minister of the Department of Regional Economic Expansion, the Honorable Mr. Donald Jamieson and the Minister of Industry and Tourism, the Honorable Claude Bennett, 1973.

Clark, S. D. *Canadian Society in Historical Perspective*. Toronto: McGraw Hill, 1976.

———. *Church and Sect in Canada*. Toronto: Toronto University Press, 1948.

Clubb, J. Earl. *A Review of the Industrial Opportunity Study for the Cornwall Area* presented in Cornwall, Ontario, 22 September 1971, Price and Waterhouse Associate.

———. *Government of Canada, Department of Regional Economic Expansion, Industrial Opportunity Study, Cornwall, Ontario,* June 1971, Waterhouse Associates.

Community Survey Report St. Lawrence Seaway Area. Toronto: University of Toronto School of Social Work, 1957.

Conklin, Paul. *American Originals: Homemade Varieties of Christianity*. Chapel Hill: University of North Carolina Press, 1997.

Cooper, Michael. Alcoa spokesman. Interviewed by author, 4 May 2000, telephone conversation.

Courtaulds Report to Department of Labor, 13 August 1936

Craig, Gerald M. *Upper Canada, The Formative Years, 1784–1841*. London: Oxford University Press, 1963.

Crawford, Craig and James Curtis, "English Canadian-American Differences in Value-Orientations: Survey Comparisons Bearing on Lipset's Theory." *Studies in Comparative International Development* (Fall–Winter 1979): 23–44.

Creamer, Daniel. "Manufacturing Employment by Type of Location," *Studies in Business Economics,* Number 106, New York Industrial Conference Board, 1969.

Cummings, Ron. *The Trail of the Past: The History of the First Baptist Church, Cornwall, Ontario 1882–1982*. Cornwall: Centennial Committee, 1982.

Curtis, Gates, ed. *Our County and Its People: A Memorial of St. Lawrence County, New York*. Syracuse, N.Y.: D. Mason and Company, 1894.

Curtis, James, Ronald Lambert, Steven Brown, and Barry Kay, "Affiliating with Voluntary Associations: Canadian-American Comparisons." *Canadian Journal of Sociology* 14 (1989): 143–161.

Damus and Smith Limited. *City of Cornwall Traffic Planning Report 1962–1985*.

Danhof, Clarence. *Change in Agriculture: The Northern United States, 1820–1870.* Cambridge: Harvard University Press, 1969.

Dawes, William G. *Changing Population Patterns in Eastern Ontario, 1931–1961*. Department of Geography, Carleton University, 1968.

Directory of Massena, New York, Volume I. Ithaca, N.Y.: Interstate Directory Company, 1901.

Dobbie, Joan, Louis Greenblatt, and Blanche Levine. *Before Us: Studies of Early Jewish Families in St. Lawrence County, 1855–1920*. Ogdensburg: Ryan Press, 1981.

Dolan, Jay P. *Catholic Revivalism: The American Experience, 1830–1900*. Notre Dame: Notre Dame University, 1978.

Donnan, Hastings and Thomas M. Wilson. *Borders: Frontiers of Identity, Nation and State*. Oxford, England: Oxford International Printers, 1999.

Drummond, Ian. *Progress Without Planning: The Economic History of Ontario from Confederation to the Second World War*. Toronto: University of Toronto Press, 1987.

Dumas, Eleanor L. and Nina E. Dumas. *History of Massena the Orphan Town*. Massena: 1977.

Dunar, Andrew and Dennis McBride. *Building the Hoover Dam: An Oral History of the Great Depression*. New York: Twayne Publishers, 1993.

Dunwell, Steve. *The Run of the Mill*. Boston: David R. Godine Publishers, 1978.

Easterbrook, W. T. and Hugh Aitken. *Canadian Economic History*. Toronto: Macmillan of Canada, 1958.

Ellis, David M., James A. Frost, Harold C. Syrett, and Harry J. Carman. *A Short History of New York State*. Ithaca: Cornell University Press, 1967.

Ellis, Ralph. "Labour and Politics in Cornwall, 1936–1939." Master's Thesis, McGill University, 1982.

Ensign Francis Mccarty Deposition, 12 January 1787.

Everts, L. H. and J. M. Holcomb. *History of St. Lawrence County, New York*. Philadelphia: L. H. Everts and Company, 1878.

Faludi, E. G. *The Making of a New Cornwall, 1963–1983: An Urban Renewal Study*, 1954.

Final Report on Courtaulds Strike 22 September 1936.

Finke, Roger and Rodney Stark. *The Churching of America, 1776–1990: Winners and Losers in Our Religious Economy*. New Brunswick, N.J.: Rutgers University Press, 1992.

First Report of the Board of Registration and Statistics on the Census of the Canadas 1851–1852. Quebec: John Lovell, 1858.

Fitzsimmons, Lowell, dragline operator. Interview by author, 25 February 1989 Alexandria Bay, N.Y., tape recording.

Fobert, Roland Clarence. *Faith Is Our Strength: The Story of St. Columban's Parish, 1829–1993*.

Foster Business Services Limited, Ottawa, Report for Eastern Ontario Development Association, 3 January 1955.

Fraser, Dr. S. B., P. S. Robertson, and F. B. Macmillan. *St. John's Presbyterian Church: A History, 1787–1975*.

French, Michael. *U.S. Economic History Since 1945*. Manchester, England: Manchester University Press, 1997.

Friedman, Saul. *Incident at Massena: The Blood Libel in America*. New York: Stein and Day, 1978.

Garraghan, Gilbert J. *The Jesuits of the Middle U.S.* Chicago: Loyola University Press, 1984.

Garreau, Joel. *The Nine Nations of North America*. Boston: Houghton and Mifflin Company, 1981.

Gates, Paul. *The Farmers' Age, 1815–1860*. New York: Holt, Rinehart and Winston, 1960.

Glazebrook, G. P. de T. *A History of Transportation in Canada*. Toronto: The Ryerson Press, 1938.

———. "The Origins of Local Government." In *Aspects of Nineteenth Century Ontario,* edited by F. H. Armstrong. Toronto: University of Toronto Press, 1974.

Gorrow, Walter, union steward for Local 322 during the Seaway construction. Interviewed by author, 8 March 1989, Massena, N.Y., tape recording.

Guillet, Edwin. *Pioneer Days in Upper Canada.* Toronto: University of Toronto Press, 1933.

———. *Early Life in Upper Canada.* Toronto: University of Toronto Press, 1963.

Harkness, John Graham. *Stormont, Dundas and Glengarry: A History 1784–1945.* Oshawa, Ontario: Mundy-Goodfellow Printing Company, 1946.

Hartz, Louis. *The Founding of New Societies.* New York: Harcourt, Brace and World, 1964.

Hatch, Nathan. *The Democratization of American Christianity.* New Haven: Yale University Press, 1989.

Henretta, James, W. Elliot Brownlee, David Brody, Susan Ware, and Marilynn S. Johnson. *America's History, Volume One.* New York: Worth Publishers, 1991.

Herrington, W. S. *Pioneer Life Among the Loyalists in Upper Canada.* Toronto: The Macmillan Company of Canada, 1915.

Hill, T. L. *The St. Lawrence Seaway.* New York: Frederick Praeger, 1959.

Hinjosa, Gilberto Miguel. *A Bordertown in Transition: Laredo, 1755–1870.* College Station: Texas A&M University Press, 1983.

History of Knox United Church, 1846–1975.

Horowitz, Irving. "The Hemispheric Connection: A Critique and Corrective to the Entrepreneurial Thesis of Development with Special Emphasis on the Canadian Case." *Queen's Quarterly* 80 (Autumn 1973): 346–366.

Hough, Franklin Benjamin. *History of St. Lawrence and Franklin Counties.* Baltimore: Regional Publishing Company, 1970.

Houston, Cecil J. and William J. Smyth. *The Sash Canada Wore: A Historical Geography of the Orange Order in Canada.* Toronto: University of Toronto Press, 1980.

Howison, John. *Sketches of Upper Canada.* Edinburgh: Oliver and Boyd, 1821.

Hudson, Winthrop S. and John Corrigan. *Religion in America: An Historical Account of the Development of American Religious Life.* New York: Macmillan Publishing Company, 1992.

Hutchinson, John. *Champions of Charity: War and the Rise of the Red Cross.* Colorado: Westview Press, 1996.

Informational brochure published by Reynolds Metals Company Aluminum Reduction Plant in 1998.

Innis, Harold. *Essays on Canadian Economic History*. Toronto: University of Toronto Press, 1956.

Internal Alcoa memo from J. H. Park, April 4, 1990 Re: Workforce History.

Internal Alcoa document provided by Kevin Cooper, Public Information Officer for Alcoa Massena, with average number of employees from 1903 to 1937.

International Directory of Company Histories, Volume V. Chicago: St. James Press, 1991.

Ishwaran, Dr. K. *Family, Kinship, and Community: A Study of Dutch Canadians A Developmental Approach*. Toronto: McGraw-Hill Ryerson Limited, 1977.

Jermyn, Chris. "Some St. Lawrence Seaway Communities, 1959–1969." *Canadian Geographical Journal* 79 (1969): 155–163.

Johnson, Paul. *A Shopkeeper's Millennium: Society and Revivals in Rochester, New York, 1815–1837*. New York: Hill and Wang, 1978.

Jones, Bryan D. and Lynn W. Bachelor. *The Sustaining Hand: Community Leadership and Corporate Power*. Lawrence: University of Kansas Press, 1993.

Kealey, George, ed. *Canada Investigates Industrialism: The Royal Commission on the Relations of Labor and Capital*. Toronto: 1973.

Keesbury, Forrest. "The Role of Dwight D. Eisenhower in the Development of the St. Lawrence Seaway." Master's thesis, Bowling Green State University, 1965.

Kerr, Donald. "The Emergence of the Industrial Heartland c.1750–1950." In *A Geography of Canada: Heartland and Hinterland*, ed. L. D. McCann, 65–99. Scarborough, Ontario: Prentice-Hall, 1982.

Ladies Auxiliary, St. John's Church. *Town of Massena, N.Y.* Camden: Moesius Phototype, 1900.

La France, Ted. *History of Massena Church of Christ, Upstate New York is Calling*.

Landon, Harry. *History of the North Country: A History Embracing St. Lawrence, Oswego, Lewis and Franklin Counties*. Indianapolis: Historical Publishing Company, 1932.

Laws of New York xxvth Session.

Laws of New York 1896, Chapter 484.

Lesstrang, Jacques. *Seaway: The Untold Story of North America's Fourth Seacoast*. Vancouver, B.C.: Evergreen Press, Ltd., 1976.

Letter from John Strachan to Dr. Brown of Aberdeen Scotland, October 27, 1803

Letter to Pastor Durst from Bill and Irene Riddle, 30 August 1977.

Letter from Reverend Earle Smith, Calvary Baptist Church, to Claire Parham, 6 October 1998.

Letter from treasurer, Jack Haworth to Claire Parham, 11 September 1998.

Lipset, Seymour. "The Value Patterns of Democracy: A Case Study in Comparative View." *American Sociological Review* 28 (August 1963): 515–531.

———. "Canada and the U.S.: A Comparative View." *Canadian Review of Sociology and Anthropology* 1 (November 1964): 173–185.

———. "Historical Traditions and National Characteristics: A Comparative Analysis of Canada and the United States." *Canadian Journal of Sociology* 11 (1986): 113–155.

———. *Continental Divide: The Values and Institutions of the United States and Canada*. New York: Routledge, Chapman, and Hall, 1990.

Lipton, Charles. *The Trade Union Movement in Canada, 1827–1959*. Toronto: NC Press, 1973.

Lockridge, Kenneth. *A New England Town: The First Hundred Years, Dedham, Massachusetts, 1636–1736*. New York: W.W. Norton, 1985.

Lynd, Robert and Helen Merell Lynd. *Middletown: A Study of American Culture*. New York: Harcourt, Brace and Company, 1929.

Mabee, Carleton. *The Seaway Story*. New York: Macmillan, 1961.

MacKesey, Thomas. *Massena Master Plan: A Report to the Town and Village of Massena.* Watertown: Sargent, Webster, Crenshaw and Folley Consultants, 1958.

MacMillan, Donald. *The Kirk of Glengarry*. Ste. Anne Bellevue, Quebec: Imprimerie Cooperative Harpell, 1984.

Malcolm, Mrs. Earl. *History of Victorian Order of Nurses*. April 1973.

Manning's Classified Business Directory. New York: H. A. Manning Company, 1933 and 1957.

Marin, Clive and Frances. *Stormont, Dundas and Glengarry: 1945–1978*. Belleville, Ontario: Mika Publishing, 1982.

Marks, Lynne Sorel. "Ladies, Loafers, Knights, and Lasses, The Social Dimension of Religion and Leisure in a Late Nineteenth Century Small Ontario Town." Ph.D. diss., York University, 1992.

Marr, William and Donald Patterson. *Canada: An Economic History*. Toronto: Macmillan of Canada, 1980.

Martinez, Oscar. *Border People: Life and Society in the U.S.–Mexico Borderlands.* Tucson: University of Arizona Press, 1994.

Marty, Martin. *Modern American Religion Volume 2: The Noise of Conflict, 1919–1941*. Chicago: The University of Chicago Press, 1991.

Massena Alcoa Operations Annual Reports, 1985 to 1990.

Massena Alcoan, 21 January 1946, 2 and 9.

Massena Alcoan, 50th Anniversary Issue, June 1952.

Massena Chamber of Commerce Brief Massena Facts, July, 1958.

Massena Manuscript Census, 1905–1925

Massena Mineral Springs Committee, *Massena Mineral Springs: A Great Natural Resource*. Massena, N.Y., 1936.

Massena Observer Progress Edition, Review and Forecast Outlook (January 1997): 1–8.

Massey, Bill, Waddington resident and tug boat operator during the construction of the Seaway. Interviewed by author, 24 February 1989, Waddington, N.Y., tape recording.

McConville, Daniel. "November Pour." *The Quarterly* (April 1988): 7.

McInnis, Edgar. *Canada: A Political and Social History*. Toronto: Holt, Rinehart, and Winston of Canada, 1982.

McKelvey, Blake. *Rochester on the Genesee, The Growth of a City*. Syracuse: Syracuse University Press, 1993.

McLoughlin, William. *Revivals, Awakenings, and Reform: An Essay on Religion and Social Change in America, 1607–1977*. Chicago: University of Chicago Press, 1978.

Memo by M. S. Campbell, Department of Labor Councillator, 31 August 1936.

Memorial to Stephen De Lancy, 18 January 1787.

Miller, Douglas T. and Marion Nowak. *The Fifties: The Way We Really Were*. New York: Doubleday, 1977.

Moodie, Susanna. *Roughing It in the Bush*. New York: G. Putnam and Company, 1923.

Murphy, Terrance, and Roberto Persin, eds. *A Concise History of Christianity in Canada*. Oxford: Oxford University Press, 1996.

Naylor, R. T. *The History of Canadian Business, 1867–1914, Volume Two, Industrial Development*. Toronto: James Lorimer and Company Publishers, 1975.

Need, Thomas. *Six Years in the Bush*. Bobcaygeon, Ontario: Bobcaygeon Public Library Committee, 1838.

New York State Census 1875–2000.

New York State Department of Commerce. *New York State Business Facts*. Albany, New York: The State of New York, 1954.

Newtown, Walter, air tamper operator. Interviewed by author, 4 March 1989, Winthrop, N.Y., telephone conversation.

Oakes, Jimmy, machine operator. Interviewed by author, 23 March 1989, Massena, N.Y., telephone conversation.

O'Brien, M. T. *Roundtable On The Impact On Human Well-Being Of A Rapidly Evolving Industrialization: Profile No.1 St. Lawrence Seaway-Cornwall.* Toronto: University of Toronto School of Social Work, 1955.

Oettershagen, M. W. "St. Lawrence Seaway—Fact and Future," May 5, 1959, 1–11.

Official Souvenir Booklet for the Stormont, Dundas, Glengarry Old Boy's Reunion, August 11 to 15, 1906.

Official Souvenir Booklet for the Stormont, Dundas, Glengarry Old Boy's Reunion, July 31 to August 7, 1926.

O'Keefe, Marian and Theresa Sharp. *Massena Historic Sites, 1803–1995*. Massena, N.Y.: Stubbs Printing, 1995.

Old Home Week Souvenir Booklet and Program, City of Cornwall and the United Counties of Old Home Week Souvenir Booklet and Program, City of Cornwall and the United Counties of Stormont, Dundas and Glengarry, 1946.

Ontario Hydro, brochure, St. Lawrence Power Project, August 1956.

Parmelee, Roy. *The Anglican Church of the Good Shepherd, Cornwall, Ontario, Celebrate the Light 100 Years.*

Patterson, William John. *Joyous Is Our Praise: Trinity (Bishop Strachan Memorial) Church 1784–1984*. Kingston: Brown and Martin, 1984.

Peer, Richard, Leonard Prince, and Nick Podgurski, eds. *The Billion Dollar Story*. Massena: Chamber of Commerce, 1955.

Phoebe Orvis Diary, 1820–1830.

Piore, Michael J. and Charles F. Sabel. *The Second Industrial Divide: Possibilities for Prosperity*. New York: Basic Books, 1984.

Podgurski, Nick, Leonard Prince, and Richard Peer, eds. *The Massena Story*.

Prince, Leonard, ed. *1802–1952: The Story of Massena*. Massena: Massena Chamber of Commerce, 1952.

Pringle, J. F. *Lunenburgh or the Old Eastern District*. Belleville, Ontario: Mika Publishing, 1980.

Rayside, David. *A Small Town in Modern Times, Alexandria, Ontario*. Montreal: McGill-Queen's University Press, 1991.

Renshaw, Edward. "Trends in Manufacturing Employment and Reflections on Infrastructure Investment, Tax and Expenditure Policy in New York State." In

Reindustrializing New York State: Strategies, Implications and Challenges, eds. Morton Schoolman and Alvin Magid. Albany, N.Y.: State University of New York Press, 1986.

Report of Ten Inhabitants of Township No. 2 on Meeting of 12 January 1787.

Report on Victorian Order of Nurses. Cornwall, 1945.

Research Report on the Children's Aid Society, 50th Anniversary.

Richards, Jerry, machine repairer and operator. Interviewed by author, 4 March 1989, Massena, N.Y., telephone conversation.

Roberts, Leslie. "Canada and the St. Lawrence Seaway." *The Canadian Letter* (December 1951): 127–129.

Royal Commission on Textile Industry, 1938.

Rumer, Thomas. *The American Legion: An Official History, 1919–1989*. New York: M. Evans and Company, 1990.

Ryan, Mary. *Cradle of the Middle Class: The Family in Oneida County, New York, 1790–1865*. New York: Cambridge University Press, 1994.

Sacred Heart Church, 100 Years of Community in Faith, 1874–1974.

Schneider, Herbert Wallace. *Religion in 20th Century America*. Cambridge: Harvard University Press, 1952.

Schneider, Mark and Florence Pellegrino, Massena residents. Interviewed by author, June 1998.

Scott, Myrla. *The Trail of the Past: The History of the First Baptist Church, Cornwall, Ontario, 1882–1982*.

Scott's Industrial Directory of Ontario Manufacturing, 1979.

"Second Stage of Massena Intake." *EM-Kayan* (June 1957): 3–4.

Semple, Neil. "The Nurture and Admonition of the Lord: Nineteenth Century Methodism's Response to Childhood." *Social History* 14 (1981): 172 and 174.

Senior, Elinor Kyte. *From Royal Township to Industrial City: Cornwall 1784–1984*. Belleville, Ontario: Mika Publishing, 1983.

Shaughnessy, Gerald. *Has the Immigrant Kept His Faith?* New York: Macmillan Company, 1925.

Smith, Elwyn. *The Presbyterian Ministry in American Culture*. Philadelphia: Westminster Press, 1962.

Smith, George. Notes from conversations with retired Alcoa Employees, Bauxite, Arkansas, 10 August 1983.

Smith, George David. *From Monopoly to Competition: The Transformations of Alcoa, 1888–1986*. Cambridge: Cambridge University Press, 1988.

Smith, Timothy. *Revivalism and Social Reform in Mid-Nineteenth Century America.* New York: Abingdon Press, 1957.

Sobel, Robert. *The Age of Giant Corporations: A Microeconomic History of American Business, 1914–1984*. Westport: Greenwood Press, 1984.

Sowell, Thomas. *Ethnic America: A History*. United States: Basic Books, 1981.

Statistics for Industrialists. City of Cornwall: Cornwall Industrial and Economic Commission, 1970.

Stein, Jeremy. "Industrializing Cornwall: Time, Space and the Pace of Change in a Nineteenth-Century Ontario Town." Master's thesis, Queen's University, 1992.

Stiles, Harlow. *The Official History of the Cornwall Cheese and Butter Board: A History, Biography and Descriptive Account of the Dairy Industry in the Cornwall District.* Cornwall: The Cheese and Butter Board, 1919.

St. John's Episcopal Church Vestry Minutes, 21 March 1956.

St. John's Presbyterian Church, A History, *1787–1975*.

St. John's Church, Massena, New York, 1869–1969.

St. Lawrence Seaway and Power Projects Facts, brochure.

"St. Lawrence Power and Seaway Projects." *New York State Commerce Review* November 1954, 1–13.

"St. Lawrence Seaway Epoch Begins." *E-M Kayan*, November 1955, 5–6.

Sufrin, Sidney C. and Edward E. Palmer. *The New St. Lawrence Frontier: A Survey of the Economic Potential in the St. Lawrence Area of New York State*. Syracuse: Syracuse University Press, 1957.

Talman, James. *Loyalist Narratives from Upper Canada.* Toronto: The Champlain Society, 1946.

———, ed. *Aspects of Nineteenth Century Ontario.* Toronto: University of Toronto Press, 1974.

The Cornwall Mill Story, a brochure published by Domtar Fine Papers.

The New York State Department of Commerce Business Fact Book, 1957.

The Souvenir Book of Courtaulds in Cornwall, 1924–1992.

The St. Lawrence-FDR Power Project. New York Power Authority, November 1995.

The Story of a Church: Congregationalism in Massena. Waddington, N.Y.: Northland Press, 1964.

The 165th Anniversary of the First Baptist Church, Massena, New York: A Celebration of Faithfulness to God's Word Since 1829.

Thompson, John H. and James M. Jennings. *Manufacturing in the St. Lawrence Area of New York State*. Syracuse: Syracuse University Press, 1958.

Traill, Catherine. *The Backwoods of Canada*. London: C. Knight, 1836.

Trinity Church Records.

Tulchinsky, Gerald, ed. *To Preserve and Defend, Essays on Kingston in the Nineteenth Century*. Montreal: McGill-Queen's University Press, 1976.

Upper Canada Returns of Population and Assessment, Volume I.

Vatter, Harold. *The U.S. Economy in the 1950s*. New York: W.W. Norton and Company, 1963.

Vecoli, Rudolph. "The Italian Americans." In *Uncertain Americans: Readings in Ethnic History*, eds. Leonard Dinnerstein and Frederic Cople Jaher. New York: Oxford University Press, 1977.

Villeneuve, Rudolph. *Catholic Education in Cornwall, Ontario: Yesterday, Today and Tomorrow.* Cornwall: The Stormont, Dundas and Glengarry County Separate School Board, 1971.

Violi, Ross, laborer. Interviewed by author, 23 March 1989, Massena, N.Y., telephone conversation.

Wallace, Donald. *Market Control in the Aluminum Industry*. Cambridge, Mass.: Harvard University Press, 1937.

Walsh, H. H. *The Christian Church in Canada*. Toronto: Ryerson Press, 1956.

Watts, H. D. *Industrial Geography*. New York: John Wiley and Sons, 1987.

WCAD, Canton, New York. Massena Broadcast transcript April 30, 1936.

WPA Writers Project. *New York: A Guide to the Empire State*. New York: Oxford University Press, 1938.

Wheeler, Orin. *Early Days of Massena*. Massena: Massena Historical Association.

Whiteley, Marilyn Fardig. "Do Just About What They Please: Ladies' Aid in Ontario Methodism." *Ontario History* 82 (1990): 292.

Wigginton, Fred, human resources specialist. Interviewed by author, 26 April 2000, telephone conversation.

Wiley, Alexander. *St. Lawrence Seaway Manual: A Compilation of Documents on the Great Lakes Seaway Project and Correlated Power Development*. Washington: United States Government Printing Office, 1955.

Willis, R. B. "The St. Lawrence Seaway: Economics for Canadians." *The Quarterly Review of Commerce* (1941): 249–303.

Willoughby, William R. *The St. Lawrence Waterway: A Study in Politics and Diplomacy*. Madison: The University of Wisconsin Press, 1961.

Wood, Harold. "The St. Lawrence Seaway and Urban Geography, Cornwall-Cardinal, Ontario." *The Geographical Review* (October 1955): 509–530.

Yaseen, Leonard. *Plant Location*. New York: American Research Council, 1960.

Yeates, Maurice. "The Industrial Heartland in Transition: Problems and Prospects of an Urbanized Region." In *A Geography of Canada: Heartland and Hinterland*, edited by L. D. McCann. Scarborough, Ontario: Prentice-Hall, 1982, 101–131.

Zieger, Robert. *American Workers, American Unions*. Baltimore: Johns Hopkins University, 1986.

Index

www.ingramcontent.com/pod-product-compliance
Lightning Source LLC
LaVergne TN
LVHW040157080826
844660LV00001B/9

* 9 7 8 0 7 9 1 4 5 9 8 1 2 *